MW00629177

PREFACE

While contemplating the possibility of applying to law school, I read a book entitled *Government Lawyer* by Malcolm A. Hoffmann. Mr. Hoffmann was not a famous lawyer. As a work-a-day lawyer, he was employed by the Department of Justice. Later he became a private antitrust lawyer, representing plaintiffs. The description of his legal work was formative. Many legal memoirs are written by lawyers who have achieved a degree of fame. Some were sufficiently well known that they could earn significant royalties from their publication. Others may have been motivated by the opportunity to develop new clients, who might retain them after reading of their successes. I do not fit any of these descriptions. My hope is that my experiences as a trial and appellate attorney will inspire others to participate in and improve our system of justice. Along the way, I have tried to provide "lessons learned" and hints to young lawyers for trial practice and career development. As an adjunct professor at two law schools, I was able to pass on the benefits of my experience to budding lawyers. This memoir is a continuation of that endeavor.

Another aim of this memoir which is personal, is to inform my grandchildren, and anyone else's children and grandchildren who read this, of the gratification and worth of a career marked by hard work, honesty, and devotion of at least a portion of one's efforts to helping others. I start with my great grandmother and grandfather, who toiled as dairy farmers and had the courage to relocate their family across an ocean to further their children's economic opportunity. In describing my own experiences, my perspectives are from the vantage points of the judiciary (as law clerk to a federal judge); voting and civil rights laws (as legislative attorney in the U.S. Department of Justice); the criminal justice system (as an Assistant U.S Attorney); the death penalty (as pro bono lawyer in the U.S. Supreme Court); the ins and outs of complex litigation (as an attorney in private practice) and the joys of teaching (as an adjunct law professor).

◆ ◆ ◆

INTRODUCTION

It is difficult to say that Covid 19, which has killed almost 600 thousand Americans, many unnecessarily, has any upside. Yet, a number of published reviews of memoirs have referred to the impact of the pandemic lockdown as providing a period for reflection. Over the past year and a half, while under Covid lockdown, I have looked back over the cases I tried and appeals I argued and selected those that I thought would be of interest. Friends, lawyers and even a federal judge, who read early manuscripts, have told me that it was entertaining. Those remarks were gratifying and I hope all readers will enjoy it. But if I wanted solely to entertain, I would have written a novel like *The World of Timothy Colt* by Louis Auchincloss, which reportedly is a fictionalized account of the author's experiences in a prominent Wall Street law firm.

In writing this memoir, I found that much of my work has a place in a continuum of developing policy on important current issues. These issues include First Amendment rights, civil rights, voting rights, mental competence and capital punishment, nuclear energy safety, antitrust, tax enforcement, and the interface of litigation and the health care system. My hope is that this history will not only portray an entertaining parade of trials and appeals but will also provide some guidance for dealing with policy issues that are important to justice and democracy.

Many of the trials, appeals and other matters described here were also in the context of outstanding events. These include the Little Rock school desegregation, the Civil Rights Act of 1960; the "Red Scare" including the conviction of Julius and Ethel Rosenberg and David Greenglass for passing atomic secrets to the Russians, convictions of members of the Communist Party for conspiring to overthrow the government, and the anti-communist investigations by the House Unamerican Activities Committee and Senator Joseph McCarthy; Alaska statehood, the 1800 Electrical Equipment Price Fixing Cases filed in 33 courts, the revival of the death penalty, the Three Mile Island nuclear plant accident; the sexual revolution fueled by the invention of Viagra; the development of generic drugs; and the rise of Managed Care in the health care system. As such, this personal memoir is also a trip through the history of the last half of the twentieth century.

Many lawyers' memoirs focus on justice. There are books entitled *Doing Justice, Pursuing Justice*, and just plain *Justice*. Justice is a noble but abstract concept. There are essential parts to justice. One of those parts leaps from the page of Justice Brennan's dissent in a death penalty case I argued in the U.S. Supreme Court, which is quoted in Chapter I. It is stated in the pronouncement of clerks throughout the land at the opening of court: "And you shall be heard." A concomitant part of the equation, as expressed by Justice Brennan, is the expectation that whoever hears you, whether a judge or jury, will be "listening." Citizens have a need to be heard and listened to by access to the courts and judges who will not be bound by preconceived ideologies. Part of the equation is the lawyer whose skilled advocacy can arouse courts and juries to listen. Importantly, apart from court proceedings, citizens have a right to be heard through the election process. These themes pervade the description of trials, appeals and cases that I describe here.

⋄　⋄　⋄

Chapter I

AND YOU SHALL BE HEARD

It was 8:30 p.m. My client, Leslie Lowenfield, who had been found guilty of murder, was scheduled for execution in Louisiana at 12:30 a.m. Following my argument before the U.S. Supreme Court, which upheld his conviction, he consented to be examined by a psychiatrist. The diagnosis was that he was paranoid schizophrenic and could not understand the consequences of his conviction and the impending death penalty. A recent Supreme Court decision had held that the Eighth Amendment prohibition against cruel and unusual punishment prohibits a State from carrying out a death sentence upon a prisoner who is insane. The Court stated that execution of an insane person was "savage and inhuman," a "miserable spectacle," and "extreme inhumanity and cruelty."

I filed briefs in the trial court and two Louisiana appellate courts, which rejected the appeals without a hearing. I then shifted to federal court. The federal district court denied a petition for habeas corpus. I alerted the United States Supreme Court that a petition was forthcoming unless the court of appeals stayed the execution. At 12:10 a.m., the Fifth Circuit Court of Appeals rejected an appeal with one judge dissenting. At 12:45 a.m., the Fifth Circuit opinions were circulated to the U.S. Supreme Court Justices. I petitioned the Supreme Court to grant a writ of certiorari so the appeal could be heard. I also asked the Court to stay the execution while the case was pending. I sought permission to argue by telephone. The request to argue was denied but the Court agreed to review briefs, which I faxed. At 1 a.m., while the defendant was strapped in the electric chair, four justices voted to grant certiorari, which was sufficient for the Court to hear the appeal on the merits. Four justices also voted to stay the execution. In support of a stay, Justice Brennan wrote an opinion, joined by Justices Marshall, Stevens and Blackmun. He reasoned:

> "Due Process means little if it requires the courts to provide an opportunity to be heard, without imposing on them a concomitant duty to listen, and where a life is at stake, to listen very carefully. Presumably, it was in recognition of the injustice that four of us (one less than the requisite five) voted to stay petitioner's execution so as to consider his insanity claim in an atmosphere that was not itself lunatic."

Did Justice Brennan's plea have an impact on any of the other Justices, at least one of whom had to change his vote and agree to a stay? Were they listening? In subsequent cases, have the courts listened to the mental competency and other claims on behalf of those on death row? Read on!

◆   ◆   ◆

Chapter II
EARLY YEARS

My mother's grandparents and her father emigrated in the late 1800s from a town called Bobrka, which—at the time—was in a province of the Austro-Hungarian Empire. It encompassed some ninety villages. My father's parents also came from the same town. My parents met at a family wedding attended by people who emigrated from Bobrka.

According to the *Boiberke Memorial Book* (Sivan Press, 1975), in 1880, the town had about 1,480 Jewish persons out of a total population of about 4,390. The industrial centers of the Empire, where young men could find work, lay elsewhere. Families did not leave Bobrka to escape persecution. Emperor Franz Joseph, of whom my grandfather talked glowingly, was kind to the Jews, who had rights in government and got along with their neighbors. Young men and their families were part of a wave of immigration by those seeking economic opportunity.

Bobrka was surrounded by forests and fields that were suitable for farming. In the late 1700s, Emperor Joseph II decreed that the Jews could engage in farming. That explains why upon arriving in America, my great-grandfather, after whom I am named, became the owner of a farm in the borough of Queens, New York. When he was sixteen years old, my grandfather, Joseph Wecker, was sent to the United States to scout out where the family might live when they emigrated to this country.

He visited Tennessee, and probably other states, but concluded that New York was the preferred location.

My mother told of her visits to the farm where she observed my great-grandmother going out at night to lock up the barn with a shotgun in her apron to protect against those who had tried to poison their cows because they did not want to have Jewish neighbors.

Correspondence with Henry Schwartz, a distant relative and the owner of the recently closed Elmhurst Dairy, revealed that his grandfather and great-grandfather also owned dairy farms in Queens, NY in the late 1880s and early 1900s. His grandfather, Henry Field, had a problem with an antisemitic neighbor who put ground glass in Henry's cow pasture. Henry told him in no uncertain terms that if it happened again, there would be serious consequences.

In Europe, at the start of World War I, Jewish people had worse concerns than protecting their cows. In 1914, on a day known as "Black Saturday," Russian Cossacks attacked the Jews, whom they regarded as their enemies. During World War II, 6,000 Jews, constituting the entire population of Bobrka, were annihilated by the Nazis, sometimes with help from the Ukranians, as the town was then part of Ukraine. As pictured in a new book by Wendy Lower, *The Ravine (Houghton, Mifflin, Harcourt, 2021)*, the victims were not shipped to concentration camps but were shot in the open and dumped into a ravine. Our families were fortunate to have left Bobrka years earlier.

Soon after arriving in New York, my grandfather realized that he was not cut out for a farmer's life so he became a tailor working at Saks Fifth Avenue in New York City. He made suits to order for Arturo Toscanini, who needed extra material in the armpits so his sleeves would not roll up while he was conducting the NBC Philharmonic. Mayor James (Jimmy) Walker of New York City was known as Beau James because of his flamboyant lifestyle, which included his extensive wardrobe as well as frequenting speakeasies (it was the age of prohibition) and consorting with showgirls. Mayor Walker would send a limousine to pick up my grandfather when he needed a suit measured to order.

A friend asked Joseph, as a favor, to accompany him to the pier where he was to meet his arranged bride who was arriving on a ship from Europe. Reluctantly, Joseph agreed, but upon arrival fell in love and ultimately married his friend's fiancée. My grandmother, Rose Wecker, had five children. Her oldest daughter, Henrietta was killed in the *Morro Castle* disaster in 1934. She was on a cruise ship from Havana, Cuba, that caught fire off the coast of New Jersey, and ran aground. It was reported that a mutiny had occurred among the crew, who took over the lifeboats. As a result, 137 passengers died.

Upon arriving in America, Jewish immigrants took care of each other by forming burial and social welfare organizations. Joseph was president of the Bobrka Lodge. Rose was a vice president who regularly addressed the association in fluent German. As such, she was an early feminist.

After high school graduation, my mother, Dorothy, wanted to attend college and become a physical education teacher, but limited finances required her to learn shorthand and work as a stenographer. She played the piano. She and I took lessons with a teacher who—unbeknown to me—taught piano to Fran, my wife-to-be.

On my father's side, my grandparents and their four children lived in a tenement on the Lower East Side of Manhattan. My grandfather worked in a sweatshop in the garment industry. He died of pneumonia when my father, Samuel Solomon Klingsberg (who was called "Sol"), was thirteen years old. In order to support his mother and two sisters, he delivered laundry and sold newspapers on the street. In later life, he generously tipped newsboys and others as he remembered his own early plight. He graduated from Dewitt Clinton High School in New York City where he excelled in mathematics and won track medals. He decided to attend New York University, which was a private college, because he thought the education would be better than at a tuition-free city school. He attended college at night while working in the Post Office to earn his tuition. Upon graduation, he informed his mother that he passed the examinations to be licensed as a Certified Public Accountant. She urged him to stay in the post office, as it was a steady job. Nevertheless, he opened his CPA office only to lose his clients who went bankrupt in the Great Depression.

Grandparents' wedding

Dad went to work for the National Recovery Administration (NRA), which was established by the National Industrial Recovery Act (NIRA). As part of the New Deal, to revive the economy during the Great Depression, President Roosevelt signed the NIRA, which allowed industries to agree on codes of fair competition. In one sense, these codes superseded the antitrust laws because they allowed agreements on fair pricing. However, the codes also addressed fair labor practices such as minimum wages, maximum hours, child labor and the right to bargain. In a case involving the Schechter Poultry Corporation, the U.S. Supreme Court invalidated the NRA regulations in the poultry industry. The Court held that the NIRA provided for an unconstitutional delegation of power without adequate standards. Roosevelt then abolished the NRA. But certain industries continued the fair labor codes.

Mom and Dad

The International Ladies Garment Workers Union and the manufacturers created a Recovery Board for their industry. Dad continued his affiliation with the industry successor to the NRA. He and his staff of accountants investigated violations of the codes including the failure to pay union dues. Disputes were resolved by an Impartial Chairman, often an ex-mayor of New York City. Ex-Mayor Jimmy Walker became an Impartial Chairman. Often, Dad and his team of accountants would find that a manufacturer had a double set of books, one for the business and one to calculate union dues. As a result, he was sometimes offered bribes, which—being scrupulously honest—he turned down. Dad inculcated me with the importance of honesty and recognized my good fortune in being in a profession where corruption was not pervasive. Dad was allowed by the Recovery Board to maintain a private practice, which he did in a minor way. However, because of his experience losing clients in the Depression, he was reluctant to give up his job and devote himself to building a full-time practice.

When World War II began, my brother, Jules, who was ten years older, enlisted in the Army Air Force even though he was only seventeen years old. He served in the Eighth Air Force as a navigator-bombardier. As such, he flew twenty-eight missions over Germany and other parts of Europe. If half of the planes returned from a mission, it was considered a success. In his book, *Slaughterhouse-Five,* Kurt Vonnegut criticizes the infamous fire-bombing of the city of Dresden in Nazi Germany. Jules, who participated in that raid, said he would do it again if asked. When he returned from the war, he attended NYU. Unlike me, he was science oriented. Upon graduation, he applied to medical school. Despite being a veteran and having good grades, he was rejected. Inquiries by our father revealed that medical schools had quotas for Jewish applicants. Jules then got a master's degree in histology. He reapplied to medical school but again was rejected. This was another exposure to anti-Semitism. He settled on going to NYU Dental School, and practiced as a periodontist. He was a scientist at heart, and did research on implanting eye tissue into the gums. He was the only dentist who had access to the Columbia Medical School eye bank.

In those days, families lived close together and helped each other out. My grandparents, Joseph and Rose, lived a city block from us and I visited them often. My mother's sister, Ida, and her family lived across the hall in our apartment house in Brooklyn, New York. Her son and my cousin, Richard Wax, and I grew up like brothers. Richard became a biophysicist with a PhD from Penn State and a postdoctoral degree from the Weizmann Institute in Israel. When Ronald Reagan was elected president, he cut the budget of the National Institute of Health where Richard was working on a cure for cancer. He lost his job and went to work for a pharmaceutical manufacturer researching how to make pigs fatter.

Growing up, a career choice was far from my mind. When I was in kindergarten, we were asked to draw a picture that illustrated our job as an adult. I drew myself as the leader of a big band. There was no tradition of practicing lawyers in my family that could have influenced me to join that profession. The only lawyer in the family was my mother's younger brother, Uncle Teddy. He graduated from St. John's Law School in the midst of the Depression but could not find employment as a lawyer. He was an avid golfer and became the manager of a public golf course and ultimately an administrator in the City Parks Department. He provided legal services for barter—if a friend owned a men's clothing store, Uncle Teddy would draft his will in return for a new suit. That was not the impetus for me to study law. However, Uncle Teddy did teach me the finer points of golf.

I attended Public School 130, which was progressive. I skipped a grade in the third year. In the fourth grade I was put into an "individual progress" class. There were selected students from the fourth to the sixth grade in one classroom. We met with our teacher, Miss Russo, in the back of the classroom to review our assignments and then worked individually at our desks. We did two years of school work in a year and a half. Report cards specified,

Young tennis player

"Excellent," "Satisfactory," "Could do better" or "Fail." Miss Russo marked me as "Could do better." When my parents inquired how this could be when my test scores were high, she said I could do even better if I tried harder. She inspired me to do my very best.

Childhood activities were unsupervised and revolved around the seasons. We played punch ball, roller skate hockey and touch football in the street, as there were few cars. We played basketball and baseball in the schoolyard. And we played ice hockey on the neighboring Prospect Park Lake when it froze, which it often did before global warming. I also learned to ride a horse on the bridle paths in the park. Nearby was a tennis club that was open to the public. There, I learned to play by filling in on doubles games with my brother and his friends. After paying a dollar for an hour, the owners, Adolph and Eudo, would let children play all day if no one was using the courts. In his thick German accent, Adolph would patrol the courts and give instructive hints to the young players: "Klingsberg, put your racket behind your back when you serve so you get more power." As a boy, I escaped the city heat in the summers and went to a camp in Pennsylvania. Those were happy times.

After World War II, my parents bought a piano so I could take lessons in classical music. My parents did not buy a television set until after I left for law school, because they thought it might interfere with my studies. We always had on hand a raft of newspapers. These included the early editions of two tabloids, The *Daily News* and The *Daily Mirror.* The *Herald Tribune* was center-Republican in its editorials and had excellent columnists including Walter Lippmann. In the evening my father brought home The *World-Telegram.* My grandfather read The *New York Post,* long before it was bought by Rupert Murdoch. He also read the Yiddish-language newspaper, *The Day* (which was conservative compared to the other Yiddish language daily, *The Forward*). On Sundays we sometimes got the *Journal-American,* a Hearst paper that had entertaining comics. As a counterbalance, we also read the left-wing *PM* whose columnists included Max Lerner and I.F. Stone. Before the advent of television, we subscribed to magazines, including *Life,* which was noted for its photographs; *Saturday Evening Post,* which had short stories and Norman Rockwell covers; *Look,* which was an imitation of

Life magazine; and *Readers Digest* and *Coronet*, which were pocket-size magazines with interesting articles.

We regularly listened to the radio. Before the war, my parents listened to Hitler's rantings. During the war, I had to be silent until the radio news announcer reported on the Eighth Air Force in which my brother was serving. There were numerous news commentators including H.V. Kaltenborn, Lowell Thomas and Walter Winchell. I was an avid reader and read many children's classics including *Ivanhoe, Robin Hood, Tom Sawyer* and my favorite, *The Count of Monte Cristo*. Although I was often late for school, I recalled that the Count always arrived at the stroke of the hour, silently so his carriage horses' footsteps were not heard. As I told my students while teaching at law school on the subject of brief writing, the key to becoming a good writer is to have read extensively as a child and thereafter.

I attended Erasmus Hall High School, which had an excellent faculty, offered honors classes and provided good training for college. In the mornings, during my freshman year, I had to go to synagogue for Bar Mitzvah lessons, and then take two trolley cars to get to school. Mom and Dad did not drive me everywhere and, indeed, we did not own a car. At Erasmus, we had a choice of language and I selected French, which I took for four years. In the last year, Madame Crawford, our teacher, sometimes wanted a day's rest so she would show a movie of *Carcassonne*, the French fortress of crusader times. One of my goals, which Fran and I fulfilled, was to visit the fortress, now sadly commercialized with shops.

I got a high grade in physics but did not take chemistry; I was told it involved just memorization. This omission turned out to be a disadvantage in patent/antitrust and product liability cases in my law practice. I took elementary biology but I never took college level microbiology, which would have been useful in pharma product liability cases. My classmates in law school majored in college in a variety of subjects including music—it is a myth that "prelaw" students must major in history and social science.

THE DUTCHMAN

"To the Victors Belong the Spoils"

Members of 1949 Net Squad: Standing (l. to r.)—Ed Yeaker, David Klingsberg, Coach Milton Huppert, Captains James Tompkins and Maynard Driver.

Kneeling—George Goodman, Sandy Schaeffer, Bernie Schwar*

Erasmus Hall High School Championship Tennis Team

I hated gym class in part because I was a year-and-a-half younger than the other boys and could not perform the gymnastics. I learned that I could get excused from gym class if I joined a team. I was too thin for football; I could not see without my glasses while playing basketball and track seemed dull. So, I joined the tennis team where the prereq-uisite was to own a racket. I practiced in the February cold at a nearby playground by hitting against a handball wall. And I made the starting team. We practiced from 2 to 4 p.m. every day. Then, I had to take two buses to get home from the public courts, leaving little time for stud-ies. Our team, together with Forest Hills High School and Bronx High School of Science, was in the city championships each year.

In the back of Erasmus Hall there was a square block of row houses. In the middle, the homeowners built a tennis court. We would practice there in March after the snow melted but before the public courts opened. Our number one and two players, Jimmy Tomkins and Maynard Driver, could beat anyone in the city. It did not matter who played number one or two. But they were excluded from Eastern Lawn Tennis Association tournaments because—like the families who built the backyard court—they were Black. There were no Black players in organized tennis until the entry of Althea Gibson some ten years later. This was my first observation of racial discrimination, which I kept in mind when I later worked at the U.S. Department of Justice on civil rights matters.

I graduated from Erasmus with a B+ average. It was not until college and law school that I turned up the heat and studied hard enough to get As. A classmate in high school who got all As went on to star at Harvard College, and then only did mediocre work at Yale Law School and got a mediocre job after graduation. Perhaps there is some advantage not to burn out too early.

• • •

Chapter III
COLLEGE AND LAW SCHOOL

New York University

I did not contemplate a legal career when I entered college. My father, brother and Uncle Teddy had attended NYU so it was preordained that I enroll there as well. Moreover, my parents and brother advised that fraternity parties at out-of-town colleges detracted from studying. Dad may have thought that if I studied accounting, I might go into practice with him, but it was not to be. My worksheets for college accounting courses rarely balanced, and were a mess with erasures. I was not particularly fond of this field which involved numbers. I preferred the written word and courses in literature, history, philosophy, psychology and economics. Being in New York City, NYU had an excellent liberal arts faculty. One English professor asked if I came from a large family because of my writing skills. My response was that I only had one brother. Early on, he introduced me to Fowler's *Modern English Usage* and Strunk & White's *Elements of Style*, which sharpened my writing skills. I studied diligently and graduated *magna cum laude,* and second in my class. In those days, class standing was measured separately for male and female students.

In senior year, I heard that you could get admitted to Harvard or Yale Law School if you had good grades. That seemed an attractive prospect, as compared with my subway commute to college over the past 3 years, as well as an alternative to getting a job. I took the LSATs without any prep course, which was not in vogue. I was admitted to Harvard and Yale. I consulted with a professor who was a lawyer. He advised that since I had attended a large college, I might like a small law school. So, I chose Yale, which had an entering class of about 125 students as compared with Harvard, which had about 400 students.

Yale Law School

Over the summer, I read a number of books to orient myself to the study of law. These included Lloyd Paul Stryker's *The Art of Advocacy,* Louis

Nizer's *My Life in Court,* and a biography of Clarence Darrow. In *Final Verdict,* Adele Rogers St. Johns's biography of her father, Earl Rogers, she wrote that he was unlike Clarence Darrow in that he usually won his trials. When someone described Darrow as an attorney for "lost causes," Earl Rogers reportedly quipped, "and lost cases." As a defender of those accused of capital crimes, Rogers was a fierce opponent of the death penalty, which he described as "inhu-

Yale Law School

man and ungodly." This was my first introduction to this subject, which was to play a large role in my pro bono activities. Rogers also was keen on getting the best press coverage for his trials, a lesson I followed during a trial involving the Three Mile Island nuclear accident.

A window into things to come in the U.S. Attorneys' Office for the Southern District of New York was a biography by Martin Mayer of a former United States Attorney and litigator in a large New York City law firm: *"Emory Buckner, The Story of a Great Trial Lawyer of the 1920's."* Later in preparation for new litigations, I recalled that Buckner always started the descriptions of his trials with a reference to the team he put together. Trial practice is indeed a team sport. Although I had not originally thought of becoming a trial lawyer or a federal prosecutor, looking back, I suppose these books were in my subconscious mind when I decided to become an Assistant U.S. Attorney and pursue a career in litigation.

The Yale Law School was, and still is, a unique institution. The faculty was diverse and inspiring. Classes were small and allowed for free discussion. There were opportunities to study philosophical (in law, jurisprudential) subjects that were not directly related to training for the practice of law. Students lived at the school in a quadrangle of three dormitories and one for classrooms, faculty offices and the law library. This setup allowed for encouragement by upper classmen and exchanges of views with classmates. The upper-class students in our corner of the dorm were helpful in explaining the ins and outs of law school. They advised that the goal was to learn logical thought processes rather than to memorize the law. There are many prominent alumni. After I graduated, perhaps the most well-known were the Clintons, who met at the law school. A number of my classmates became federal and state judges.

Arriving at Yale Law School was a daunting experience. Many of the students in the first-year class had come from Harvard, Yale and other Ivy League colleges. One student, with whom I became friendly, had a master's degree from the Wharton School. Another was first in his graduating class at UCLA. Of some comfort was that in a class of about 125, with wide geographic distribution, there were five students from my high school, Erasmus Hall, in Brooklyn. I was greeted on the first day at a cocktail party in the courtyard of the quadrangle. A student pointed to the pleats in my trousers and asked me if I was going to take off like an airplane. Soon thereafter, I went to J. Press clothing store in New Haven and purchased the uniform of pleat-less oxford gray slacks with a drab tweed sport jacket. I asked the local barber to trim my wavy hair, and left with an Ivy League crew cut.

We were not aware that the five women in our class were having an even more difficult time. At a recent reunion, Alice Hartman gave a heart-rending description of problems that she had encountered. She decried the fact that one professor even asked her to sit in the back of the classroom so the male lawyers could sit up front. This has all changed now.

My roommate, Shale Stiller, was involved in an ongoing student poker game. Sometimes, the poker players would play all night before an exam and walk into the exam without sleep. Late one night, his poker partners came into our dorm room to remove the furniture as payment for his losses. Shale became managing partner of his firm in Baltimore and a successful tax attorney. He also was awarded two honorary degrees.

Classes were taught by the Socratic method. Professors would ask questions and prod the students on their inadequate responses. Lectures were not the norm. The Yale faculty was a colorful group. In first year, Fowler Harper taught a class in Torts. He was a frequent debater taking the left position against William Buckley, a Yale College alumnus, who became editor of the conservative *National Review.* Our contracts professor was Friedrich "Fritz" Kessler. Unlike so-called strict constructionists, he taught that without express language, a contract could be "instinct with an obligation." We learned that the casebook used at Harvard Law School, *Williston on Contracts,* was focused on language rather than intent, as compared with our *Corbin on Contracts* casebook.

Fleming James, who taught Procedure, represented the New Haven Railroad. As a lesson in how not to overprepare a witness, he related the story of the young girl who was the only witness to an accident in which a train hit a car that was on the tracks. When the railroad lawyer, who had prepared her, called his young witness to the stand, he began by asking, "Young lady, please tell the court and jury your name." She quickly replied, "The gate was down and the bell was ringing . . . the gate was down and the bell was ringing . . . the gate was down and the bell was ringing." Our federal practice professor, J.W. Moore, was editor of the classic reference in the field, *Moore's Federal Practice.* At our last class, Professor Moore predicted that most of the graduates would become what he called fat cats, engaging in business-oriented law practices. He said he hoped that some would become lean cats, meaning trial lawyers. I often thought back on these words as I made career choices. In some respects, I became a fat cat, and in others a lean cat.

Yale Law School enabled me to pursue some of the philosophical subjects that I missed in college. I took a course with F.S.C. Northrop who taught at the college as well as the law school. The course was *"Philosophical Foundations of Jurisprudence."* I wrote a paper on the influence of Roman law on modern legal principles. I also read Northrop's book, *East Meets West,* in which he proposed to bridge the gap between Asia and the West by finding commonalities between the two cultures. I took two jurisprudence courses, one with Professor Kessler and one with an Oxford University professor. None of these courses were career-oriented but I found them intellectually stimulating.

I attacked my studies vigorously. I took copious notes in class and outlined the cases that we were assigned to read. The editorial board of the Yale Law Journal was selected in first year based on grades. To my amazement, I was selected. The first assignment was to write a Note, which was a short article on a reported case. Next was a Comment, which was a longer piece. My draft Notes were consistently preempted by other articles that were published before I could complete mine. So, I jumped to preparing a Comment. My topic was a case that the Supreme Court had agreed to hear entitled *NAACP v. Alabama.*

Law Journal—NAACP v. Alabama

Alabama sought numerous documents from the National Association for the Advancement of Colored People (NAACP). The Association produced the documents except it refused to produce information on its rank-and-file members for fear of reprisals. Alabama sought to ban the NAACP from doing business in that state because it would not provide its membership list. A state court issued a temporary restraining order against the Association's continued activities. An Alabama appeals court threatened the Association with fines and other penalties if it did not comply. The NAACP filed suit to protect its membership information. The Association claimed that the document demand was a harassing tactic that was unconstitutional and a violation of the rights to association and privacy. The Alabama Supreme Court dismissed these claims.

To begin the assignment, I visited the NAACP headquarters in New York City where I met Thurgood Marshall and Robert Carter. I did not know then that Marshall was the leading civil rights litigator in the nation, who ultimately argued thirty-two civil rights cases in the U.S. Supreme Court and won twenty-nine of them. I also did not know that he would become the first Black Justice of the Supreme Court or that later in my career I would argue before him in that court on three occasions. I also did not know that Robert Carter would become Justice Marshall's law clerk on the Court or that later I would appear before him when he became a federal judge in the Southern District of New York. Thurgood Marshall was the chief counsel. They provided me with a draft brief that was in its early stage. I wrote the law journal Comment in a way that mimicked a Supreme Court brief. The Comment was published and we provided a copy to the NAACP lawyers who adopted our arguments. The Supreme Court ruled in favor of the NAACP. Although the Court did not cite my Comment, it followed the line of argument I presented. In a unanimous opinion, Justice Harlan stated:

The NAACP's members' right to pursue their lawful private interests privately and to associate freely with others in doing so come within the protection of the Fourteenth Amendment.

The Court held that freedom to associate with organizations dedicated to the "advancement of beliefs and ideas is an inseparable part of the Due Process Clause of the Fourteenth Amendment." The Court distinguished earlier cases banning association by members of the Communist Party. Justice Harlan wrote that there was a right to association for legal and ethical purposes. This right was implicit in the First Amendment's rights to free speech and assembly as well as the right to "liberty" in the Fourteenth Amendment.

For more than a half century, the Supreme Court's decision in *NAACP* v. *Alabama* was the foundation for Supreme Court decisions balancing First Amendment rights to freedom of association with regulatory needs for disclosures of various kinds. These cases included striking an Arkansas statute that required teachers to list their organizations, and sustaining a Washington law requiring disclosure of those signing election referendums. In a case decided on the last day of the 2021 term, a Supreme Court decision changed the calculus. Two conservative advocacy organizations, *Americans for Prosperity* and the *Thomas More Law Center*, challenged California's requirement that charitable organizations disclose to the State Attorney General's office the identities of major donors. The Attorney General said that the information is needed to facilitate fraud investigations. Chief Justice Roberts, writing for the six-judge majority, ruled that the statute violated the First Amendment right to freedom of assembly. The NAACP and the American Civil Liberties Union filed a joint brief urging the Court to hold the California law unconstitutional "as applied" because of evidence of widespread leaks of private information by the California Attorney General's office. Justice Sotomayor, in her dissenting opinion, said she could live with that result. But this limitation was not adopted by Justice Roberts' opinion.

In *NAACP* v. *Alabama,* the Supreme Court invalidated Alabama's disclosure law based on evidence of "an uncontroverted showing that on past occasions, revelation of the identity of its rank-and-file members has exposed these members to economic reprisals, loss of employment, threat of physical coercion and other manifestations of pubic hostility." But Justice Roberts held that in this case such a showing was not essential. Rather the disclosure provision was subject only to a facial challenge, which did not require proof of any significant burden on the members. The dissenting opinion concluded that "the Court discards its decades-long requirement that, to establish a cognizable burden on their associational rights, plaintiffs must plead and prove that disclosure will likely expose them to objective harms, such as threats, harassment, or reprisal." The dissent concluded that there would be no burden so long as the information could remain confidential, as the Ninth Circuit Court of Appeals found it would under new, tighter security precautions.

Interestingly, a Yale Law School institute, sponsored by Floyd Abrams, a prominent First Amendment lawyer who was at law school with me, filed a brief asking the court to consider, without taking a position on the outcome, whether there is a First Amendment interest in knowing the source of speech on matters of public concern. Without this element, which the Court did not mention, a concern is whether the Court's rationale could call into question the validity of statutory requirements for disclosure of the sources of election-related spending that were recognized in the *Citizens Union* decision. Finally, both the NAACP and Justice Roberts' decisions mention a "right of privacy" as inherent in the express freedoms in the First and Fourteenth Amendments. Today, in attacking *Roe v. Wade*, right-to-life advocates argue that the right of privacy is not expressly provided for in the Constitution.

An apt target for Justice Robert's facial challenge is a recently enacted Florida law that was proposed by Governor DeSantis, a loyal supporter of our former president and a potential candidate for president himself. The law requires public university teachers and students to declare their political beliefs in an annual state-mandated survey. Under the statute, the results could result in defunding the school. On its face, this law does not reflect a legitimate government interest in the required disclosure, and it could burden the students by depriving them of scholarships, and put the teachers' employment at risk.

Job Hunting

At the end of second year, I was ranked eighth in the class. I set about interviewing for a summer job at a New York City law firm. I was interviewed by Sullivan & Cromwell, a staid Wall Street firm. The interviewer asked me what prep school I attended. When I responded that I graduated from a New York City public high school, the iron curtain came down between us. That was essentially the end of the interview. I was turned down by a number of similar law firms. Classmates who had mediocre grades, were not Jewish, and attended prep schools and Ivy League colleges, got those jobs. Since then, all of the law firms in New York City have begun hiring diverse applicants. The in-house corporate attorneys, who retain those law firms, have monitored the diversity of the outside law firms they can choose to retain. I suspect that the application of this openness to partnership opportunities has lagged behind the hiring practices.

I did get a summer job with a small firm, Gilbert & Segall, where the partners were of mixed religious background and favored Yale Law graduates. I worked mainly with Harold (Ace) Tyler, a litigator who later became a Justice Department official and a federal judge. Since it was a small firm, it only needed one litigator, so in later years Mr. Tyler's movement in and out of the firm did not coincide with my interest in entering private practice. Phil Gilbert represented Rolls Royce for whom I worked on litigations. Every two years, Mr. Gilbert ran for Congress on the Democratic ticket in Westchester County, New York, and lost. The year after he came close to winning, he stopped running. It was a good summer and I learned a lot from Phil and his partner, Harold Segall. The dark, shadowed streets of the Wall Street area were depressing in what was otherwise a sunny summer. That feeling may have dissuaded me from returning to Wall Street later in my career.

• • •

Chapter IV
ROMANCE

In my day, law students did not always get jobs in law firms until they finished the second year of law school. One year of law school does not qualify a student to do much valuable legal work. Today, most law students get summer jobs with law firms after the first year of school. Law firms are motivated to offer summer jobs to first-year students with high grades or law review experience as a way to entice them into coming back after the second year of law school and after graduation. The summer after my first year of law school seemed to be a good opportunity to spend one last summer engaging in joyful and outdoor activities. I got a job as a tennis instructor at a summer camp where I met my wife-to-be, Fran Sue Morganstern. The camp had a canteen where counselors congregated in the evening. The first night I was sitting at a table chatting with my friends when I noticed a very pretty girl across the crowded room. What followed is exemplified by the song in the musical *South Pacific* which describes how you may find your true love across a crowded room and even then you know you will see her again and ultimately never let her go. At a recent wedding anniversary party of our children and grandchildren, accompanied by my grandson, Judah, on the piano, I sang this song to Fran:

That summer in camp, I was the envy of my fellow counselors who complained that the "Ivy League guys get the prettiest girls." When we were not on duty, I taught Fran to play tennis, which she says is why she has a weak backhand to this day. Fran and I soon realized that years earlier we had studied with the same piano teacher. Upon returning home that summer, Fran told the piano teacher, Mario Pariante, that we were dating. He suggested that we had different personalities and would never get along. We have been happily married for sixty-two years.

During the next two years at law school, I often commuted on weekends to see Fran, who was attending Brooklyn College. In turn, Fran came to the law school for social events where we danced to standards like *Ain't She Sweet* and *Dancing Cheek to Cheek*. In April, as my stint in the Justice Department in D.C. was winding down, we were ambling through Gramercy Park, a small and charming park in New York City where I proposed. We were married in August. New York City experienced a brownout that night, and the next day it turned into a blackout, but we were in the air flying to San Juan, Puerto Rico, and the Virgin Islands for our honeymoon.

Our Wedding

Fran majored in statistics and psychology, which—after graduating from college—enabled her to get a job with a large Madison Avenue advertising agency, Young & Rubicam. She did motivational research, testing ads for effectiveness and analyzing the results. Fran resigned when we had our first child. She became active in community affairs, being a trustee of our synagogue, chair of the religious school board, president of the PTA, and president of the Sisterhood. When the children were older, Fran obtained a graduate degree in computer science. She mastered the difficult higher mathematics needed for programming and outshone her younger classmates. She then taught the teachers of our local high school about computers, which were just coming into serious use. As the description of my various litigations will show, I was often in court out of town. So, Fran was often alone to raise our three sons, keep track of our finances, pay the bills and maintain the household.

The family tradition of being a lawyer began with me. Our oldest son, Ethan, graduated from Yale Law School, and is a partner in a large international law firm specializing in corporate law. Our

middle son, Jordan, graduated from Georgetown Law School where he earned a master's degree in Taxation. He is a partner in a tax boutique where he specializes in estate and trust planning and administration. Fran told our youngest son, Matthew, that she did not want to live through a fourth bar exam so—being more mathematically talented—he earned an MBA at NYU and is a Director of Finance at a

Young family

large corporation. All of our sons are happily married to accomplished women, who are also great mothers. Lauren is an active member of the New York branch of the National Audubon Society and a progressive political activist. Debra is a busy litigating lawyer. Stephanie has a doctorate in psychology and was captain of the Princeton tennis team. We are blessed with seven grandchildren, who are among those for whom I have written this volume.

We were also close with Fran's mother and father, Sylvia (nee Gurfein) and Harold Morganstern (who our children fondly called "Pop.") When she was nine years old, in the 1920s, Sylvia emigrated with her parents and five siblings to escape the pogroms in Eastern Europe. She quickly learned English, Hebrew and enough Spanish to help Fran with her schoolwork. She worked at polling sites for the Democratic Party and kept up with politics, which we discussed avidly during the five years she lived with us, until she passed away at age ninety-three. Pop grew up in St. Louis, Missouri. His father, who was a mohel and successful real estate investor, sent him to New York City when he was ten years old to attend a yeshiva. He was learned and observant, but did not wear his religion on his sleeve. Our families had Friday night dinners together to welcome the Sabbath with prayers over candles, wine and challah bread, a tradition that our sons have continued.

Fran's Mom and Pop

• • •

Chapter V
JUDICIAL CLERKSHIP

Based on my academic background at NYU, tax law seemed a good fit. I enrolled in all of the tax law courses in law school, and did well. However, as students started applying for jobs in third year, a judicial clerkship presented a more exciting option. I received three offers: one from a Second Circuit Court of Appeals judge, Carroll C. Hincks, and two from district judges in the Southern District of New York. As a general matter, appellate court clerkships were considered to be more prestigious. However, I consulted with the Dean of the law school, E.V.D. Rostow, who suggested that my writing for the Yale Law Journal was similar to the work I would be doing for an appellate court. In contrast, clerking for a district judge would provide a window into what actually goes on during a trial in a courtroom. Thus far, my exposure to courtrooms had been a mock trial exercise and a moot court appellate argument at law school. The Dean advised that Judge Edward J. Dimock was an excellent writer from whom I would learn a valuable skill. I also had an offer from Judge Edward Weinfeld, who was known as a superstar district judge. Later, I tried a criminal case before Judge Weinfeld, and we crossed paths at several resorts where we played tennis. But at that time, Judge Weinfeld was about to embark on a long antitrust trial involving a merger of two major steel companies, and I did not want to get bogged down in a single antitrust case.

As it happened, Judge Weinfeld asked his current clerk, Martin Lipton, to stay on for another year. Marty went on to found the firm of Wachtel, Lipton, and to become a well-known mergers and acquisition lawyer. One day, at lunch, he complained that Judge Weinfeld was unhappy with his work. Marty replied that he came in at 6:00 a.m. when the judge arrived and stayed until 10 every evening, so what else could he do? Judge Weinfeld peered at him through his deep-set eyes and admonished him to "become more efficient." In retrospect I made the right decision in choosing to clerk for Judge Dimock.

An Old-fashioned Gentleman and Outstanding Jurist

Judge Dimock called his secretary, of some ten years, Mrs. Goldman. He called his bailiff, Mr. Garlinge. And he called his clerk Mister, Mrs., or Miss (Ms had not been invented yet) until the day his or her clerkship was over; then he shifted to a first-name basis. The judge spent his career at a small but prestigious firm specializing in municipal bond offerings. Yet he had an amazing knack for dealing with lawyers in trials and writing opinions. Some judges frequently interject questions to relieve their boredom or because they approach the case differently than examining counsel. Of course, a judge should intervene and ask a question if it is critical to the outcome and the lawyers missed the point. A court reporter complimented Judge Dimock in this regard, saying that he had judicial *sitzfleisch*, meaning the patience to sit quietly. He let the lawyers be heard, and he listened carefully.

The judge was a Democrat and his stately wife, Constance Bullock Dimock, was a Republican. He lived on the Upper East Side of Manhattan from which there was probably an oversupply of potential Democratic candidates for judgeships. Judge Dimock had a country home upstate in Sullivan County where he was probably one of few Democrats interested in a judicial appointment. He lived a relatively simple life, ice-skating at his country home when the lakes froze. He told me that he had never gone to a warm climate for a winter vacation.

Many judges employed two law clerks, each for two years, so that there was always a clerk with a year's experience. Judge Dimock believed that from the point of view of the recent law graduate, one year as a clerk was sufficient. Judge Dimock's clerks could write memoranda to the judge, but were not allowed to draft opinions until they learned to write in the judge's style. That did not happen until ten months into my clerkship in the summer of 1958. This practice gave the law clerks more writing experience than Judge Dimock's friend, Learned Hand, who sat on the Second Circuit Court of Appeals in New York. Judge Hand had a partner's desk in his chambers. The clerk sat opposite the

Edward J. Dimock, U.S. District Judge, SD

judge. The clerk orally reported research results to Judge Hand and they exchanged views. But the clerks were not permitted to put pen to paper, lest they put their stamp on Judge Hand's unique writing style.

In those days, district judges periodically sat in what was known as "motion part." At the end of a day of argument, there would be a stack several feet high of motions to be decided. The judge suggested that we each take some motion papers home to work on overnight. The next morning, I had notes on one motion while the judge had handwritten opinions deciding ten motions. After that, I learned to be more efficient. For example, most summary judgment motions could be denied on the ground that there were genuine issues of fact. The judge had one Second Circuit decision that he always cited to support that legal conclusion.

The judge and I worked six days a week. On Saturdays, we went to lunch with Judge Weinfeld and Judge McGohey together with Weinfeld's clerk and Weinfeld's son-in-law who clerked for Judge Palmieri. Our fare was modest; we lunched at the Automat restaurant near City Hall. There were no waiters at the Automat—you put a quarter or two in a slot and out came your sandwich or slice of pie.

Judge Dimock was known as a kind judge when it came to sentencing. For example, many cases involved petty crimes such as theft from a mailbox by young heroin addicts. Judge Dimock would typically give them probation or light sentences. But to the surprise of some defense lawyers who tried to steer their cases to him, Judge Dimock was tough on white-collar crime. I recall one long trial of a physician convicted of tax evasion. The stacks of paper recording stock transactions were overwhelming and seemingly beyond the ken of a physician. Yet, Judge Dimock imposed a sentence of five years in prison. The law required a mandatory minimum of five years imprisonment for narcotics offenses— possession or sale; the judges had no discretion. The judges complained that, for example, a musician in possession of a marijuana cigarette was sentenced to five years in prison. At our Saturday luncheons, the judges expressed concern about the number of cases involving the drug heroin, including prosecutions for possession and sale as well as petty crimes committed by addicts. Judge McGohey opined that the addiction was similar to his own addiction to cigarettes, and difficult to overcome. Back then, the judges, who sentenced offenders who were guilty of the possession or sale of illegal drugs, were discussing decriminalization of drug possession, which recently has been adopted by Oregon and Washington.

As a law clerk, I worked on cases involving admiralty, trademarks, copyrights and patents, none of which I studied in law school. We had a trial regarding a trademark dispute between the owners of the Dunlop Tobacco shop and Dunlop clothing. Several trials involved musical copyrights including a dispute as to the rights to the Pepsi-Cola jingle touting that it hits the spot.

I learned a lesson that I put to use later in private practice—that a litigator could master a subject sufficiently to argue in court without having studied the subject in law school. If a judge could understand a case without previous knowledge of the legal specialty, so could a practicing lawyer, who typically would have more time than the judge to devote to studying the law. Another lesson learned was the need to provide judges with the law and the facts in a way that was easily accessible. At the end of one legal argument, a lawyer handed Judge Dimock a list of cases with citations. When we got back to chambers, the judge threw the paper in the trash. He said that if a lawyer wants a judge to consider a reported case, he would need to file a brief that spells out what the case held and why it is relevant. When confronted with a citation to a case without further explanation, judges could not be expected to figure out for themselves why a case was pertinent to the issues before the court.

District judges are sometimes asked to sit "by designation" as appellate court judges. When Judge Dimock was designated to sit on the Second Circuit, I gained insights into the appellate process. After argument, the three judges on the court would huddle to critique the arguments and give their tentative decisions. On one occasion, they opined that a well-known appellate lawyer and partner in a leading Wall Street law firm, who was in his seventies, had lost a step in his advocacy skills. I recalled that when I retired in my seventies. In another case, a railroad worker had sued claiming injury from the lack of toilet facilities at the workplace. As a result, after he had used the facility on a train, which had been idled in the station, he headed to the exit. The train pulled into the station, and boarding passengers, who did not expect anyone to be exiting the train, knocked him down and injured him. His attorney cited an earlier decision in which the court allowed a claim by a railroad worker who, while using the facility on an idled train, was injured by a flying object when the train suddenly started. Chief Judge Lumbard recommended ruling against the plaintiff in the case before the court on which Judge Dimock sat, because in the prior case the plaintiff was "on the pot," and in the current case he was "off the pot." Even the awesome Second Circuit was not averse to some humor

The Disappearance of Flight 2501

Judge Dimock allowed his clerks to observe court proceedings so long as we were willing to work nights to complete research and memo writing assignments. Observing court proceedings was useful in putting our work in context. A trial that stands out in my mind was a lawsuit by the estates of four individuals who were among fifty-eight passengers who perished in a Northwest Airlines crash in Lake Michigan.

Northwest Airlines Flight 2501 was scheduled to fly from LaGuardia Airport in New York City to Seattle with a stop at Minneapolis. According to the Federal Aviation Agency (FAA) Accident Investigation Report, weather forecasts before takeoff indicated moderate to severe turbulence in thunderstorms. Well before the crash but after the flight had left Flight Control, a revised forecast predicted widespread thunderstorm activity with a squall line at the time of the accident. Air Route Traffic Control (ARTC) did not warn flights of the squall line. That night, three flights that took off from Detroit returned due to turbulence from the storm. During the flight, ARTC refused requests to fly at a lower altitude due to other air traffic. At 5:30 a.m. CST, the aircraft was declared missing. What followed was an extensive search by the Air Force, Navy, Coast Guard and state police. But apart from floating fragments, the aircraft was never found.

Presumably, most of the estates of the deceased passengers settled with Northwest. But suits were filed on behalf of three passengers who had wealth and apparently desired a greater recovery than the airline was offering. Unfortunately, none of the plaintiffs' attorneys were specialists in airline negligence. One lawyer was the estates lawyer for his client; another was an automobile negligence attorney who analogized the flight into a thunderstorm as going through a red light. Northwest's lawyer was an experienced airplane accident lawyer nicknamed "Eyebrows Riley" for his bushy red eyebrows. He was a large man who was bombastic in his delivery. His presence dominated the courtroom. One of Mr. Riley's tricks was to speak *sotto voce* to the jury out of the hearing of the judge and plaintiffs' lawyers. Later on, as an Assistant U.S. Attorney trying criminal cases, when defense counsel used the same tactic, I learned how frustrating that could be.

A prospective juror, who had a pilot's license, had not been challenged during jury selection. Plaintiffs' lawyers argued that the airline was negligent in allowing a plane that had no radar to fly in a thunderstorm with squall lines. In his summation, Riley addressed the pilot on the jury. With dramatic gestures, he urged the pilot to tell the other jurors that radar was not essential because a pilot could see the storm clouds out of his window and steer around them. The jury rendered a verdict for Northwest. The judge and I were sympathetic to the plaintiffs. I was tasked to research the motion to set aside the verdict. While plaintiffs did not argue the point, the judge and I were skeptical of the propriety of Riley addressing the pilot on the jury. I found a case where a judge set aside the jury verdict on the ground that the defendant's lawyer urged a nurse on the jury to use her expertise to inform the other jurors. This violated the right to cross-examine expert witnesses and was my early contribution to a cause for justice. On this basis, Judge Dimock set aside the verdict. I learned that the case was retried before another judge and jury, and Riley won again.

Learning to "Play Judge"

Toward the end of the clerkship, Judge Dimock took a summer vacation at his home in Sullivan County. By that time, I was sufficiently experienced to draft opinions rather than just memoranda. I drafted two opinions. One dealt with an issue in admiralty law. The admiralty case related to the law of triage, that is, how to divide liability for losses when a ship is sunk or damaged. There was a 1926 U.S. Supreme Court decision in point. But the case law in England had developed a different solution over subsequent years. I opted to apply the British rule. When he returned from vacation, Judge Dimock rewrote the decision so as to follow the old Supreme Court rule. On appeal, the Second Circuit reversed and applied the British rule.

The second case involved a challenge to the development of Lincoln Center, a series of buildings in New York City, which included the Metropolitan Opera House and a concert hall for the Philharmonic. Plaintiffs argued that government funding of the center violated the First Amendment's prohibition on establishment of religion because Fordham University, a Catholic institution, was being subsidized as a part of the complex. The plaintiffs had argued and lost that argument in New York State court. I wrote a decision analyzing the law of issue preclusion, or as it is commonly called, *res judicata.* Applying this principle in the opinion I drafted, plaintiffs were barred from asserting the claim in federal court that they had lost in state court. Plaintiffs argued that they were not barred because the issue involved the federal constitution. I rejected plaintiff's contention that a state court could not render a decision on a federal constitutional issue that would bind a federal court. This time, Judge Dimock endorsed my draft. The court of appeals affirmed, and Chief Judge Clark, a Yale Law School professor and author of *Corbin on Contracts,* complimented the district court's decision as being "well-reasoned."

After the clerkship ended, the judge's former law clerks took turns making an annual dinner party for all the clerks and Judge and Mrs.

Dimock. The judge gave us a martini shaker for our dinner party. The Dimock clerks were an impressive group, which speaks to the Judge's perspicacity in selecting us. Bob Ehrenbard, the first clerk, was a litigating partner in the Kelley, Drye law firm and became a companion to Miriam Cedarbaum, a later clerk, after their spouses had passed. Miriam became a federal judge in the Southern District of New York., fulfilling her dream to follow in Judge Dimock's footsteps. George Zeidenstein, the second clerk, devoted his career to public service, having been Peace Corp director in Nepal, Ford Foundation representative and President of the Population council. Gerry Walpin served with me as an Assistant U.S Attorney, was a partner in the Rosenman firm and was appointed an Inspector General in Bush administration. He went so far as to name his son after the judge and called him by the judge's nickname, Ned. The last reunion was held at the judge's home in Sullivan County, New York. At that time, he was in a wheelchair and it was sad to see him in his aged state. He died at the age of ninety-six.

◆   ◆   ◆

Chapter VI
U.S. DEPARTMENT OF JUSTICE

A Career Crossroad

As my clerkship was coming to an end, I turned to the next step in my legal career. Judge Dimock told a story, which may have been apocryphal, of an applicant for a legal position at his old law firm. The applicant had good grades from a good law school, was the son of an important client and presented well. After positive interviews by most of the partners, he saw the head of the firm. Then, the other partners asked if he had been given an offer. The answer was no—because he was not wearing a hat. "Hat" referred to a fedora. I had one of those hats when I was in law school, but after my experience interviewing for a summer job, I was not anxious to get into that scene.

On the advice of Judge Dimock, I rejected an offer from a firm specializing in corporate transactions, Berlack, Israels (which years later retained me to try a case involving the Three Mile Island nuclear plant accident). The offer was for $7,500 a year, which was more than the going rate for new lawyers. Parenthetically, that amount adjusted for inflation would be worth today about $55,000, which is the lowest salary that most any NYC firm pays. Large firms today are paying $160,000 and more for graduating lawyers. The judge advised me that if I found that offer attractive, I should consider a career in investment banking where I would earn more money and not work as hard. But if I wanted to be a "real lawyer," I should become a trial lawyer. He suggested that I train in a prosecutor's or public defender office to develop the necessary litigation skills. I took his advice.

During my clerkship, I observed young prosecutors trying criminal jury cases. This seemed exciting and good training for trial practice. The huge courtrooms were poorly heated so the Assistant U.S. Attorneys (AUSAs) wore three-piece suits with vests. They strutted about the courtroom with confidence. This seemed like an important and challenging place for a young lawyer. I asked Judge Dimock if he could get me into the U.S. Attorneys' Office for the Southern District of New York. He replied that it was political; we had a Republican president, Eisenhower, and the judge was a Democrat. I did not know then that my dream of becoming an AUSA would be fulfilled in a year.

Judge Dimock was sitting on a three-judge court together with District Judge Lawrence E. Walsh and Circuit Judge Hincks. A three-judge court can be convened under special circumstances, particularly when there are constitutional issues. This case involved the Alleghany Corporation, which was in the process of acquiring the New York Central Railroad System. The court's earlier opinion was written by Judge Dimock and joined by Judge Walsh, with Circuit Judge Hincks dissenting. The Supreme Court reversed. A second opinion was written by Circuit Judge Frank, a professor at Yale Law School, and joined by Dimock and Walsh. The Supreme Court again reversed and remanded for consideration of whether the transactions complied with the Interstate Commerce Act which regulated railroads. I worked with Judge Walsh who wrote a third opinion remanding the case to the Interstate Commerce Commission to consider whether the transaction was in the public interest. To support his opinion, Judge Walsh dispatched his law clerk, Myra Shubin (wife of Milton Shubin, later to be my law partner at Kaye Scholer,) and me to travel to Washington to find regulatory opinions in the Interstate Commerce Commission library in support of his views. Judge Walsh was not one to take a Supreme Court reversal lightly. When we reported that we could find no railroad cases in point, he directed us to find trucking cases that could be cited by analogy. Judge Walsh's opinion also was reversed by the Supreme Court. In his memoir, Judge Walsh ascribed the Supreme Court's reversal to inadequate legal representation by the party that was favored by Judge Walsh's ruling. Bad lawyering can result in bad law.

Office of the Deputy Attorney General

Judge Walsh offered me a position on his staff at the U.S. Department of Justice, where he had just been appointed to be Deputy Attorney General. I jumped at Judge Walsh's offer as it postponed going to a law firm and enabled me to continue government service. As occurred at future stages of my career, I just happened to be in the right place at the right time, and took advantage of an opportunity that fate presented. A career, like life, cannot always be carefully planned, and happenstance often presents a happier result.

I moved to Washington. D.C., where I rented an apartment on the sixteenth floor in the Arlington (Virginia) Towers, overlooking the Iwo Jima memorial. The apartment was in the flight path of airplanes taking off from National Airport. The lights shined into my apartment as the planes lifted off and just missed entering my room. One evening, Fran's brother, Dr. Jay Morganstern, stayed with me as he attended a dental convention in D.C. When the first plane approached, he jumped under the bed.

I worked with a law school classmate, Victor Friedman, who was to have been Walsh's law clerk but had to serve in the army reserves. Miriam Goldman Cedarbaum, who later became a federal judge in the Southern District of New York, was the third officemate. Miriam had been a law clerk for Judge Dimock several years before me. During the week, Judge Walsh was often on the road for speaking engagements. We had to work weekends preparing his speeches. Before he left, we would remind him to take the speech we had written. He would simply tap his head and say it was all there.

Our immediate supervisor was Assistant Deputy AG Leon Silverman, a litigation partner at Fried, Frank, a large New York law firm which had given me an offer. Leon was designated by Judge Walsh to oversee all of the Justice Department's litigation. Judge Walsh had an affinity for relying on his personal staff rather than the permanent government lawyers. As a result, when case files were sent up from the divisions for review, we started from scratch. This provided broad experience on matters relating to civil, criminal, antitrust, and civil rights litigation.

As a break from our legal work, there was a poker game at what was then the Woodner Hotel (ironically the hotel was built by Ian Woodner whom I would later prosecute for tax evasion). Hayden Crawford was part of the Deputy AG's group and supervised the U. S. Attorneys around the country. He claimed that he knew nothing about poker and had to keep a piece of paper with the order of the suits. Yet, he won every week. I also played on the Department of Justice tennis team in the late afternoons. As we lacked sufficient players, we partnered with the Internal Revenue Service. The Weather Bureau was the champ of the intergovernmental tennis league.

Little Rock School Desegregation

The court order in 1957 to integrate a high school in Little Rock, Arkansas, was a historic event. Before I arrived in D.C., Governor Orval Faubus encouraged protesters who physically threatened the young black students. He called out the Arkansas National Guard ostensibly to prevent violence, but actually to prevent the students from entering the school. President

Eisenhower nationalized the guard and instead sent in the 101st Airborne Division to protect the students.

In 1958, there was further litigation over the desegregation order in Little Rock. Faubus closed the schools for a time. When I arrived at the Justice Department, the Deputy Attorney General's office was gearing up for what became Little Rock II.

Judge Lawrence E. Walsh, Deputy Attorney General, U.S Dept. of Justice

In September, 1958, shortly after I arrived in D.C., the Supreme Court, in *Cooper* v. *Aaron*, rejected the Little Rock's school board's request to delay integration of the high school. In a case that had been argued by Thurgood Marshall, the Court reasoned that "The constitutional rights of respondents are not to be sacrificed or yielded to the violence and disorder which have followed upon the actions of the Governor and Legislature."

President Eisenhower told Attorney General Rogers that he intended to withdraw military forces, which had been involved earlier in enforcing the desegregation order. Our office was command central for fast moving and dangerous events. Walsh, Silverman, Cedarbaum, Friedman and I regularly met to strategize the alternatives. Judge Walsh, who was adept at thinking outside the box, came up with the idea of asking a federal court to impose a million dollar a day fine on the state for every day in which the governor interfered with integration. We concluded that this was too radical an approach.

Without the troops that the president had withdrawn, and considering Faubus' control over the Arkansas National Guard, there was a problem as to how to protect the children and get them safely into school. The U.S. Marshal suggested a solution. We learned that the U.S. Marshal had relatives and friends in the Ozarks where desegregation was not such a controversial issue. If they could be deputized, and thus able to carry weapons and wear badges, they could protect the children. This was not the official duty of U.S. Marshals, which was to protect the federal courthouses and those in them. Nevertheless, with the approval of Attorney General Rogers, fifty men were trained and deputized as marshals to safely enforce the Little Rock school desegregation order. During the crisis, we monitored the tense situation in which the children approached the school, and, under the protection of the U.S. Marshals, safely gained entrance.

Subsequently, Judge Walsh extended the training of U.S. Marshals to enforce desegregation orders in other parts of the country. Today, there is a question as to the desirability as well the legality of using federal officers to keep the peace at the state level. Recently, employees of the Immigration Service and the Homeland Security Department were brought to Washington, D.C. to put down peaceful demonstrations that protested police misconduct. Images on television news showed men in unmarked uniforms putting protesters into unmarked vans to be taken for arrest. The tactic inflamed the protestors and was criticized as violating the protesters' First Amendment right to peaceful assembly. We applauded President Eisenhower's deployment in 1957 of U.S. Army troops, and our Little Rock team's deployment in 1958 of specially deputized U.S. Marshals, to facilitate compliance with the desegregation order. But, at Little Rock, the governor was himself violating the law and could not be depended on to keep the peace. Moreover, the U.S. Marshals were enforcing a federal court order. On January 6, 2021, a delay in calling the National Guard allowed extremists to invade the capitol and almost succeed in interfering with certification of the Presidential election. However, a countervailing concern was that premature deployment might have enabled the President to enlist the military to further the insurrection. Yet, National Guard troops were needed to protect the inauguration of President Biden. In the end, we must look to history, which teaches that whether the military is to be used for protection or insurrection is dependent on whether the electorate chooses an Eisenhower or a Faubus as commander in chief.

Voting and Other Civil Rights

Our Little Rock experience sparked the need for federal legislation to protect children in these situations as well as to proscribe other deprivations of civil rights, particularly in regard to voting. Leon Silverman was in touch with Roy Wilkins, the head of the NAACP, who was advocating additional civil rights legislation. We were tasked with drafting a new civil rights bill. Although I had many duties, my title was "legislative attorney." Miriam Cedarbaum was the senior attorney of the three of us, and was tough on the drafts that Vic Friedman and I prepared. The three of us prepared a draft bill, and submitted it to Leon Silverman and Judge Walsh.

In order to properly draft a civil rights bill, we looked to the past to study the history of civil rights legislation. And we considered current events and circumstances to focus on the protections that were needed. To put our bill in context, it was the second civil rights act since a series of such laws that had been enacted during the Reconstruction era beginning in 1866. The first of such laws provided for rights of citizenship but, according to the legislative history, was not intended to affect voting rights, which were believed to be the province of the states. Subsequent acts required states, which had seceded, to provide for male voting rights as a condition of reinstatement to the Union. The Fifteenth Amendment, adopted in 1870, provided that the right to vote shall not be abridged "by reason of race, color, or previous condition of servitude."

The pronouncement of the Fifteenth Amendment was insufficient to ensure voting rights. Nor was the U.S. Supreme Court of help. In *Giles*

v. *Harris*, decided in 1903, suit was filed on behalf of more than five thousand African Americans, citizens of the county of Montgomery, Alabama, to require that all qualified members of the plaintiff's race be entered on the voting rolls, from which they had been excluded. The eminent jurist, Justice Oliver Wendell Holmes, who was famous for pronouncing that "hard cases make bad law," wrote the majority opinion, which rejected the application for relief. While Justice Holmes recognized that the complaint "imports that the great mass of the White population intends to keep the blacks from voting," he found the courts to be impotent in addressing what he recognized as a "great political wrong." Technically, the court concluded that equity does not address political wrongs. From a practical point of view, Justice Holmes opined that merely ordering the plaintiff's name on the voting rolls would not solve the problem. Rather, the Court decided that only the legislature and political department of government could right the wrong. Justices Harlan, Brewer and Brown dissented on the ground that the plaintiff was entitled to relief from the court "in respect of his right to be registered as a voter."

This decision was a severe blow to the enforcement of voting rights. As a result, for years thereafter, Jim Crow obstacles continued to be successfully placed in the way of Black peoples' ability to vote. Yet, from the point of view of our drafting effort, the decision demonstrated how essential it was to incorporate relief from voting obstacles in federal legislation, as Justice Holmes suggested.

After legislation during the Reconstruction era, following the end of the Civil War, there were no further civil rights laws until President Eisenhower signed the Civil Rights Act of 1957. That act created the position of Assistant Attorney General for Civil Rights, which led to establishment of the Civil Rights Division of the Justice Department. A U.S. Civil Rights Commission was authorized to investigate allegations of voter infringement. The Commission consisted of six members appointed by the President. It was to be bipartisan with no more than three members from one political party. The Commission was authorized to call witnesses, conduct hearings and issue a report. Unfortunately, the Act provided that the Commission shall "cease to exist" sixty days after the submission of its report. The bill also authorized the Attorney General to seek injunctive relief against anyone who interfered with the right to vote. Contempt proceedings could be filed against anyone who violated the court order but punishment was limited to a $1,000 fine and six months imprisonment. The bill, as originally proposed, had stronger provisions that were eliminated under pressure from southern Democrats including a lengthy filibuster by Senator Strom Thurmond of South Carolina. Thus, for example, the 1957 Act did not ban literacy tests, which were prevalent in some southern states as a requirement for voting. It is a reflection of our society that today, the threat of filibuster is impeding enactment of a voting rights bill. After eighty-seven years of inaction in the face of denials of voting rights for minorities, the 1957 act was groundbreaking. But clearly further legislation was needed to ensure voting rights and well as to effectuate the Supreme Court's desegregation decision.

At the time we drafted our bill, President Eisenhower was surrounded by a number of Southern politicians as advisors. A problem was to get the president to support the bill we drafted. That was the task of the Attorney General, William Rogers. Walsh also had good relations with Senator Eastland of Mississippi who headed the Judiciary Committee. He told us that Eastland regarded Rogers as "slick as a shithouse rat." Rogers, who had been a name partner in a prestigious New York law firm, was a skillful politician as well as an honorable Attorney General. He was known to always have a clean desk, which enabled him to concentrate on policy issues.

Rogers waited until the president's southern advisors were away. He then made a personal trip to the White House during which he gained the president's support for our bill. Despite opposition by the bloc of Southern Democrats, the bill was passed by Congress with some amendments. No Republicans voted against the bill. The contrast between the alignment of the two major political parties on voting rights today and in 1960 is striking. At that time, the parties were motivated by their racial attitudes. Today, the Republican Party is admittedly fearful of losing elections where minority voting in enabled. The Act was signed by the president on May 6, 1960.

To remedy the problems at Little Rock, the Act provided for criminal penalties for obstruction of court orders. To avoid the need for criminal prosecution and lengthy jury trials, the Act provided a remedy of injunction for interference with desegregation orders. The bill enabled district judges to appoint Special Masters to engage in factfinding for desegregation orders. While drafting the bill, we followed civil rights news that might be relevant. We subscribed to publications by the Student Non-violent Coordinating Committee (SNCC), which sponsored student actions to secure voting rights and other civil rights activity. Often the students were subject to violent attacks including murder. There were bombings of Black churches and fires set by the Ku Klux Klan. In 1957, Montgomery, Alabama, was the scene of a bus boycott and the attendant violence. The bombings were not within the scope of federal jurisdiction but were only a state crime. To address these concerns on a federal level, the Act, which we had drafted, outlawed fleeing a state to avoid prosecution for damaging or destroying property, illegal use of explosives and threats to use fire and explosives.

J. Edgar Hoover, the longtime head of the FBI, was not happy with this provision, as he expressed the view that the FBI's mandate was to catch criminals like the Mafia and not get involved in civil rights disputes. Walsh had good relations with Hoover and convinced him not to oppose this provision. There was no separate FBI building then. The FBI shared space in the Justice Department building.

Hoover's private elevator to his office was a sign of his power within the Department.

Most significant in regard to plugging the gaps in the 1957 Act, the bill we drafted had a provision that those given the right to vote shall not be deprived of that right on account of race or color. Those who engaged in acts to deprive that right could be held in contempt of court. The courts were given authority to appoint voting referees to report on infringement. The referees also could help African Americans to register and vote. "Vote" was defined to include registration, casting a ballot and having the ballot counted. Another section of the Act provided criminal penalties for failure to preserve voting records including records of poll taxes. Voting records in federal elections had to be preserved for twenty-two months. Anyone tampering with the records was subject to a fine and imprisonment. Recently, the Attorney General sent a letter warning so-called auditors in Arizona, who were not qualified for the job, that they might be violating federal law; but no legal action has as yet been filed.

Finally, the Act empowered the Civil Rights Commission to examine witnesses under oath. The Civil Rights Commission has had a checkered history relating to the makeup of the commissioners who were appointed by presidents whose support for civil rights enforcement varied. Its role has been limited to investigating and reporting without enforcement powers. In 2018, the Commission issued unanimous findings and recommendations that found undue restrictions on minority voting rights from strict id laws, closing polling places, cutting early voting and purging voter rolls. But Congress did not respond to the Commission's urging to enact legislation which would be more effective than individual lawsuits. Later, during the last administration, the Commission prepared another report detailing violations of voting rights but the Republican commissioners hand-picked by the president blocked its release.

At the time, the 1960 Act was controversial, but its enactment led to an increasing concern over the preservation and enforcement of voting rights, which led to additional legislation in 1964 and 1965. While I was not involved in subsequent civil rights legislation and court decisions, I am constrained to comment on what has followed from what I participated in beginning. In his address to Congress near the end of his presidency, Eisenhower proposed civil rights goals. Several of those goals were achieved by the 1960 law. At the time our bill was submitted to Congress in 1960, then Senator Lyndon Johnson had his own bill, which we concluded had too many holes. But after he became President, Johnson was responsible for the Civil Rights Acts of 1964 and 1965, which had a tremendous impact. These Acts banned poll taxes, literacy tests and other devices to inhibit voting. Also included was a provision extending the ban on voting rights discrimination based on national origin.

A key provision of the 1965 Act required that states, which were designated because of a history of voting discrimination, had to preclear with federal authorities any changes in their voting laws. In 2013, in an opinion authored by Chief Justice Roberts, *Shelby County v. Holder*, the Supreme Court held that this provision was based on data that was out of date, and was unconstitutional. When Congress renewed the Act in 2006, it rejected suggestions to update the states that would be subject to the preclearance provisions. As a result, the Supreme Court held that Congress needed to revisit the issue. In the meantime, preclearance was held to be unconstitutional. Justice Ginsburg dissented analogizing the decision to saying that when out in the rain you should put down your umbrella because you had been dry. Justice Ginsburg's dissenting opinion was prescient in expressing concern with "backsliding" when the preclearance procedures were eliminated by the Court's opinion.

In *Shelby*, Chief Justice Roberts wrote, "Section 2 forbids any "standard, practice, or procedure" that "results in a denial or abridgement of the right of any citizen of the United States to vote on account of race or color, and that "injunctive relief is available in appropriate cases to block voting laws from going into effect." Section 2 was at issue in *Brnovich v. Democratic National Committee*, a case decided along party lines by the Supreme Court on the last day of the 2021 term. If you thought that *Giles* and *Shelby* undermined voting rights, this recent decision, written by Justice Alito, outdoes them both by what the dissenting opinion characterized as "eviscerating" what remains of the 1965 Voting Rights Act. In a concurring opinion in *Shelby*, Justice Thomas took the position that the entire 1965 Voting Rights Act was unconstitutional. While Justice Alito did not go that far, the wide berth he gives to allowing voting restrictions imperils pending lawsuits challenging state laws and could be the basis for a challenge to any new federal voting rights law. Several major corporations have announced their opposition to the new restrictive state laws, which state legislatures have ignored. In 2006, an impetus for the renewal of the 1965 Act was the support of corporations, including one of my former clients, Pfizer and its Chairman, Henry McKinnell. Similar actions by corporate America today could impact the chance of enacting the new federal voting rights legislation; but there is no sign of any such widespread support. To the contrary, major corporations, whose names are publicly available, have contributed millions—directly and through PACs—to the six senators and 147 Congress persons who voted to reject certification of the results of the election of President Biden.

Recent efforts to "stop the count," by the past president and his supporters to set aside the election results include his attempts to influence the Justice Department to undermine the Georgia election results, and efforts to induce the Georgia Secretary of State to find votes that did not exist. These actions appear to warrant investigations into whether the perpetrators violated federal laws including the civil rights acts that are described earlier, as well as election laws. For example, the

Federal Election Campaign Act of 1971, which supersedes state laws, contains provisions that protect the integrity of the political process.

McCarthy

My time at the Justice department was during the era of Senator Joseph McCarthy, a Republican from Wisconsin, who was obsessed with rooting out Communists, or those he suspected of being Communists, from the government. President Eisenhower was criticized for having been an enabler for not having taken down McCarthy before he destroyed so many lives and careers. Other commentators have praised the president's decision, made in light of Republican senatorial support for McCarthy, to operate behind the scenes in ways that eventually resulted in McCarthy's political demise.

We were assigned to review files at the Defense Department of employees who had been identified as potential Communists. For this, we had to get a high security clearance. My parents' neighbor expressed concern that I was in trouble because the FBI was making inquiries as part of my security clearance. While we had to do our assigned jobs, we did our best to be reasonable in the degrees of separation that warranted singling out anyone as a Communist sympathizer. Thus, for example, we concluded that an employee should not be tarred as a Communist sympathizer merely because his uncle had been identified as a Communist.

D.H. Lawrence

The Post Office wanted to ban the importation and mailing of the classic novel, *Lady Chatterley's Lover* by D.H. Lawrence, as being pornographic. I purchased and read the book. I brought it into Judge Walsh's office and suggested that he read it before taking a position of the Postal Service's ban. His response was that he did not want to read that "trash." Thereafter, a district judge ruled against the government and allowed the book to be imported and mailed. Judge Walsh persuaded President Eisenhower to allow the Justice Department to refrain from appealing the decision. I assume that Judge Walsh ultimately read the book, or at least the court's opinion.

Puerto Rico and Alaska

I was assigned to work with the Office of Legal Counsel in the Justice Department to assess the status of Puerto Rico as a Commonwealth. Apart from Puerto Rico, the status of other American entities was independent, statehood, or territory. A question arose as to whether Congress could change the status of Puerto Rico even though previous legislation designated it as a Commonwealth. Supreme Court Justice Frankfurter, when he was a Harvard Law professor, wrote an article concluding that the initial status bestowed by Congress could not be changed. I differed. After I left the Justice Department, the office of Legal Counsel called me back to provide further advice on this issue. Commonwealth status remains an issue to this day. In light of the prior administration's recent failure to provide sufficient aid to Puerto Rico after devastating hurricanes, statehood is being seriously advocated.

We were involved in issues relating to Alaska statehood. John Sheneman, a New York admiralty lawyer, was designated by Walsh as Assistant Deputy Attorney General for Congressional liaison. He was sent to Alaska to deal with statehood issues. Upon his return he complained that it was so cold you had to leave your car engine running whenever you stopped at a store, which resulted in numerous auto thefts. We were tasked with the selection of a federal district judge to replace the three territorial judges. Being a lawyer was not a prerequisite for territorial judges, and two of the three candidates were not lawyers. There was a bitter fight among the three territorial judges, which included accusations of sexual misconduct against one of them. We were bombarded with photographs of a candidate with his paramour. Ultimately, we recommended that the new federal district judgeship should go to the only one of the three territorial judges who was a lawyer.

Judicial Appointments and Pardons

One of our jobs was to vet potential federal judicial appointments, which the Attorney General would recommend to President Eisenhower for nomination to the Senate. Since the dawn of civilization, a just system must include fair and honest judges. That means judges who will listen to both sides of an issue with an open mind, and not be bound by preconceived ideology. Our instructions were to read all that the candidate had written in order to assess intelligence and reasoning ability. The Deputy Attorney General also relied on the assessments of the American Bar Association standing committee, whose members were from every circuit. No judges were recommended who were rated as "unqualified." Most were rated "well qualified" or "exceptionally well qualified." This is in contrast with the experience of the past four years when an "unqualified" rating could be superseded by the candidate's preconceived philosophy. Unfortunately, newly elected President Biden announced that he would not be guided by the ABA rankings apparently because of the resulting delays. We were not asked to consider political leanings, or opine on how the future judge would decide particular issues that might come before the courts. In other words, we were looking for judges who would not only hear, but also listen.

The Deputy AG made recommendations to the president on pardons of those convicted of federal crimes. We reviewed the files and made recommendations based on the merits, irrespective of any political influence or the wealth of the person. Pardons were not recommended based on friendly or political contacts with the president. Pardons were handled as a regular routine after study and recommendation. The president granted pardons that passed through the regular Department procedure, which was a review by my two officemates and me. Typically, Eisenhower issued pardons at Christmas time, often of those who had already served their time, and in some instances, to reduce a death penalty to a life sentence. He began the practice of issuing pardons in a batch and leaving it to the

Deputy Attorney General to sign the individual warrants. Our practice was in sharp contrast to the recent administration's grant of pardons based on the president's desire to help his friends and contributors. While our pardon process was honest, it was not the best system. We were only recently graduated from law school. We had no experience or training on the subject. And we had other responsibilities that took up our time. Recently, a better system has been proposed. A bipartisan board could be appointed consisting of persons with knowledge of records of prison time, rehabilitation, and reentry into society. This board would not only bring expertise to bear on who should be pardoned and what sentences should be commuted, but also it would have the time and resources to deal with the many thousands of prisoners who deserve consideration.

◆　◆　◆

Chapter VII
THE U. S. ATTORNEY'S OFFICE FOR THE SOUTHERN DISTRICT OF NEW YORK

After a year in the Justice Department, Fran and I were married and decided to live in New York City, where Fran was employed at Young & Rubicam. At first, and perhaps jokingly, Judge Walsh said he did not give me permission to get married and move in the midst of a Congressional session. Nevertheless, at my request, he recommended me to the U.S. Attorneys' Office in the Southern District of New York where I became an Assistant U.S. Attorney in the criminal division. My salary at the Justice Department, of $5,500 annually, was reduced to $4,500 when I moved to the Southern District. Fortunately, Fran's higher salary at Young & Rubicam sustained us. We ate many meals at our parents' homes. We had no car and no TV, but we were happy and enjoying our work.

Trial by Fire—the Education of a Prosecutor

The experience to become a prosecutor with minimal supervision was trial by fire. The Executive Assistant of the U.S. Attorney's office was Jerome Londin, who reviewed our trial prep notebooks. He taught me the ins and outs of trial practice, including, for example, how to introduce a business record in evidence: Ask:

"Was this document made in the regular course of business?"

"Was it the regular course of business to make and keep such documents?"

We prepared trial notebooks in which we wrote the expected answers to questions. But we did not write the questions because that might be seen as a transcript of prior questions and answers that would have to be produced to defense counsel. We had to extemporize in framing questions based on the answers we had written. That was good training because at trial there are always instances where you have to deviate from the script and frame questions on the spot.

U. S. Attorneys' Office Under S. Hazard Gillespie. I am 7 in from the right in the 3rd row.

Judge Thomas Murphy was a giant of a man with a handlebar mustache. He was known to have been a tough New York City police commissioner. I first appeared before him to report on a guilty plea agreement. Criminal defendants have a right to have a grand jury vote to indict for a felony. But where a guilty plea was negotiated, the defendant usually waived indictment so the government would just file charges in a document that was known as an "Information." In my first court appearance, I announced, "The government wishes to proceed by way of waiver of indictment and information." Judge Murphy responded sardonically that if the government waived both information and indictment there would be no basis for a criminal charge. I apologized for my ambiguous request and rephrased, "The government would like to proceed by way of information and waiver of indictment."

Immigration cases were assigned to the new Assistants. In one case, the defendant, who illegally entered the U.S. from Jamaica, claimed he was a U.S. citizen from the territory of Virgin Islands. On cross-examination, I asked him if he knew Charlotte Amalie, which I recalled from our honeymoon there was the capital city of St. Thomas, VI. He said he did not know her. This was some evidence of guilt. A problem was that the immigration officer had misstated the defendant's height on the record. In order to identify him as the same person who had previously been deported, I retained a fingerprint expert who submitted a report which found that the defendant's fingerprints matched those of the person previously deported. After admonishing me for not calling the expert as a live witness, the judge accepted the report in evidence and convicted the defendant.

The immigration defendants typically were sentenced to probation on condition that they not attempt to reenter the country illegally. In another case, after a trial and conviction, the judge imposed a sentence of five years' probation. The defendant asked the court: "How can I get five years' probation on a two-year max?" that is, a maximum jail time of two years for the offense. Neither I, nor the Legal Aid defense attorney, knew the answer, so the judge reduced the probation time to two years.

During the summer, most judges went on vacation, as there was no air conditioning in the federal courthouse at Foley Square in Manhattan. Judge Murphy and Judge Weinfeld stayed in town to clean up the criminal docket, sometimes requiring us to try cases back-to-back. In a case before Judge Murphy, the defendant was accused of paying workers below the minimum wage. In the grand jury, I had questioned one of the workers. She testified under oath to her illegal low wage. Her boss had apparently threatened or bribed her and she testified at trial, to my surprise, that she was paid a proper wage. I paused to review my notes to impeach her new story with her grand jury testimony. When I looked up, I saw that Judge Murphy had excused the witness and told the jury that the district attorney (which is what he called us) apparently had no further questions. He granted my request to recall the witness. This was a lesson in speeding up my cross-examinations.

In another trial before Judge Murphy, the defendant was charged with selling stolen auto parts across state lines. The case stemmed from an FBI investigation of a ring of employees at a Ford auto plant in Mahwah, New Jersey. Employees, some of whom were ex-convicts, smuggled auto parts out of the plant under their clothing. The company could not search the employees under union rules. The stolen parts were then sold to a fence in New York City. The FBI video taped the movement of the parts from the plant across the river to New York. This evidence induced the perpetrators to plead guilty.

I told the management of the plant that I had just purchased a Ford Falcon, which was one of the first "compact" cars. They said that I should have told them in advance so they could have given me a car built for an employee—that is, where 4 bolts were needed, the workers would often put in one bolt, but for a fellow employee, they would put in six bolts.

In this case, there were two witnesses: an accomplice and the fence, that is, the person who had purchased the stolen parts, and had pleaded guilty. The accomplice was reluctant to testify and I tried to scare him with the prospect of being prosecuted and jailed. He failed to show up the next day for further questioning. I learned that he wrapped his car around a telephone pole on the Southern State Parkway. I wondered if I had scared him too much or he was afraid the defendant would take revenge if he testified. The federal criminal law permits conviction based on the testimony of one witness (unlike the Torah which requires two witnesses). At trial on direct examination, I followed the usual practice of asking the fence to describe his prior convictions. This tactic was to take the steam out of the defense counsel asking the same questions in order to impeach the witness' credibility. Defense counsel then asked the witness if he had pleaded guilty in this case and why he had not so stated in his direct testimony. Judge Murphy immediately called counsel into chambers. I could only say that the witness' guilty plea in this case was clearly a "prior conviction," and I inadvertently neglected to elicit that information on direct examination. Judge Murphy angrily told me, in curse words not appropriate to write here, that if I were not a newcomer he would have had me disbarred. He instructed me in harsh terms never to make that mistake again—another lesson learned in trial by fire before Judge Murphy.

In a case that same summer before Judge Weinfeld, the defendant was accused of participating in the theft of a safe from a post office, which contained valuable bonds. The defendant's role was to lift the two-hundred-pound safe out of a six-foot-high window. When he was arrested by NYC police, he tore the police station apart, throwing desks and chairs. He was committed to a federal mental institution. Upon his release, the psychiatrists noted that he was dangerous. Yet, Judge Weinfeld let him out on bail. I arranged for extra U.S. marshals to attend the trial. After the first day of trial, everyone had left the courtroom except the defendant and me. He was standing over my table and asked whether I had told the marshals to search him. I replied that I did not. I grabbed my papers and ran out of the courtroom. Judge Weinfeld found the defendant guilty and sentenced him to time he had already served and probation on condition that he get further treatment for mental illness. One evening I noticed the defendant following me down Chambers Street after work. I paused to look in a store window and he did the same. Then I ran down the steps to the subway station, and jumped on a train as the doors were closing. I was not bothered thereafter.

Tax Evasion

After a year of short trials, I graduated to more complex cases. Ian Woodner had degrees in architecture and had been involved in the design of the Central Park Zoo and an exhibition at the World's Fair. In the 1940s, he formed a construction company which was known for building the Woodner Hotel in Washington, D.C. After a divorce from his wife, Woodner dated the actress, Magda Gabor. He sent her flowers, which he charged as an expense of his construction company. Other personal expenses for luxury items also were charged to the business. That practice is common among business people but seemingly unnecessary to someone like Woodner who was independently wealthy. I noticed over the years that acquaintances often charged personal expenses, such as automobile lease charges, as business expenses. I would tell them that I used to prosecute such cases criminally.

Woodner had been in a child custody fight with his wife, Ruth, during divorce proceedings. He hired detectives to follow Ruth in an effort to prove infidelity. He charged the cost of the detectives as a corporate business expense disguised as guards on his construction projects. This activity formed the basis of the first count of an indictment for tax evasion. The second count was based on a deal where one of Woodner's corporations negotiated a construction loan for a project near an air force base in Illinois. The interest on the loan was initially 3.5 percent. At Woodner's request, the bank agreed to charge 4 percent and rebate 1/2 percent, in the form of checks to Ed Jasen, an employee and friend of Woodner. Jasen cashed the checks and put the cash at first in a briefcase in Woodner's living room. Later, the funds were put in a safe deposit box to which only Woodner and Jasen had access. Jasen, whom I called "steady Eddie" in my jury summation, was a prime witness. He testified that Woodner commingled the rebates with his personal funds. Woodner failed to report the rebates on his personal tax return.

Two key witnesses were the Special Agent of IRS, who would describe the evidence of criminal intent, and a Revenue Agent, who computed the deficiency in the taxes paid. The evening before he was to testify, the Revenue Agent developed cold feet. He was reluctant to testify in a case that might result in the defendant going to jail. So, we had to work into the night to educate the Special Agent on the tax computations. I have been in few trials that did not develop last-minute hitches.

Defense counsel was Louis Bender, a former college basketball player and Assistant U.S. Attorney, who was one of the two most prominent tax evasion defense lawyers in the Southern District of New York. The other attorney known for defending criminal tax evasion cases was Boris Kostelanitz. His clients were often spared a trial when he presented a physician's diagnosis of a physical illness. Bender was more of a trial lawyer. He used all the tricks in the book including talking *sotto voce* to the jury so that the judge and I could not hear his remarks. He liked to stand behind me and bellow in my ear. I despised him during the trial although we later became friends.

One of the defendant's main witnesses was his marital lawyer, Samuel Gottlieb. He testified that Woodner's wife was threatening to take over the corporations so the detective fees were properly charged to the company. During his direct examination he frequently checked written notes before framing his answers. He must have been nearsighted because he held the notes up close to his thick eyeglasses. On cross-examination, he exhibited the same mannerism. I asked the court to direct the witness to hand over his notes based on the evidentiary rule that opposing counsel is entitled to see whatever a witness uses to refresh his recollection. Bender strenuously objected that the notes contained confidential and privileged attorney-client communications. Judge Palmieri ordered that the notes be handed over to me. I reviewed the notes during a short recess and found that the notes contained admissions that supported conviction. I proceeded with cross-examination in which I framed each question as a statement from the notes with a question mark. There was no way that Mr. Gottlieb could avoid answering accurately and completely.

A challenge was drafting proposed jury instructions that Judge Palmieri would read to the jury. I interacted with the judge and his law clerk, the future Supreme Court Justice Ruth Bader Ginsburg, to clarify the legal standards that the jury had to apply. After a long trial, the jury could not agree. Judge Palmieri declared a mistrial. Interviews of the jurors revealed that they did not understand the complexities of the case and the tax code. In a second trial, for some reason, Bender decided that he could win if he had a blue-ribbon jury of high caliber persons. This jury ended up having some corporate managers.

In those days, there were no computers on which to design visual aids. Fran came up with the idea that she could ask the art department of her employer, Young & Rubicam, to prepare visual aids for the second Woodner trial. The visuals, which Y & R prepared under Fran's supervision, depicted green arrows to show the path of the funds rebated by the bank to Jasen and ultimately to Woodner personally. There were sheets to tear off to make the presentation dramatic. And it worked. In the second trial, the jury came back with a guilty verdict in 15 minutes. As the lawyer in the musical show *Chicago* sang, you need a little "razzle-dazzle." The jury convicted on the second count relating to the rebates. One juror held out on the first count. When asked, she said it was because the defendant was Jewish. Ironically, Woodner's birth name was Israel and he changed it to

Ian, a fact not presented to the jury. He was sentenced to two and a half years in prison. I later heard that he cooperated in an unrelated criminal investigation, and was released earlier.

After I left the office, an appeal was argued by Sheldon Elson who was a good friend, and succeeded me as Chief Appellate Attorney. Woodner's principal argument at trial and on appeal was that the amounts were small in light of the large amounts involved in his construction businesses so he could not have intended to evade taxes. The appellate court rejected this contention in light of the evidence of concealment of the scheme and the way in which the funds were kept and spent. The court of appeals affirmed the conviction, noting "the essential fairness of the long and strenuously contested trial."

A case referred by the IRS involved a furrier who fired his secretary. The disgruntled secretary told the IRS that her boss hid cash that he received from customers under the cushion on his desk chair. That raised suspicion, but was not enough to convict. The IRS agent in charge of the case did a net worth computation. This analysis showed that the taxpayer's net worth increased more than his reported income during the tax year. However, I found that this computation was based on estimates that would be difficult to prove beyond a reasonable doubt at trial. We accepted a plea from the defendant's business entity.

I tried a case in which a restaurant owner named Russos Zobanakis had failed to file tax returns for several years. His accountant presented purportedly retained copies of tax returns, which stated that no payment or refund was due. As a result, there was no check written to or from the IRS to provide evidence that the returns were actually filed. The IRS had no record of the filing. The restaurant owner was a Greek immigrant who spoke broken English and might not have understood what his accountant was doing. As a result, I asked the grand jury to vote to indict the accountant. At trial, the accountant took the stand, which defendants do not often do. On cross-examination, I got him to admit his wrongdoing. In his closing statement, defense counsel appealed to the sympathy of the six-woman jury, arguing passionately that "the poor man" only received ten dollars per month and a turkey sandwich while he was working on the books. The jury voted to acquit. Judge Irving Kaufman presided over this trial. He was the judge who sentenced the Rosenbergs to death for giving the Russians atomic bomb secrets. After the verdict, Judge Kaufman called me to his chambers and chewed me out for not indicting both the restaurant owner and the accountant. He thought that since the jurors were sympathetic to the accountant, they might have convicted the taxpayer. Some weeks later, he called me back to tell me that rough justice was probably done.

Tax evasion indictments were frequently brought and publicized just before April 15, when tax returns were due to be filed. I believe that the publicity of indictments and jail sentences had a positive impact on potential tax evaders and increased tax revenues. Today, the IRS no longer follows that practice because of budget cuts. The Woodner case illustrates the resources needed to investigate potential tax evasion schemes, to marshal the evidence and bring cases to trial and argue appeals. Special Agents must have the investigative skills of FBI agents together with thorough knowledge of tax law. Revenue Agents must be able to compute tax liability absent the evasion, which is more difficult than a straightforward tax computation from an accurate set of records. And these agents must be assigned to work with AUSA's to indict, try, and handle appeals in tax evasion cases in the federal courts. The IRS has said that its lack of resources to enforce the tax laws has led to revenue losses of $1 trillion a year. Substantial budget cuts to the IRS have led to loss of a third of the agency's enforcement staff and a 25 percent reduction in criminal tax prosecutions since 2010. Recent high profile tax prosecutions arose from federal investigations of nontax offenses. President Biden has asked Congress to allocate $80 billion for tax enforcement, which is expected to reap $700 billion in additional revenue. Under the new administration, the Treasury has proposed a substantial budget increase to update its technology and enable the IRS to conduct additional audits. Unfortunately, as I write, Republican legislators have objected to provisions in a bipartisan infrastructure bill that would provide these resources to the IRS. While it is understandable that some legislators would object to tax increases, it is hard to believe that they would try to help donors who are tax cheats. To achieve effective deterrence of tax evasion, the public needs "to be heard" from the government as to its vigorous enforcement and prosecutions.

Pursuing Justice

The Chief of the Criminal Division and later Chief Assistant U.S Attorney was Silvio J. Mollo. He was a career assistant who was rough around the edges, but knew everything about running the office. In honor of his service, the federal building in Manhattan was named after him. When Robert Morgenthau was elected District Attorney of New York County, Sil followed him there. In deciding whether to prosecute, we tried to do justice. I had a referral from the Veterans' Administration to prosecute an elderly woman who got a job in Woolworth's Five and Dime store, which paid more than she was allowed in order to be eligible for payments for her late husband, who had been killed in WWI. I asked Sil Mollo what to do, as I did not want to prosecute. He told me to present the case to the Grand Jury without a recommendation (in contrast to most cases where the Grand Jury mechanically went along with the Assistant's recommendation to indict). The Grand Jury voted not to prosecute and almost recommended indicting me for presenting such a case.

A similar experience involved the annual prosecution of temporary Christmas postal employees who lied on their applications. One young man did not state that he had a record of a felony conviction. He explained that since he pleaded guilty and did not go to jail, he thought it was not a conviction. He also was the sole support of his quadriplegic, diabetic father. Again, I did not prosecute. Another case involved a company that supplied the Veterans' Administration with African coffee mislabeled as Colombian coffee. The defense counsel threatened to have jurors do a taste test. So, I agreed to take a plea from the company.

The Secret Service of the Treasury Department referred a case for prosecution of a defendant who allegedly passed a counterfeit $20 bill at a store in Chinatown, near the courthouse. The only witnesses were the storeowner and his ten-year old son. Before trial, I asked the storeowner how he came to identify the defendant in a lineup. He said that while standing in front of his store, he saw the defendant being escorted to the courthouse by a Secret Service Agent. On cross-examination by me before trial, he said that he was not sure if the man he identified was the man who came into his store, or the man being arrested. I dropped the case.

◆ ◆ ◆

Chapter VIII
CHIEF APPELLATE ATTORNEY

The U.S. Attorney for whom I worked in 1959–60 was S. Hazard Gillespie, a former partner in the law firm of Davis Polk & Wardwell. Eisenhower was president. As the 1960 election approached, John F. Kennedy was running against Richard M. Nixon for president. I was concerned that a Democrat-appointed U.S. Attorney would clean house. After Kennedy was elected, he appointed Robert M. Morgenthau as U.S. Attorney. Morgenthau kept the job throughout Kennedy's and Lyndon Johnson's presidency and then was elected District Attorney of New York City, a position he held until he was eighty nine. To my surprise, Morgenthau appointed me to be Chief Appellate Attorney with supervision over all criminal and civil appeals. At the age of twenty-six, and four years out of law school, I was flabbergasted and delighted. I had a huge office in the courthouse, my own secretary, and a big American flag behind my desk.

The appellate organization was such that each assistant handled appeals from his or her own trial court cases. Some assistants were better trial lawyers than they were brief writers. For briefing, with the help of three assistants, I was in charge of editing all appellate briefs, which sometimes had to be rewritten by our team. As for advocacy, if an assistant was not up to the job I would hear from the Chief Judge, Edward Lumbard. On one occasion, one of the few political appointees in executive positions argued a complicated civil tax appeal. Judge Lumbard called to berate me for assigning the appeal to someone who was incapable of making a comprehensible argument.

U.S Attorney's Office Under Robert M. Morgenthau. I am 5 in from the right, 2nd row.

In the Second Circuit Court of Appeals

During the course of my career, I argued appeals in each of the eleven circuit courts, which are the intermediate, federal appellate courts between the district or trial courts, and the United States Supreme Court. As Chief Appellate Attorney, I cut my teeth in the Second Circuit Court of Appeals, which covered New York, Connecticut and Vermont. The judges of this court were among the most distinguished in the nation.

Early on, I had the honor of arguing before Judge Learned Hand, whom many lawyers believed should have been on the Supreme Court. I met Judge Hand when I was a law clerk. Judge Dimock drove him home every evening. While waiting for his lift, Judge Hand and I would have jurisprudential discussions. Hand was a Harvard Law graduate and advocated following "the law" wherever it went. I was a Yale Law graduate and was taught that policy considerations influenced how the law should be interpreted. Hand argued, "I like peaches; you like apples—who can say who is right?" One day, Judge Dimock asked me to bring Judge Hand a copy of a new statute entitled the Senior Judge Act, which enabled judges over a certain age to continue hearing cases. Judge Hand leaned back in his chair and laughed, saying they should call it the "Senile Judges Act." I read with interest Hand's inspiring book, *Spirit of Liberty*.

Another judge before whom I appeared in the Second Circuit was Charles Clark, one of the authors of the groundbreaking federal rules of civil procedure, and a former Dean of the Yale Law School. During one argument, Clark interrupted and told the lawyers to write him a letter with the rest of their argument because he had to catch a train to New Haven so he could teach a course at Yale Law School.

I describe here my argument, which involved one of the defendants in the Communist Smith Act cases, before Thomas Swan, another Second Circuit judge who had been Dean of the Yale Law School. I also argued before Harold Medina, a professor at Columbia Law School. Judge Medina succeeded Judge Hand on the Second Circuit, after having been the district judge who conducted the 1948 Act trial of alleged Communists who were convicted of conspiring to overthrow the government.

Jumping ahead to my years in private practice, I argued before Justice Sonia Sotomayor, when she was on the Second Circuit, before she was appointed to the Supreme Court. She was well prepared with questions on the cases I had cited in my brief. Continuing the tradition of appointing Yale Law deans to the circuit court, I argued several times before Judge Guido Calabresi. Guido was in the class just after mine at the law school and we knew each other well. He went on to become a distinguished professor at the law school writing about tort law theory and the impact of the social sciences. On the bench, he was a more formidable adversary than some of the lawyers I was arguing against. Unfortunately, my respect for this court demands that I point out that the qualifications of appointments by the prior Republican administration have not followed the tradition of excellence.

Narcotics

My first assignment, to myself, was to oppose an appeal from an order that denied a postconviction motion to set aside the conviction of Vito Genovese, who was said to be the number one Mafia don. Genovese was represented by Edward Bennett Williams, who was reputed to be the best criminal lawyer in America. I had earlier made it a point to watch Williams give his closing argument in a tax evasion case against Congressman Adam Clayton Powell of New York, who was acquitted. I tried to learn from Williams's friendly but convincing style. Williams made it look as if he was extemporizing, but in fact, he had probably prepared and memorized his text beforehand. I recommend that budding litigators learn trial techniques by watching trials conducted by skilled lawyers like Williams.

The files of the Genovese case trial filled every empty table in my office. I had help in plowing through the huge record from a summer assistant, Charles Stillman, who later became a well-known criminal defense counsel. The issue involved insufficiency of evidence, as the only witness was a low-level operative named Nelson Cantellops. He testified to a meeting, at which Genovese was present, where he overheard a discussion about dividing territory for narcotics distribution. During the preparation, Fran and I received threatening phone calls, and we had to unlist our telephone number. After a vigorous oral argument, the Second Circuit Court of Appeals affirmed the district court's denial of the petition to set aside the conviction.

The U.S. Attorneys' office, Criminal Division, had a narcotics section, called the "junk unit," to which, thankfully, I was not assigned. The head of the group was a tough, career prosecutor named Bill Tendy, who, together with his assistants, worked on a regular basis with undercover agents from the Drug Enforcement Administration (DEA). The junk unit lawyers were adept at inducing potential witnesses to "rat on" their coconspirators and coaxing them through their testimony. This was often rough stuff. During a jury trial of narcotic dealers, in which I was not involved, the jury foreman allegedly fell—but actually was thrown—down the stairs of his home and broke his back. A mistrial was declared. Another jury was impaneled and sequestered in a hotel for the duration of the trial. In order not to dissuade jurors from serving, there was no publicity for this event.

My earliest contact with those accused of selling or possessing narcotics was on Saturday duty. We learned that heroin addicts had to be interviewed and arraigned quickly or they might get sick and mess up your office. The DEA agents told me that heroin addicts could be cured of their addiction by cold turkey treatment at the federal prison hospital in Lexington, Kentucky. Even though they were cured of their addiction, they often resumed their abuse of heroin when they were released. This regressive behavior was to escape from their squalid living conditions. In contrast, the DEA agents advised that once cocaine addicts "get the itch," they remain addicted, and are hooked for life.

At times, Saturday duty could be exciting, as when a notorious person was arrested and brought in for arraignment. It was the office practice that if you handled the arraignment, you also handled any related press conference, even if you were a recently appointed Assistant. That policy changed with at least one subsequent U.S. Attorney.

Early on, I was assigned to brief and argue appeals from convictions for narcotics offenses in cases tried by lawyers in the junk unit. I assume that my background on the Yale Law Journal and as a judge's law clerk qualified me for these assignments, which in turn led to my appointment as Chief Appellate Attorney. While there were few legal errors in the narcotics trials, the defendants were motivated to pursue appeals so that they could remain out on bail during the proceedings. The appellate lawyers were imaginative in finding arguable issues. One appeal, which I argued successfully, involved a challenge to the trial judge's instruction to defendant's witness, that he was entitled to remain silent and to get his own attorney. Upon hearing the judge's advice, the witness refused to testify. The defense counsel complained that by his action, the judge precluded the witness from testifying in favor of the defense. Defense counsel argued that the judge should have first stated the grounds for the need to give the witness that advice so defense counsel could challenge it. The Second Circuit rejected that argument because imposing such a requirement would undermine the protection to which the witness was entitled under the Fifth Amendment.

Canadian Court

There was a problem with bail jumping (not showing up to serve a prison term) by narcotics defendants who were released on bail pending appeal of their convictions. They sometimes would go to Canada where the extradition treaty with the U.S. covered narcotics offenses but not a general conspiracy violation, which was typically the charge in our indictments. I was assigned to go to Canada, supervise our Canadian counsel, and testify as an expert in American law. I took the train to Montreal and changed for a train to Ottawa, the capital. This gave me uninterrupted time to prepare.

I arrived at our Canadian counsel's office and asked to see his brief. He replied that in Canada, unlike the U.S., written briefs were only submitted in cases before the highest appellate court. I inquired how he would present the case law to the judge. He guided me to his law library where his clerk had lined up casebooks on a dolly with markers for the cases to be used in argument. The trial lawyers, called barristers, wore gowns, as in England, but not wigs. I took the witness stand and testified that we typically secured indictments for conspiracy to violate the narcotics laws. In our practice, that was a narcotics offense and therefore covered by the extradition treaty. The wily defense barrister began by asking, "Son, how long are you out of law school?" I replied, "Five years, sir." The barrister then sarcastically retorted, "Five years, and you're an expert already (huff)!" Our barrister then presented his legal argument. When he relied on a published case, he handed the book to the judge who paused to read the case. At the end of the hearing, the judge ruled in our favor. He read into the record a learned opinion that included quotations and cites to the cases that our barrister had handed him earlier. From then on, those convicted of conspiracy to deal in narcotics were unable to escape their jail sentences by fleeing to Canada while out on bail pending appeal.

The Canadian procedure was far more efficient than our American practice. American judges typically reserve decision after argument and often, weeks later, render a written decision after studying lengthy "moving" briefs, "answering" briefs, and "reply" briefs submitted by the lawyers. The slowness of our system was illustrated at a recent presidential impeachment hearing. The president's defense counsel argued that Congress should have first sought documents and testimony by enforcing subpoenas in the court system. The Democratic impeachment managers explained that it would take months to get the courts to enforce Congressional subpoenas for testimony and documents. Under the Canadian system, such delays would not have been an obstacle. A judge in the Southern District of New York, Archie Dawson, aptly stated that the priority of trial judges was to be fast rather than right; if the decision is wrong, the appellate court will correct it.

I had hoped to stay in Ottawa the rest of the day to tour the impressive architecture of the parliament buildings, but I had heard that the last person to be extradited to the U.S. had become a human torch in Rochester, N.Y. Many of the bail jumpers, who looked like the defensive line of an NFL football team, were in the audience. So, I grabbed a taxi and went right to the airport.

Appellant's Counsel

I wanted experience representing an appellant, that is, the attorney filing the appeal. In criminal cases, the Assistant U.S. Attorney always represented the Government as appellee, to oppose an appeal from a conviction. The government had lost a patent case in the district court relating to the Sperry gunsight used in WWII. I divided the argument with David Hyde, who had been with the law firm of Cahill Gordon. He joined the office at about the same time as I did, and—following the path of appointing nonpolitical capable lawyers—was named by Morgenthau to be Chief of the Civil Division. Sperry's attorney was a patent lawyer and seemingly not a litigator. During oral argument, he brought the gunsight, which was about six feet high, into the courtroom. He demonstrated how effective it was by rotating the apparatus and the attached gun to the tune of rata-tat-tat. I objected that the gunsight had not been in evidence at the trial. The court ordered that it be removed immediately. Without going into detail, we had a tenuous argument, which I advanced as best I could. The appellate court ruled in the Government's favor. But then the patent owner asked to be heard *en banc*, meaning before all the judges of the circuit. After hearing argument, the *en banc* court ruled against the Government.

The Red Scare

Following the end of World War II, when the United States and the Soviet Union entered the cold war stage of their relationship, there developed widespread fear that Communists were infiltrating the federal government and other segments of society such as the movie industry. The fear was stoked by events, including the conviction of Julius and Ethel Rosenberg for spying for the Soviet Union and providing it with atomic secrets. I have already described by experience in the Justice Department with Senator McCarthy's investigation into alleged Communists in the Defense Department. As Chief Appellate Attorney, I had additional involvement with cases that related to the concerns of this era.

Judge Irving Kauman sentenced the Rosenbergs to death and they were executed. David Greenglass was Ethel's brother-in-law who was also convicted but was sentenced to imprisonment. I wrote the briefs and prepared Morgenthau for his argument in opposition to a motion by Greenglass to set aside his conviction. He argued that Judge Kaufman erred in instructing the jury that they could consider as evidence of guilt that Ethel had refused to answer questions based on the right in the Fifth Amendment to remain silent and not incriminate oneself. Greenglass urged that the case law, which had developed after the Rosenberg's execution, rendered it error to consider a refusal to testify on Fifth Amendment grounds as evidence of guilt. We argued successfully that the erroneous instruction had been given regarding Ethel's guilt, and did not affect Greenglass' conviction. There was a lesson, however, which I recalled later when I represented defendants in death penalty cases, that the finality of an execution could preclude reliance on later recognized constitutional rights.

In 1948, a trial was held in the Southern District of New York before Judge Harold Medina, who I appeared before when he was a Second Circuit judge. Ten members of the Communist Party were convicted of advocating the violent overthrow of the government and were sentenced to jail. After the trial, four defendants absconded and their bail was forfeited. The rest served prison terms.

I argued against an appeal by the former Chairman of the Communist Party, William Z. Foster, who, due to a heart condition, had been severed from the 1948 Smith Act trial. Foster moved to expand his bail limits ostensibly to get free medical treatment in the Soviet Union, which he said had better climate. More likely he wanted to die in the Soviet Union where he could have a hero's funeral. His heart condition could only worsen so it was unlikely that he could ever be tried in the U.S. But the House Un-American Activities Committee, which was rabidly anti-Communist, insisted that we oppose the motion. HUAC was formed in 1938 to investigate subversive activities. The Committee's hearings were in the forefront of the Red Scare era. People from various industries, including the movies, were called before the committee and asked whether there were or had been members of the Communist Party, and whether they could identify others who were members. While I did not personally favor opposing Foster's application to extend his bail limits, it was my duty to follow the Justice Department's orders to oppose the appeal.

At the argument, Judge Swan asked me whether the court would have the authority to dismiss the case if the defendant were deceased. I took the position that only the U.S. Attorney had that authority. But that was not the deciding issue. The court of appeals held that the District Judge, David Edelstein, did not abuse his discretion in denying the motion to extend bail limits. There was no applicable extradition treaty with the Soviet Union, and Foster did not represent that he would return after his medical treatment. Nor did he show that adequate medical treatment was unavailable in the United States. Foster's claim that he would never recover from his heart ailment was found to be inconsistent with his claim that medical treatment in the Soviet Union might provide a cure. Following an appeal to the Supreme Court, the Solicitor General in the Department of Justice decided to drop the opposition. The Second Circuit judges were angry that I had led them down the path of ruling against Foster only to be undercut by the Justice Department. As it turned out, Foster died in the Soviet Union where he was given a state funeral in Red Square. He became an icon for American Communists.

More recently, on January 6, there was another "Red Scare" by rioters with red baseball caps, inspired by others wearing red neckties. Recalling these experiences made me think that the Smith Act might apply to those who inspired and contributed to the January 6 attack on the Capitol in an attempt to block certification of the presidential election results. Another applicable statute provides that "Whoever incites, sets on foot, assists, or engages in any rebellion or insurrection against the authority of the United States or the laws thereof, or gives aid or comfort thereto," is subject to fine or ten year imprisonment as well as being banned from public office. In *Dennis v. United States*, The Supreme Court adopted Judge Learned Hand's rationale for the Second Circuit's affirmance of the Smith Act convictions—that there was a "clear and present danger." While *Dennis* was weakened in subsequent decisions, *Yates v. United States*, an actual attack would still seem to violate the law, Hopefully, in addition to prosecuting the hundreds of people who physically participated in the attack, the Justice Department will present the prospect of indicting those who planned and incited the attack on the Capitol.

The Independence of the S.D.N.Y.

In addition to briefing and arguing appeals, I had other duties. The office formed a unit that for the first time would concentrate on violations of the securities laws. These cases involved insider trading, providing false or misleading information to shareholders, and failing to inform stockholders of pertinent information. Arthur Liman, a classmate at law school, was in charge of the unit. As a partner in the Paul, Weiss law firm, he later represented Michael Milliken who was sentenced to jail for insider trading (buying or selling securities based on knowledge not known to the public). I was tasked with reviewing each of the indictments prepared by the securities law unit. That introduction to securities law came in handy in securities litigation that I later handled in private practice.

There was a dock strike that threatened the economy. Before the date for argument, we had visitors from the Department of Justice in D.C., who said they were taking over the case. The U.S. Attorneys' Office for the Southern District of New York was proud of its independence from the Justice Department. Morgenthau told the Justice lawyers that he had been a lawyer in the Navy. He defended a sailor who was accused of beating up some soldiers. The sailor testified that he didn't mind when the soldiers knocked him off a bar stool, or when they pushed him to the ground or kicked him. But when they pissed on him, he really got mad. Morgenthau loudly pronounced that: "You guys are pissing on me. So, go back to D.C. We are keeping this case." And we did. This event stands in contrast to recent attempts by the Attorney General in the prior administration to interfere for political reasons with prosecutions in the Southern District of New York, including an attempt to replace the sitting U.S. Attorney.

· · ·

Chapter IX
FAREWELL TO GOVERNMENT SERVICE

After a year as Chief Appellate Attorney, it was time to move on to private practice. Fran and I were going to have our first child. Fran would leave her job at Y&R, and we needed more than the $9,000 a year I was earning. I really enjoyed my stay in the government and was reluctant to leave. Fran jokingly suggested that she ask a law firm when making me an offer to put an American flag in my office to remind me of my U.S. Attorneys' experience. In August of 1962, I submitted my resignation to Robert Kennedy, the U.S. Attorney General. He had visited the U.S. Attorneys' office to address the staff. We all stood around in the office library where he spoke from the middle of the crowd. He was electrifying in his presentation. In my letter of resignation, I expressed my gratitude for the opportunity to serve the country and the wish that someday I would get to return to public service at a higher level. I never had that opportunity.

Looking back, I marvel at the importance to society of our federal civil service. Some of my conservative friends complain about what they call the evils of "big government." Yet those who have been a part of that government uniquely appreciate the federal agencies' contribution to the well-being of our citizens. Under the prior Republican administration, civil servants have come under fire for doing their jobs in the face of undemocratic policies imposed by their politically appointed superiors. The Justice Department has been infected with political appointees who lack competence and experience. Department heads did the bidding of the president who is not supposed to interfere with Justice Department business. Hopefully, the Department's long reputation for honesty and excellence will be restored by the new administration.

The law firm of Kaye, Scholer, Fierman, Hays and Handler was actively recruiting lawyers from the U.S. Attorneys' office. A partner in the firm was Milton Wessel, a former AUSA who had prosecuted a famous case where mafia leaders had a meeting at a cabin in the Appalachian Mountains and were charged with conspiracy. One of my colleagues at the U.S. Attorney's office, Paul Curran, who later ran for governor of New York as a Republican, had moved to that firm as well. These recruits made the firm attractive for me. The firm made me an offer. The firm asked for recommendations by Judge Walsh (who by this time had gone back to his old firm, Davis Polk & Wardwell) and S. Hazard Gillespie, who was the U.S. Attorney when I was an Assistant in the Criminal Division, and also a Davis Polk partner. Walsh and Gillespie called and invited me to come to Davis Polk. This was a prestigious white-shoe law firm and I was honored by the offer. But I still recalled the poor reception I encountered when I was applying to such firms while in law school, so I turned them down. I agreed to associate with Kaye Scholer.

Political Campaign

I was scheduled to start with Kaye Scholer after Labor Day. After a vacation in Bermuda, Fran and I were about to leave our apartment in Brooklyn to spend the weekend at the cottage of her aunt and uncle, which was upstate in Congers, New York. As we were walking out the door, I received a telephone call from Robert Morgenthau informing me that he was about to announce his candidacy for governor of New York. That day he was to give a three-minute address to the media making this announcement. And he wanted me to come immediately to the offices of CBS television to help write his speech. I sent Fran off to the cottage by herself. I proceeded to CBS where I met Morgenthau, Lou Harris, who was one of President Kennedy's pollsters, and the WNEW radio station space correspondent. Together we drafted the statement that Morgenthau read to the press and on television. Morgenthau explained to us that he was chosen by President Kennedy to run on the Democratic ticket against Nelson Rockefeller, who was a popular incumbent governor and a center-leaning Republican. Morgenthau's father, Henry Morgenthau Jr., had been Secretary of the Treasury and a close advisor to President Franklin D. Roosevelt. Kennedy thought that Robert's name recognition would help the Democratic ticket in the election. Morgenthau asked me to become his chief speechwriter. I asked Jim Hays, the managing partner of Kaye Scholer, for permission to delay my start with the firm. He declined, stating that Morgenthau had no chance to win so I was wasting my time.

I did, however, get to spend considerable time with the campaign as a speechwriter. It was my first experience with politics. Despite the odds against a victory at the polls, it was exhilarating. Morgenthau easily won the primary against Howard Samuels, a businessman who had been President of Off-Track Betting. The New York State Democratic Party lacked research memoranda that were needed to provide a factual basis for the campaign platform and speeches. Fortunately, Samuels had hired a number of college professors to prepare position papers for his campaign, and he was gracious enough to make them available to us after the primary.

I wrote some dynamic speeches for Morgenthau. But he was soft spoken and shy. His delivery was decidedly less exciting than the texts we provided. He had a staff of experienced political operatives, and it was fascinating to watch them in action. The hotel workrooms were always busy, and tension filled the air. One of the events that Fran and

I attended was President Kennedy's birthday party in Madison Square Garden where famously, Marilyn Monroe, wearing a tight-fitting white glittery dress, sang "Happy Birthday Mr. President." Rockefeller beat Morgenthau handily, which was expected. After the election, I was concerned about the disadvantage we had at the outset of our campaign due to the lack of position papers. I volunteered to work with the State Democratic Party to rectify that situation by updating and drafting position papers for future use.

Law Firm

My principal mentor at the firm was Professor Milton Handler. We called him "the Professor," as he was on the Columbia Law School faculty. At the law school, Handler taught antitrust law. For many years he was regarded as the premier antitrust expert in the country. He delivered a lecture annually at the City Bar Association in which he commented on the past year's antitrust decisions. The lecture was well attended and the audience included most of the antitrust lawyers in the city. He also published numerous articles, some of which he coauthored with lawyers in the firm.

Professor Handler was demanding. If he thought a draft brief was not up to par, he would say that I must have been tired when I wrote it, and suggest that I rewrite. He taught me to put away the final draft of a brief for a day. Then, reread the draft, and make it clearer and more persuasive. The professor encouraged his protégés to lecture and write. Often, he would offer me the opportunity to lecture in response to some of the many invitations he received.

Handler and I had a sometimes symbiotic and sometimes strained relationship. He maintained a personal relationship with his younger colleagues. Early on, he held a working meeting of young associates for dinner at his home. He went around the table and asked each of us about our family. Others told about their children. I said we had no children and likely would not have any if I were at work every evening. He tartly responded that, "they will come." And they did. We were invited to his annual birthday party at his apartment on Park Avenue where his nieces and nephews extolled his accomplishments in poetry. In the summer we attended poolside barbeques at his home in Yorktown Heights. One summer when we rented a house in Southampton, his wife Miriam asked us to watch over him while she traveled to Chicago for a charitable event. At dinner, he relived his entire career, while Fran and I did not get a word in edgewise. He took us out on his speedboat. Our young son, Matthew, sat in the front with the captain. The professor and I sat in the middle of the boat where he opined on strategy in litigations on which we were working. Fran sat in the stern and got soaked whenever the boat turned. Handler's solution was not to change seats, but to hand her some rain gear. When Fran and I had a baby boy who died of a heart malfunction at the age of two months, he sympathized, and suggested I deal with my grief by diving into a daily work routine.

Handler encouraged us to actively seek to develop new business. Yet, when years later I told him that I was the largest biller in the firm, he insisted that was due to his reputation. I wrote his biography for the *Yale Biographical Dictionary of American Law*. Together with his daughter, Carol, also an attorney, I delivered a eulogy at his funeral. He always said he was taking early retirement at ninety, but when he turned ninety, he changed his mind. In retrospect, I survived his harsh demands and I owe him much. The lesson is that if you can find a mentor early on, or a mentor finds you, take advantage of that opportunity.

In contrast to Handler, Milton Kunen, the firm's senior litigator, imparted practical approaches for dealing with the courts. Kunen did not attend law school; he studied law as a clerk in a law office and passed the bar. He was a savvy trial lawyer. He believed that judges had no time to read briefs, and therefore we should present arguments in summary form on page one. He advised us to avoid long quotes, as judges may not read them. But if you do include a quote, explain before and after the quote what the point is. Judges often do not read footnotes, so do not present essential arguments in footnotes. Apart from these hints, if you tried to show Kunen a draft brief, he would reply that if you graduated from law school, he assumed you knew how to write a brief.

To improve my advocacy skills, I took a course designed for trial lawyers, given by a drama coach. He taught us that in order to keep the judge's or jury's attention, we should alternate between speaking slowly and more quickly, and in low and louder tones. We were taught breathing exercises and how to speak from the abdomen. The most useful lesson was to practice one's presentation in full voice in front of a mirror. In that way, you could single out words and phrases that did not flow easily.

•   •   •

Chapter X

THE MOST CELEBRATED PRICE FIXING CASE OF OUR TIME

Introduction to Plaintiffs' Antitrust Litigation

One of the reasons that Kaye Scholer was heavily recruiting from the U.S. Attorneys' Office is that the firm was retained by fifty-five investor-owned electric utilities to file complaints seeking damages from electrical equipment manufacturers for price fixing, in violation of the antitrust laws. During my interviews at the firm, I expressed a desire to try cases, and not get bogged down in a huge antitrust litigation. One of the managing partners, Stanley Waxberg, who represented banks, assured me that "they would bring my lunch pail down to the courthouse." When I arrived at the firm, however, I was called into the office of Professor Handler. He told me about his clients, including Texaco and PepsiCo, and the opportunities open to me if I worked for him. He told me that he was about to undertake depositions of marketing employees of General Electric, and in view of my trial experience, which most associates lacked, he wanted me to help him prepare for the examinations. I mentioned the promise made when I was hired, and he assured me that this was a temporary assignment. Five years later, I emerged from what had been a full-time assignment on these cases, but without regrets.

I was given an office to share with a summer associate. That was more than I could take, having had my own huge office as Chief Appellate Attorney. When the summer associate left to go back to law school, I piled the other desk with documents needed to prepare for the depositions that Handler had assigned. When the office manager told me that I would soon have another officemate, I threatened to tell Handler that the manager was interfering with my preparation—I maintained my private office.

If I had been asked during law school whether I was to specialize in antitrust law I would have said a resounding "no." I graduated high in my law school class; however, in third year, when I was concentrating on writing my law journal comment, I got Cs in two courses. One was Negotiable Instruments. I simply did not have a head for the technical intricacies of the Uniform Commercial Code. The other "C" was in antitrust. The course was an experiment in multi-discipline. Dean Rostow reigned in front of the classroom and conversed with Ward Bowman, an economics professor at the University of Wisconsin, over the students' heads, literally and figuratively. There was no casebook, which would have contained abbreviated case reports and explanatory notes to make the case reports readable for students. Instead, we used a thick paper-bound book of leading Supreme Court antitrust cases in small print. As I previously noted, I avoided a clerkship with a judge who was going to devote the year to the trial of a steel industry merger case. Yet, fate led me into the field of antitrust, under the tutelage of Professor Handler. Who would have predicted that I would soon be conducting trials and arguing appeals in major antitrust cases, advising Fortune 500 corporations, lecturing and writing on antitrust issues, and teaching a course at Columbia Law School on how to conduct the trial of an antitrust case?

Plaintiffs' Counsel in the Electrical Equipment Cases

The electrical equipment manufacturers' price fixing conspiracy has been described as the most celebrated price fixing antitrust case of modern times.

The civil litigation grew out of indictments returned by a federal grand jury in Philadelphia and filed by the Justice Department in 1960 against the manufacturers for price fixing from 1956 to 1959. The indictments alleged that the companies held secret meetings, at which they conspired to raise, fix, and maintain prices of equipment used to generate and transmit electric power. The corporations and a number of officers and marketing personnel pleaded guilty to the more serious charges and *nolo contendere* to others. In February 1961, seven executives were sentenced to jail. Twenty-three others were given suspended jail sentences. The companies were fined nearly $2 million.

Investor-owned (private) utilities formed The Antitrust Investigation Group (ATIG), which in turn retained Professor Handler to oversee economic and legal studies in order to determine if they were damaged by paying inflated prices. Handler retained Jerome Cohen, an economist, and John Firestone, a statistician, both professors at City University in New York, and Robert Eisner, an economist at Northwestern University graduate school. For each product, they published reports that contained charts that illustrated the uniformity of increases in book prices. There were also "scatter charts" that portrayed the actual purchase prices, which were discounted from the book prices. In order to show that the utility purchasers were injured and could recover damages, they would have to prove that the prices they paid were higher than what would have been charged if there were no conspiracies. The charts showed an overall increase in prices during the conspiracy period, and a price drop when the conspiracy was uncovered. A rough method of establishing injury from overcharges caused by the price fixing conspiracy was to draw a straight line back from the lower postconspiracy prices and measure the difference from each of the higher prices paid during the conspiracy period.

The utilities accepted the Antitrust Investigation Group's recommendation to file suits for damages. Various groups of plaintiffs were formed in different areas of the country, each represented by a different law firm. Kaye Scholer was retained by fifty-five utilities in the northeast known as the Atlantic City Group, being the name of the first utility company on the list alphabetically. Kaye Scholer was also retained by American Electric Power, which had plants in Michigan, Indiana, West Virginia, and Kentucky. AEP sold the most electricity of any utility in the world except for the Soviet Union government-owned facilities.

As a former prosecutor, suing manufacturers who had pleaded guilty to criminal price fixing was up my alley. It turned out to be a welcome assignment. I made many contacts with lawyers all over the country with whom I kept in touch as we referred matters to each other. I conducted and defended depositions, drafted briefs on groundbreaking antitrust and evidentiary issues, and I was heavily involved in one of the three cases that went to trial. I also developed relationships with utility CEOs and general counsels, whose companies I got to represent in other important cases. So, the moral is to take advantage of the opportunity that is given to you, and make the best of it even though it was not what you may have sought.

Approximately 1,800 cases were filed in 33 federal district courts. In order to deal with the burdens on the federal court system, the Chief Justice of the U.S. Supreme Court appointed Chief Judge Murrah of the Tenth Circuit to devise a solution for managing the cases. The products included steam turbine generators, circuit breakers, transformers, condensers, meters, insulators, power switchgear, and other large and small equipment. The business generated more than $2 billion in sales, and the potential for damages was huge. The plaintiffs included investor-owned private utilities as well as municipal and state-owned entities. The defendants included General Electric, Westinghouse, Allis-Chalmers, Federal Pacific, ITE Circuit Breaker, Carrier, and many others.

Judge Murrah divided the cases by product line and—in order to expedite rulings—assigned each product to a trial judge who would preside over depositions (which were normally conducted without the presence of judges). Each product line also had a lead plaintiffs' counsel. Kaye Scholer was assigned to take the lead against General Electric (GE) who, together with Westinghouse and Allis-Chalmers, manufactured large steam turbine generators, the largest of the equipment involved. A panel of judges was appointed to oversee the process. Later this process was codified in legislation creating the Judicial Panel for Multidistrict Litigation. The Panel consisted of district and appellate judges who were authorized to transfer similar cases, which had been filed in different districts, to a single judge for pretrial proceedings. Later, I participated in a number of such cases and presented arguments before the Panel.

Handler first called me in to prepare for the deposition of John Peters, a GE marketing manager. The challenge was that the defendants' employees were reluctant to admit to outright price fixing agreements. There was evidence that for certain equipment, the manufacturers secretly met at airport motels or even had discussions at major league baseball games. For one product, there was evidence that the conspirators set price changes to occur with phases of the moon. Most often, the defendants met at trade association events, which were legitimate. But there were so-called rump or unofficial sessions. In the depositions relating to turbine generators, our goal was to show that at these rump meetings the marketing personnel talked about price. Based on Supreme Court authority, this evidence combined with uniform increases in list or book prices following the meetings could lead to an inference of a price-fixing conspiracy. Evidence of express agreements was not essential to proof of a combination and conspiracy. I thought of this recently when Special Counsel Robert Mueller concluded that despite numerous contacts with Russia, followed by Russian interference in the 2016 election, there was insufficient evidence to support a charge of collusion with Russia by the presidential campaign. Applying the antitrust rulings by analogy, there seemed sufficient circumstantial evidence to charge the campaign with conspiracy with Russia to interfere with the 2016 election.

I and others on the team prepared notebooks with questions and the possible answers for Handler to use at the depositions. Handler was tough on the associate lawyers with whom he worked, as well as other employees. When we came back from court, he would often say: "I am going to my club for a steam and a nice dinner. I will return at 6:00 a.m. tomorrow morning. Have everything on my desk for the next day in court." We would work until the wee hours to prepare.

Handler employed one of his students to drive a limousine, which would pick him up at Columbia Law School, where he taught an early morning antitrust course. Then, he would pick us up at the office to go to court. If the driver went too fast, he would admonish him by saying: "Driver, we are working back here," which we were—on the deposition scripts. If the driver got stuck in traffic, he would say: "Driver, your job is to study the city maps to avoid traffic jams." There were no GPS devices in cars then. At one point, I consulted a cardiologist to complain about pains in my chest. After a cardiogram and a chat, the doctor attributed the pains to Handler, and told me simply that life is tough.

After a time, Handler tired of taking depositions, and I moved to the front lines traveling around the country examining the defendants' managers and marketing personnel. One issue was whether the statute of limitations, which limited damages to a four-year period, was waived by the defendants' fraudulent concealment of their collusion. At their depositions, I represented the utilities' executives who testified that before the criminal indictments, they had no knowledge of the sellers' price-fixing conspiracy.

One of the utility executives, whom I prepared and defended at deposition, was Phillip Sporn, the president and CEO of American Electric Power. He was a genius and innovator, both in utility engineering and finance. He also was one of the few, if not the only, Jewish top utility executive. Sporn pioneered the construction of 1300-megawatt turbine generators, which were the largest of their kind. These plants were powered by coal from the fields in states where AEP operated including West Virginia and Kentucky. I met with Sporn at his country home in Connecticut. I recall his commenting on the impact of environmental change on the frogs in the stream on his property. Back then, global warming and pollution from coal-fired plants was not a major concern. Rather, having enough electric power for the nation's economy was a goal that Sporn urged me to pursue in my career. He had a modern home with everything but the bedrooms in one huge room. On coffee tables and in bookcases were numerous books and learned journals on everything from economics to engineering, domestic as well as foreign, including the Soviet Union's electrical grid.

I began the preparation by telling Sporn that I would ask the questions that we anticipated opposing counsel would ask. I first asked: "State briefly your education and background." A half hour later, he concluded his answer. While the exegesis was much too long for a deposition, the content was fascinating. Over time, I regularly reported to Sporn on the progress of the litigation and we had many enlightening discussions not limited to the cases.

I noticed that often our witnesses would be induced to answer questions as if they were having a friendly conversation with opposing counsel. In order to avoid trick and misleading questions, I devised a preparation method. I instructed witnesses to first repeat the question silently in their mind. Then frame an answer in their mind. At that point, the witnesses should turn to the reporter, who was recording the testimony, and dictate their answer slowly and clearly, as if they were dictating their last will and testament. This technique resulted in accurate, clear and responsive answers, while driving the examining counsel to distraction.

Depositions on both sides were taken in various parts of the country under the supervision of a district judge who ruled on objections on the spot. There were depositions in Miami, Florida. We stayed at the Key

Biscayne resort where President Nixon had a winter White House at the home of his friend Bebe Rebozo. In the morning before leaving for court, we often played tennis with the lawyers from the law firm of Winthrop Stimson, who had the lead in examining Allis-Chalmers' witnesses.

Fran and I traveled to San Francisco where I had to coordinate with later-to-be Mayor Joseph Alioto, who represented municipal utilities. His office door listed Joseph Alioto Enterprises, and below it, Joseph Alioto, attorney at law. He graciously welcomed us to his city and appreciated my help. Chicago was the hub for much legal activity. Judge Edwin Robson, who was designated by the judicial panel, presided. Often, he would hear us in the morning when he opened court by saying in a hoarse voice: "Welcome to Chicago." After a morning session, he would adjourn for other court matters. Then the lawyers would go to watch the Cubs who only played baseball during the day; Wrigley Field did not have lights.

But it was not all fun and games. Chicago was the location of a depository where the defendants were to place their responses to document requests. Most of the drudgework of reviewing the documents was left to younger associates. I decided to visit the depository to get the lay of the land. It appeared that the defendants reproduced documents on copiers that were short of ink so the documents would be hard to read. In addition, they eliminated all file folders, clips, staples and other materials that would make it easier to identify the context of any particular document. Instead, we were presented with reams of seemingly unconnected, dimly printed pieces of paper.

In between depositions in the Electrical Equipment cases, I worked on some smaller antitrust litigations. We represented Anchor Hocking, a glass manufacturer, in an antitrust suit. While I was taking a deposition, the phone rang. It was Fran. A partner answered and told her that I could not be disturbed. She insisted and told me on the phone that she was feeling labor pains. During the lunch break, the waiter told us that President Kennedy had been shot. All the phone lines were tied up so I hailed a taxi and rushed home. Our son Ethan was born the next morning. We were elated but the rest of the world was in mourning. Television just showed a burning log. Fran came home from the hospital on the Wednesday before Thanksgiving. On Friday, I flew to Ohio for a deposition of Cleveland Electric.

Over time, the evidence against the electrical equipment manufacturers mounted and they settled almost all of the cases. The settlements covered damages from 1956 to 1959, the period of the four-year statute of limitations and the time period during which the indictments charged the existence of a price-fixing conspiracy. The guilty pleas in the criminal case were admissible in evidence and raised a legal presumption of liability in the civil cases. This presumption dimmed the defendant's chances of succeeding at trials and encouraged settlements.

The OVEC Trial

Only three of the eighteen-hundred electrical equipment cases went to trial. I was fortunate to play a major role in such a trial in the Southern District of New York. As part of our representation of AEP, we were counsel to two related companies, Ohio Valley Electric (OVEC) and Indiana and Kentucky Electric (IKEC). These companies were established at the request of the Atomic Energy Commission to provide power for the reduction of uranium used to make atomic bombs. AEP owned the most shares; other investor-owned utilities from nearby states also had shares. In 1952, OVEC and IKEC purchased seven large steam turbine generators from GE and four from Westinghouse. Philip Sporn negotiated the purchase prices. The price-fixing conspiracy alleged by the Government's indictment, to which GE and Westinghouse pleaded guilty, did not begin until 1956.

Suits against GE and Westinghouse filed by these two utilities were part of the original filings by Kaye Scholer in the Electrical Equipment cases. In order to succeed we had to prove with independent evidence that there was a conspiracy as early as 1952, when the units were purchased. There was no presumption of guilt for that period, as it was not covered by the government indictments. Moreover, the four-year statute of limitations precluded claims prior to 1956, unless we could prove that during the earlier time period, the defendants fraudulently concealed their collusion from the utilities. In order to recover damages, we had to establish that the prices that OVEC paid for its turbines were higher than prices that would have paid absent collusion. For the post-1956 purchases, the usual way to prove damages was to compare the high prices in the conspiracy period with lower prices after 1960 when the indictments were filed and the conspiracy ended. That was simple and fairly easy to prove. However, the prices of OVEC's early purchases were lower than prices after the conspiracy ended some eight years later. Over that long period of time, prices for bread, milk and most commodities increased in the normal course. Damages would be hard to measure.

The law firms of Cravath Swaine and Moore, which represented Westinghouse, and White & Case, which represented GE, smelled blood. After settling numerous cases for millions of dollars, they sought to be vindicated by a victory at trial in the case filed by OVEC and IKEC. They refused to settle and the case was set for trial in the Southern District of New York before Judge Wilfred Feinberg, who at one time had worked in the Kaye Scholer labor department. Handler, who spent his career as a professor at Columbia Law School, had no experience in organizing the prosecution of a complex trial. So that task fell to me. Also, on the team was Michael Malina, a longtime Kaye Scholer associate, and who—like me—later was made a partner in the firm. Mike was an excellent brief writer who wrote his drafts carefully with an old-fashioned fountain pen, so that little editing was needed. He drafted briefs for most of the motions and aided with trial preparation as well. James B. Henry, who had come over from the Cahill Gordon law firm, was a descendant of

President James Buchanan. Jim was quiet and not much of a trial lawyer, but, as was shown later in the trial, he had a talent that proved invaluable.

Shortly before trial, the attorney for GE, had to withdraw as he developed Alzheimer's disease. His illness was revealed when he voiced an objection in court followed by his saying "objection overruled." White & Case was replaced by a Chicago firm, Chadwell Keck, which had been in the cases in other capacities. Tom Leary of White & Case, who was a friendly adversary in this and future cases, also participated in the trial. Allis-Chalmers was represented by Hazard Gillespie of Davis Polk, who had been U.S. attorney when I served, and by Robert Fiske, who headed up an organized crime unit in the Gillespie U.S. Attorneys' office and was to be my opponent in a trial relating to the Three Mile Island nuclear accident. While Allis was among the defendants who had pleaded guilty and settled its civil cases with the utilities, it was dropped as a party in the OVEC case as it did not sell any turbines to OVEC. It was, however, named as a coconspirator.

At trial, Handler and I divided the witnesses and we prepared examination scripts for him. Unfortunately, he was quite hard of hearing so when the witness answered a question, Handler would turn to me and ask what the witness replied, and what Handler should do next. I would tell him to ask the next written question. At this point, Judge Feinberg called Handler to the bench and told him that he thought the young man whispering in his ear was delaying the trial. Handler replied that this was not so; that I was telling him to shut up and sit down. We all had a laugh and Judge Feinberg told this anecdote for years thereafter.

Prior to trial we sought to take the deposition of Robert Neblett who had been a GE marketing manager starting in the late 1930s. Neblett was GE's chief negotiator for the turbine generators at issue in the lawsuit. Indeed, he was the person who, in negotiations with Phil Sporn, refused to grant further discounts even if OVEC agreed to purchase all eleven of its units from GE instead of just seven. GE's attorneys pleaded that he was old and not well. But we got permission from the court to conduct the deposition in ten-minute sessions.

Mr. Neblett was a gentleman and honest. He actually was proud of his knowledge of steam turbine technology and the complications of the published price book, which he explained to competitors. In his deposition, he described meetings with Westinghouse and Allis-Chalmers, as early as 1939, at which he explained GE's new price book. Employees of Westinghouse and Allis-Chalmers confirmed the existence of these meetings. Later, Neblett introduced Peters to the competitors' meetings. At trial, John Peters, whom the conspirators called GE's "price guy," at first denied attending these early meetings but he had admitted his participation in his deposition. Thus, we were able to prove from depositions and trial testimony that there were collusive meetings starting in 1939, which continued in 1952 when OVEC purchased its turbine generators, and thereafter until the units were shipped in 1956.

Injury and damages posed a difficult burden. The sellers' book or published prices were uniform. But neither OVEC nor other buyers paid the book price. The defendants pointed to Sporn as a known skillful negotiator who secured deeper discounts than other utilities by playing GE and Westinghouse against each other. The defendants argued that the amounts of discounts varied due to the buyers' size and bargaining skill.

It took several years to manufacture a steam turbine generator so there were uniform escalation clauses that increased the price agreed at the time of purchase to a higher price at delivery time. The amount of the increase was based on Bureau of Labor Statistics (BLS) indices. We contended that the uniform escalation clauses were also a subject of the conspiracy.

Our economists were Jerome Cohen and Bob Eisner, who had advised on the ATIG studies. Our statistician was John Firestone, a pipe smoking, unassuming colleague of Dr. Cohen at City University. They analyzed the pricing data in charts that showed step by step uniform and closely timed increases in book prices. And as shown in the charts, under the book prices were the different purchase prices, which were called "scatter" because of their lack of uniformity. However, it appeared that as book prices were increased, the cluster of scattered actual prices followed the book prices upward. And the cluster of purchase prices was continually in a range of no more than 10% of the book prices. But we needed proof that this configuration was a goal of the conspirators. We dispatched a bright young lawyer named Steve Banner to Chicago to search the document depository for proof. Bingo! Steve found a document, authored by John Peters, when he was marketing manager of GE, that spelled out the purpose of the price fixing meetings. The conspirators not only agreed to create identical book prices and uniformly raise such prices, but—according to this newly discovered document—they also aimed to maintain discounts within a 10 percent range of the agreed-upon published prices.

The documentation led to confirming testimony. In early 1955, before the OVEC turbines were delivered, GE Turbine Division General Manager, G.B.Warren, testified in deposition that he told Charles Mauntel, Westinghouse's turbine Sales Manager, that GE was going to maintain prices very close to the handbook prices. Neblett explained the other companies' reaction: " . . . they said 'Thank G-d.'" At trial, Peters admitted to this critical purpose of the meetings:

> *Q.* . . . In principle, your objective was to keep order prices as close to book prices as you could?
> *A.* That's true.
>
> . . .
>
> *Q.* Was that Westinghouse's position also?
> *A.* Yes, we all believed that we should quote as close to book.

Sensing the critical nature of this line of inquiry, Judge Feinberg jumped in and asked the deciding question:

The Court: That idea was discussed and expressed at your meetings?

The witness: That's correct."

All of this illustrates the importance to the outcome of the trial of my very first assignment at the firm—to prepare for the deposition of John Peters of GE.

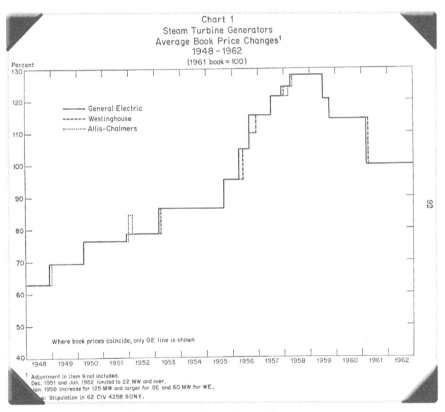

OVEC Trial Exhibit Showing Uniform Price Changes

At trial, we adduced evidence that the collusion was concealed so we could overcome the statute of limitations. The conspirators altered their expense account records, made calls from public telephones, and destroyed their notes in order to conceal their illicit discussions. The defendants contended that their marketing personnel concealed their activity from their own management and that the buyers would not have known about the collusive meetings even without these efforts. The judge did not buy this excuse.

We decided not to put our economists on the witness stand where they would be subject to vigorous cross-examination. Rather we called our statistician, Dr. Firestone, who presented the simple math to show the range of discounts from published prices, and how that translated into 10 percent damages for our clients. When asked on cross-examination why he did that computation, Firestone replied that the plaintiffs' lawyers asked him to do so. When asked if he agreed that this was an appropriate way to compute legal damages, Firestone replied that he was not an economist and was merely presenting the computation. Al Connelly, an experienced and eminent trial lawyer at Cravath, was outraged. His attempts to cross-examine and undermine the basic theory met with a brick wall from Firestone. Connelly argued angrily to the court that the "expert" witness was just doing simple arithmetic and his testimony should be rejected. This attempt to preclude plaintiff's lawyers from being heard on their damage theory did not succeed. Judge Feinberg allowed the testimony, which established our damages claim.

The defense relied mainly on their economic expert witnesses. Handler was to cross-examine the GE expert and I took the Westinghouse expert. The GE expert was Morris Adelman, a distinguished oil economist at MIT. Westinghouse's expert, Dr. John Corson, was an economist on the Princeton faculty. In his direct testimony, Professor Adelman described a ten-step regression analysis from which he derived a competitive price that—absent collusion—would have theoretically been charged to OVEC. The so-called competitive price was higher than that provided for in OVEC's purchase contract. In today's practice, we would have received the defendants' expert reports well in advance of trial. Based on later Supreme Court authority in a case called *Daubert*, trial courts would hold a pre-trial hearing to determine whether the expert's report satisfied certain criteria that demonstrated whether the expert's conclusions were sufficiently reliable to give to the jury or trial judge who was deciding the fact issues. As explained later, I followed this procedure to advantage in obtaining dismissals of product liability suits where we showed expert reports to be "junk science."

We learned of Adelman's complex analysis on the eve of his testimony. At the end of the court day, we went to dinner with our economic and statistical experts who sadly informed us that they could find no errors in Adelman's analysis. It seemed that all was lost. Jim Henry, after enjoying two martinis and a beer with dinner, confidently volunteered to take on the preparation of the cross-examination overnight. At the opening of the court session the next day, Adelman greeted Handler by asking whether "the condemned man had a hearty breakfast."

Early that morning Jim Henry reported that he found a flaw in Adelman's regression analysis. Adelman had compared the contract purchase price with his hypothetical competitive price at the time of purchase. But the price actually paid by OVEC was subject to an escalation clause that raised the ultimate price based on rising BLS indices. Jim, using his mathematical skills as applied to Adelman's methodology, recalculated a competitive price at the time of delivery. Jim's hypothetical competitive price was 10 percent lower than that paid by OVEC at the time of delivery of the units. Handler asked Adelman how he could explain the differential. His reply was that there must have been an "X" factor present in the marketplace. Next question: "Could the X factor be collusion among the bidders?" Answer: "Yes." The 10 percent number was precisely what our statistician, Dr. Firestone, had testified was the amount of the price discounted from the collusively set published price. The actual prices followed the published prices upward, as John Peters' memo stated was the intent of the collusive meetings.

Dr. Corson's methodology was to take the prices starting in 1940 and extrapolate forward based on economic factors, such as Bureau of Labor

Statistics indices, to find that the OVEC purchases were below the prices that would have occurred in a free market. In my cross-examination, I pointed Dr. Corson to the evidence of collusion starting in 1939, of which he was apparently unaware. He conceded that this undermined his conclusions:

> Q. If the prices in 1940 were affected by collusion . . . then in evaluating the prices in 1952 in the light of economic forces that prevailed between 1949 and 1952, you would have used an invalid base year, would you not?
> A. It follows that if in 1940, the prices were affected by collusion, that year would have been an invalid base year.

Then to drive home the point, a bit of repetition:

> Q. You cannot evaluate the effect of collusion on a price in one year by comparison with a price in another year, which was also affected by collusion, can you?
> A. No, you cannot.

In my cross examination of the Westinghouse expert, I also tried a few questions in which I posed an alternative to the BLS indices that he used in his calculation to show that the purchasers were not injured. He answered that he disagreed with that approach. My questions were based on the factors in the methodology used by GE's expert, Dr. Adelman. Apparently, the GE and Westinghouse trial counsel had failed to coordinate their respective expert's testimony. In our posttrial brief, I referred to the "battle of the experts"—not our experts versus the defendants', but between the two defendants. I argued, "We are content to let defendants' experts fight it out, save to note that they expressly impugn the validity of each other's use of BLS indices."

To put the final nail in Corson's coffin, I used Corson's own methodology to undermine his conclusion. I measured the increase from his base year to the final delivery price in 1955, rather than the 1952 order price. This computation showed that the defendants' published prices increased by 56 percent in comparison to the BLS indices that Corson used which increased by only 36 percent.

Judge Feinberg wrote a learned opinion finding that GE and Westinghouse conspired to fix prices starting in 1939 and continuing thereafter; that they fraudulently concealed their collusive activity; and they overcharged OVEC and IKEC. The judgment awarded damages after trebling of $16.8 million.

OVEC Power Plant

Continued Pursuit of Price Fixers

Price fixing was not limited to electrical equipment. Following on government indictments, we represented investor-owned utilities in claims for treble damages from price fixing against manufacturers of aluminum conductor cable and brass mill tubing. These cases were settled without extensive discovery or trial.

After Phillip Sporn retired, AEP had a new CEO, Donald Cook, who had been Chairman of the United States Securities and Exchange Commission (SEC) and later a member of the SEC. Cook was aggressive and frustrated by his inability to negotiate steam turbine generator prices significantly below book or published price or to get different prices from the two domestic sellers—GE and Westinghouse. In addition to ordering from a Swiss company, Brown Boveri, he asked us to recommend further legal action, as the results of the previous round of lawsuits did not sufficiently improve competition in pricing.

Following the conclusion of the criminal cases in 1963, GE announced a new pricing policy. Westinghouse followed with a similar policy. Book prices were published and they were about the same for all sellers. One company would lead. And the other would soon follow with the same increases. In addition, GE and Westinghouse decided to publish the prices of all orders and deliveries. GE also announced a "price protection policy" whereby the buyer could get the benefit of any lower price quoted by a competitor. Westinghouse did the same. This joint policy would in effect result in each company punishing itself if it lowered prices in the market. That would dissuade the two companies from engaging in competitive price negotiations.

On behalf of AEP, we filed another complaint in the Southern District of New York alleging that price fixing continued. In our strategy discussions, I posed the question of whether the manufacturers could get away with fixing prices if they announced their collusive intent openly on television rather than in secret meetings. Essentially our argument was that collusion need not be arrived at by meeting at an airport motel in the middle of the night. Rather price-fixing collusion could be achieved by open and public communications. This approach was a major step beyond existing case law in proving a conspiracy to fix prices.

GE decided to switch defense counsel and retained the law firm of Weil, Gotshal & Manges, and particularly Ira Millstein, who was a well-known antitrust lawyer. Millstein was not known as a trial lawyer but he directed his litigation team to be aggressive in pursuing burdensome pretrial discovery. His first action was to file counterclaims against AEP followed by extensive discovery requests by way of depositions and document requests. It soon became apparent that pursuing the litigation would be too time consuming and expensive. So, we took another tack.

Handler and I flew to Washington and met with the Justice Department officials who had negotiated a civil injunctive decree following the criminal indictments. We convinced the Justice lawyers that the consent decree was being evaded by the revised pricing policies. The Justice lawyers issued a memorandum adopting our theory and concluding that the 1963 pricing policies were part of a successful attempt to eliminate price competition. The Justice memorandum found that GE's initiative and Westinghouse's response were devices to achieve adherence to the same price not by secret conspiratorial meetings but by public communications. Based on our arguments, the price protection policy was seen by Justice as a way for GE to increase its costs whenever it deviated from quoted prices, thereby discouraging such deviations. The Justice Department imposed changes in the consent decree that were designed to eliminate the non-competitive aspects of the companies' pricing practices. Hopefully, the results we achieved provided a disincentive to future price fixers, whether by secret collusive activity or public signaling.

Under Sporn's leadership, AEP broke barriers by building 1300-megawatt coal-fired steam turbine generators. Over time, due to environmental and other considerations, the era of large coal-fired steam turbine generators waned, and smaller gas-fired turbines replaced them. Today, GE is pioneering the construction of wind generators sunk offshore. These are 26-megawatt generators, but a hundred of them in one farm will have more power than the old polluting coal-fired generators.

AEP was our largest client and the one that I principally worked for in my early years in private practice. One of my contacts at AEP was John Tillinghast, a senior vice president. One early morning, John telephoned me at home. Fran answered the phone, and told John that I was in the shower. John replied abruptly: "Well, get him out of there."

There came a time when we worked with Simpson Thatcher, AEP's corporate counsel, to secure SEC approval for AEP to acquire Columbus & Southern, a utility based in Columbus, Ohio. As a condition of approval, the SEC required AEP to move its headquarters from New York City to Columbus. I recall arranging to meet Tillinghast at LaGuardia Airport for a trip to Columbus. With two minutes to take off, I observed John buying a newspaper at a booth at the entrance to the departure gates. We boarded with a minute left. John told me that Sporn advised his employees that if they didn't miss a few planes a year, they were spending too much time hanging around airports. Over time, new CEOs took over, distance led to fewer contacts, and the relationship with AEP petered out. My continuing to keep busy in the ensuing years demonstrates that a successful practice should not and need not depend on any single client.

◆ ◆ ◆

Chapter XI

THE U.S. SUPREME COURT AND THE DEATH PENALTY

Every appellate lawyer's dream is to appear before the United States Supreme Court in Washington, D.C. With few exceptions, the Supreme Court has total discretion as to whether to take a case on appeal from a state high court or a federal circuit court of appeals. The process to get to the Supreme Court requires the filing of what is called a *writ of certiorari*. The writs are initially reviewed by the Supreme Court law clerks who may be only a few years out of law school. The clerks prepare memoranda that analyze appeals, which are then reviewed by the justices. Four justices must agree to grant *certiorari*. The chances that a writ will be granted are slim. About 7,000 writs are filed each year. The court only grants about 1 percent of these writs. Most of the cases for which certiorari is granted involve appeals from federal courts. Many of these cases involve serious conflicts in decisions by two or more of the eleven federal circuit courts. Writs from state courts that are granted often involve challenges to state legislation as contrary to federal constitutional requirements.

Few lawyers, including capable litigators, get the chance to argue in the Supreme Court. Apart from the difficulty of getting one's writ to be granted by the Court, there is a coterie of lawyers in Washington, D.C., who do little else but argue in the high Court. These lawyers generally had been employed in the Solicitor General's office of the Department of Justice where all they did was prepare briefs and argue in the Supreme Court. I was fortunate to be able to argue three cases in the high court.

In the late seventies, I participated in a panel at Columbia Law School on science and the law. At the luncheon I was seated next to Jack Greenberg, who was counsel to the NAACP Legal Defense Fund. He told me that he had some seventy-five clients on death row, each of whom needed counsel. I offered to take one of those cases. Shortly thereafter, I received a file in *Beck v. Alabama.* The case was referred by the Southern Poverty Law Center who advised that the New York law firm, Cravath, Swaine & Moore, had given up on the case as hopeless. I put together a team including John Herfort, a bright young lawyer who was Handler's nephew.

"Kill 'Em or Free 'Em"—Alabama's Death Penalty Law

Our client, Gilbert Beck, was a White male of very low intelligence. In a rural area of Alabama, Beck and another man broke into the home of an elderly couple. The husband, Roy Malone, was a retired veterinarian. Malone was killed in the course of the robbery. And the two men got away with seventy dollars. These facts were not appealing, but the procedural aspects of the case were unusual. In a practice going back at least as far as the 1700s at common law, juries had been instructed that they could find what is called a lesser included offense, that is to find the defendant guilty of a crime that is not as serious as the one charged. Providing this instruction was the law in all fifty states. The only exception was that Alabama provided for the instruction in all cases except death penalty trials.

The Beck jury was given a choice between finding the defendant guilty of murder, which carried the death penalty, and letting the defendant go free, even though he clearly committed a serious crime. The jury in the Beck case did not have the option of finding the defendant guilty of noncapital offenses such as robbery without intent to kill or felony murder. Intent to kill was not an element of felony murder in which a victim dies during commission of a felony such as armed robbery. The trial judge instructed the jury that if the jury acquitted Beck of the capital crime of intentional killing in the course of a robbery, he "must be discharged" and "he can never be tried for anything that he ever did to Roy Malone." The jury did not have much of a choice with this instruction.

We filed a petition for a writ of certiorari. Despite the odds against us, we secured the right to be heard as the high court granted our writ. Argument was set for the spring of 1980. During the school winter vacation, we took our three boys to California. After driving down the scenic Pacific Coast Highway, we arrived in Newport Beach from which we could visit Disneyland. At the hotel, we luxuriated in a hot tub and then a cold tub. I contracted pneumonia and bed rest was ordered. I used this absence from the office to prepare for the argument. While physicians may often deal with life-or-death situations, having a client's life at stake presented a scary challenge for a lawyer. Friends suggested that I read *The Brethren–Inside the Supreme Court* by Bob Woodward. But I was not interested in the personalities of the justices. Instead, I read Norman Mailer's *Executioner's Song,* which portrayed the anguish of Gary Gilmore. Gilmore had been sentenced to death by the state of Utah in what was to be one of the first executions after the revival of the death penalty in the 1970s. This book put me into the mind of someone about to be executed, which was a strong motivation to prepare thoroughly. Considering that I had never defended a criminal case, no less a death penalty case, I decided to delve into the constitutional provisions on which we relied. I ordered from our law firm library Harvard Law Professor Lawrence Tribe's multivolume treatise on constitutional law.

While I had argued many appeals, I knew that the Supreme Court was unique. For one thing, there would be nine judges whereas only three judges preside on federal circuit courts of appeal. I arranged for a moot court (practice argument) with an all-star team at NYU Law School. Tony Amsterdam, a professor at NYU, was most helpful. He devoted his professional life to defending those on death row. He had a coterie of law students who monitored and worked on capital cases throughout the nation. He was also known for his willingness to help others, like me, who were novices at death penalty litigation but willing to pitch in. It was said that Amsterdam worked on death penalty cases around the clock, and, when he collapsed, he checked into a hospital and then resumed his efforts upon his return. Amsterdam wrote me a letter succinctly summarizing the argument I should deliver. It was helpful to my preparation. Stephen Gillers, an ethics professor at NYU Law School, also participated in the moot court and later attended the argument. After the argument, he sent me a copy of an article he published in the University of Pennsylvania Law Review entitled, "Deciding Who Dies." He inscribed it by saying "he enjoyed the argument."

I arrived in Washington with Fran and two of our boys. Entering the huge courtroom, I was immediately impressed with its majesty. There are twenty-seven marble columns. The walls, ceiling, and floor are all made of marble. On the attorney's desk in the courtroom was a feathered pen souvenir, which attests to the historic nature of the proceedings. The court clerk sits on one side in front of the justices' bench. On the other side is the monitor for the timing of the argument. A green light is the signal to proceed with argument. A yellow light indicates that time is almost up. The red light means stop even if you are in midsentence. The atmosphere can only be described as awesome. The bench where the nine justices sit seemed higher and further removed than in federal circuit courts.

As the petitioner, I argued first. I moved from the attorneys' table to the lectern in the center. John Herfort sat at counsel table ready to help but that was not possible. You are on your own in responding to the court's questions. I had a three-holed notebook with my prepared argument and a section with potential questions and answers. I never got to open the notebook. At the outset of the argument, Chief Justice Berger graciously welcomed me and asked for a summary of the facts of the case. My basic argument was that the court's instruction to the jury unfairly tilted the jury's fact finding toward the capital murder verdict. After the Supreme Court's decision, CBS news reported that Alabama had a "kill 'em or free 'em" statute. One of our elements of proof was that there was evidence of a noncapital offense that the jury might have found if the court's instructions had allowed it to do so. Although Alabama had conceded that point, the Court asked questions about this element.

While defendants do not ordinarily testify, I explained that here, Beck testified that he did not murder the victim and had no intention of doing so. He said he thought that tying up Mr. Malone with a rope would facilitate the robbery. He testified that while attempting to tie up the victim, his partner accidentally killed Malone. Justice Thurgood Marshall, who never voted in favor of the government in a capital case, roared with laughter and asked: "You mean a man that holds a victim while he is stabbed can be acquitted of homicide?" I responded: "He can be acquitted of robbery with intent to kill if the only basis for his holding [the victim] was, as he testified, to tie up the victim rather than to cause him harm or kill him." While the facts were not pretty, it was essential to show that there was sufficient evidence to have supported conviction of a noncapital offense.

In my briefs, I presented a wealth of prior case law dealing with the lesser included offense instruction. Nevertheless, the justices harped on the fact that no case had held that the jury's ability to find guilt of a lesser included offense is a constitutional requirement. Justice Byron White, a Kennedy appointee, who rarely if ever voted in favor of a criminal defendant, asked me to specify the constitutional provisions on which I relied. I replied that I relied on the Sixth Amendment right to jury trial, the Eighth Amendment ban on cruel and unusual punishment and "I believe" the

Fourteenth Amendment right to due process. To that, White sarcastically interjected: "Counsel, we don't care what you believe." Fran later observed that White had guests sitting next to her in the gallery and they seemed delighted to hear his taunting remarks. In subsequent court appearances, I always avoided saying what "I believe", and I instructed students I taught in law schools to do the same.

As will be seen in the Lowenfield case, which is described here, there are two phases to a death penalty trial: a guilt finding trial and a sentencing proceeding. Previous Supreme Court precedents had focused on protective procedures in the sentencing phase. Justice White asked me whether it was not sufficient for the judge in the sentencing proceeding to ignore the jury's recommendation if he thought the death penalty was inappropriate. I responded that the same standards and careful scrutiny that the Court had applied at the sentencing stage of a death penalty case, should be applied to the guilt-finding trial.

Charles Graddick, the Attorney General of Alabama, was known as "bloody Charlie" for his vigorous and frequent prosecution of capital cases. While Graddick was on the briefs, one of his assistants argued the case. The Alabama Assistant Attorney General contended that the jury could simply have ignored the court's instruction, found the defendant guilty of a lesser offense and thus caused a mistrial. In the three minutes I had for rebuttal I responded to this contention. I stated:

> "Mistrial is not a substitute for the lesser included offense procedure. This postulates a situation where the jurors would say to each other, 'We really think the defendant is guilty only of a lesser included offense. So, what we will do is we will go and tell the trial judge that some of us vote to convict, some of us vote to acquit. Then there will be a mistrial. Then maybe . . . there will be a reindictment, and maybe that reindictment will [charge] the lesser offense, and maybe there will be a conviction

of the lesser offense.' That sort of speculation on such a tenuous chain of events cannot be a substitute for a proper instruction in the first instance."

In its opinion, the Court summarily rejected this argument by the State. The State also argued that juries are reluctant to apply the death penalty so the absence of a lessor included offense instruction would actually tilt the jury in defendant's favor. On rebuttal, I pointed out that the historical data on which the State relied to show jury reluctance to convict of a capital crime were from an era where the imposition of the death penalty was mandatory.

I told the Court:

"The implication of the argument is that there should be reduced standards, reduced procedural protections in capital cases. And the Court has consistently said that because of the irreversibility and the absence of any opportunity for correction of error, that there should be greater standards and that there should be greater procedural protections and more reliability in a capital case."

In any event, Bloody Charlie's 96 percent conviction rate in death penalty cases put the lie to that argument.

The State pointed out that sometimes the prosecution asked for the lesser included offense instruction so it could obtain a conviction even if the jury did not find that all of the elements of the higher crime were present. The Supreme Court held that whether the instruction helped the prosecution or the defense, its absence injected an improper element into the jury's fact finding.

The Court held that the "unavailability of a lesser included offense instruction enhances the risk of an unwarranted conviction," which in a death penalty case rises to the level of a constitutional deprivation. The Court concluded that the Alabama statute encouraged a jury to convict of a capital offense for "an impermissible reason—its belief that the defendant is guilty of some serious crime and should be punished." The Court's opinion, written by Justice Stevens, overturned the Alabama capital punishment statute. I learned that in addition to Beck, some eighty defendants on death row would be entitled to have another sentencing hearing.

Justice Rehnquist, joined by White, dissented on the ground that the Alabama lawyers representing Beck did not preserve the constitutional argument in the state court proceedings. Beck's lawyer had raised the issue in the Alabama trial court and the intermediate appellate court. But in the Alabama Supreme Court, while Beck's lawyers cited all the constitutional provisions that I argued had been violated, they did not explicitly raise the "lesser included offense" point. I wondered whether if the two dissenting justices were in the majority, they would have sent a man to his death because of a lawyer's omission.

Rolling Back a Death Penalty Case Protection

After the Beck case, I encouraged others in the law firm to undertake pro bono representation of defendants on death row. In one case, in which I was not involved, our lawyers upset the death sentence of a woman who had been physically abused by her husband. She complained to her brother-in-law who said he would "take care of it." Although she said she did not know that he meant he would murder her husband, she was sentenced to death. Her attorney failed to offer in evidence hospital records to prove the abuse she had endured.

An associate in the firm had volunteered to represent a prisoner named Leslie Lowenfield who was on death row in Louisiana. Shortly before the July 4 weekend, in 1987, I learned that Lowenfield was about to be executed. The attorney handling that case had gone to Fire Island, a beach resort. There were no cell phones in those days, and there were no phones at the resort. I put together a team and we worked over the holiday weekend to prepare a motion to stay the execution, which was granted. I petitioned the Supreme Court for certiorari. The court decided to hear the case. The defendant had been found guilty of murdering his ex-girlfriend, who was a court deputy sheriff, her four-year old child, her new boyfriend and her father. In order to focus on the defendant's constitutional right to counsel and the legal arguments that were appropriate, it was necessary to put out of my head the horror of the crimes involved. Moreover, there was solid evidence that Lowenfield was guilty as charged. Among other evidence, the rifle used in the murders was found under Lowenfield's bed. There also was testimony in regard to motive, as he was upset about breaking up with his girlfriend who had a relationship with another man.

Although this was my second Supreme Court argument, the prospect of being before the nine justices was no less awesome. As with the Beck case, I had a moot court at NYU with Tony Amsterdam and others. I received two warnings. The first was that the Supreme Court did not decide to take the case because of a perceived error at the trial. Rather Chief Justice Rehnquist probably wanted to use this case to roll back a requirement set forth in prior Supreme Court precedent. Specifically, the moot court team focused on Justice Rehnquist's possible attack on prior case law that required a separate sentencing hearing at which the jury must find an aggravating factor that would distinguish this case from other murder cases and thus warrant the death penalty. Second, I was told that Justice Antonin Scalia, who had not been on the court for the Beck argument, would likely dominate the argument with questions. He would not vote in my favor no matter how I answered, so I had to respond to his questions briefly and move on to my argument before the other justices. Both warnings were prophetic.

We had two legal grounds for alleging error. First, at the sentencing hearing, after nine hours of deliberation, the jury sent a note to the trial judge saying that they disagreed as to whether to impose the death penalty. The trial judge gave the jury an instruction, known as an *Allen* charge, named after a case that upheld its use. Usually, when jurors report that they are unable to agree on a verdict, the judge admonishes them to listen with an open mind to the views of fellow jurors, and to try again to reach a verdict. I argued that while this instruction was commonplace in ordinary criminal cases, it should not be allowed in a sentencing hearing where the death penalty is at stake. Moreover, the trial judge polled the jurors twice as to whether each of them thought that further deliberations might result in a verdict. I argued that the judge's action was inherently coercive and put pressure on the jurors to vote for the death penalty. In response to the first poll, four jurors responded in the negative; in response to the second poll, one juror said no. I argued that this juror, who had to write his vote on a piece of paper, was likely to have been opposed to the death penalty. The public nature of this procedure could have pressured that juror to abandon his antideath penalty principles. At oral argument, Justice Scalia pressed me with machine gun questions insisting that there was no way of knowing what this or any other juror was thinking. I responded that in a death penalty case, the issue is not what jurors actually thought, which could not readily be proven; rather the issue should be whether there was a risk of coercion.

The Court held that a capital punishment case did not warrant deviation from the traditional rule allowing trial judges to admonish a jury that reported a disagreement to deliberate further in order to render a verdict. Justice Marshall wrote a dissenting opinion that was joined by Brennan. Justice Stevens joined the dissenting opinion with regard to the judge's instructions when the jurors could not agree. The dissenting opinion criticized the court's opinion for not focusing on the totality of the way in which the trial judge handled the instructions after the jurors were in disagreement. The dissent pointed to the fact that after the jury found the defendant guilty of murder, the judge had the jury go right to deliberations on sentencing at 8:00 p.m. on a Saturday night, and sit until almost midnight. This rush to judgment put pressure on the jurors to reach a decision. Justice Marshall also stated that the trial judge tilted the jury's deliberations by telling them that if they did not reach a verdict on the death penalty, the court would impose a life sentence without parole. Absent that information, the jurors might have concluded that if they failed to reach a decision now on the death penalty, there would be another sentencing hearing.

The second legal ground I presented was that the trial court did not satisfy the Supreme Court's requirement that the jury be instructed at the sentencing hearing to find an aggravating factor that justified the death penalty in this particular case. The trial judge had concluded that the aggravating factor of killing more than one person was proven at the guilt phase of the trial. The trial court held that this was sufficient to invoke the death penalty without considering the presence of an aggravating factor in the subsequent hearing on whether to sentence the defendant to death. My point was that the jury might be more willing to find that aggravating factor in the context of whether the defendant was guilty than in deliberating as to whether he should be put to death.

While counsel for the Louisiana Department of Corrections was making his argument, I took copious notes and indicated in the margin of my notepad what I might say in the few minutes I had for rebuttal. Upon being called on by the Chief Justice, I rose and informed the Court that I intended to address a court case on which the State relied. But once on your feet, you do not control the issue to be addressed. Rather, I was asked the following:

". . . I would think you would delight in the fact that the jury cannot consider aggravating circumstances."

In other words, the justice was suggesting that if counsel were required to inform the jury of the aggravating circumstances of the murder, those

facts would only influence the jury to impose the death penalty. So, what
was I complaining about here where aggravating circumstances were
not considered at the sentencing phase? Here is my response:

> *Mr. Klingsberg:* "The basis for our claim, Your Honor, is that
> the jury did not meaningfully undertake to engage in a fresh
> finding of fact regarding this aggravating circumstance . . .
> [W]here you have a jury which deliberated for ten hours,
> it certainly cannot be a foregone conclusion that—if they
> had been directed to make a meaningful finding and hadn't
> been told by the prosecutor that they had already found that
> [aggravating circumstance] so they don't have to bother with
> it again—what that result might be . . . [W]here there is a legal
> element that is lacking in the procedure, particularly in a death
> sentence case, . . . that is so basic . . . it should not be treated
> as a harmless error . . ."

The Supreme Court affirmed the conviction in an opinion by Justice
Rehnquist. The heart of my argument was that the court's suggestion
would in effect read out of the law the requirement that at the sentencing
phase of the trial, the jury is required to find an aggravating circum-
stance, as defined by the state statute. The purpose of that condition is
to distinguish this case from others in a way that warrants the death
penalty. The majority opinion held that it was sufficient for the jury to
have found an aggravating factor at the guilt stage of the trial. As my
moot court panel had predicted, Justice Rehnquist used this case to roll
back the requirement in death penalty cases for a separate sentencing
hearing in which an aggravating factor must be found. In essence, an
exception was created where a statutory aggravating factor was proven
at the guilt phase of the trial. In dissent, Justice Marshall, citing prior
precedent, concluded that relying on the evidence in the guilt trial should

not satisfy the requirement to find one or more aggravating factors that would distinguish this crime as deserving the death penalty.

Insanity and the Death Penalty

Working with the New Orleans Capital Punishment Project, we had previously sought to have the defendant examined by a psychiatrist to determine if insanity precluded him from understanding the proceedings, and therefore precluded execution. He refused and maintained his innocence. For example, he urged that the police planted the murder weapon that they found under his bed. After the Supreme Court decision affirming the death sentence, Lowenfield agreed to a psychiatric examination. In Chapter 1, I described the events that followed. Justice Brennan did not convince a fifth justice to hear and listen to our argument. Lowenfield was executed and pronounced dead at 1:25 a.m., twenty-five minutes after the Supreme Court had agreed to hear the case but refused to stay the execution. Despite having granted the petition for certiorari to take the case on appeal, the Supreme Court did not hear argument and render an opinion on the insanity issue. We were not "heard" or listened to.

Dale Brown was a Hall of Fame basketball coach for Louisiana State University. He also was an inspirational speaker and a devout Catholic. Brown visited and corresponded with Lowenfield while he was on death row. According to the transcript of an interview of Brown by Robert Siegel of National Public Radio on *All Things Considered*, one of Brown's students alerted him to Lowenfield's imminent execution. Brown rushed to his cell to be with Loewenfield during his last hours. Lowenfield continued to deny his involvement in the murders and Brown declined to judge whether was guilty or not. Brown found it a "nightmare" to contemplate the execution, which was an hour and a half away, as well as the suffering of the relatives of those who were murdered. While they were waiting, the warden picked up the ringing phone. Brown thought: "They're going to stop the execution." The warden announced that there is going to be a delay. Ten minutes later the phone rang again and the warden announced that the court made a decision. "Proceed." Brown describes his shock as the prisoner "walked to be executed with the shackles and the shaved head and the pants that were ripped up." Lowenfield smiled and said, "Thank you, Coach Brown." Siegel reported that prior to the execution, Brown favored capital punishment as a deterrent. "Now he says that he's not so sure anymore." Since I was on the front line filing motions and briefs, I never experienced the "nightmare" of observing an actual execution.

Some years later, I received a letter from someone who identified himself as a Louisiana attorney. He wrote that he had read the record in the Lowenfield case. He proceeded to ask why I had not made a certain argument which he presented. I scanned the rest of the letter, which was not immediately comprehensible. I decided that I really did not want to delve any further into the letter. I had done my best to represent the accused and so did the lawyers who helped with the briefs and conducted a moot court oral argument. Public Defenders who regularly engage in death penalty defense have warned that looking back will drive you crazy.

Postscript on the Death Penalty

In 1998, a ceremony was held at the Association of the Bar of the City of New York. Former Governor Mario Cuomo gave an impassioned speech condemning the death penalty, which was courageous for a politician. I and others were given the Thurgood Marshall Award for "in the highest and noble tradition of the legal profession," having "served as pro bono counsel to a human being under a sentence of death." At an informal Saturday night service at our synagogue, I delivered a d'var Torah (a kind of sermon commenting on portions of the Bible) relating to capital punishment. Before I rose to speak, one of the congregants whispered: "You know it's allowed. An eye for an eye!" That was literally true. But in the Jewish religion, guidance flows from the rabbis' commentary, not by literal biblical commands. Indeed, the rabbis of old took full advantage of the written obstacles to imposing the death penalty so—according to the commentary—it was rarely invoked.

In my capacity as a director of the Legal Aid Society of New York, I observed the activities of the death penalty division, which was staffed with social workers who would track down all of the infirmities in defendants' upbringing and background that might explain their aberrant behavior. Many jurisdictions lack the facilities and staff to develop such evidence so it is not heard when it should be presented by counsel in the sentencing phase of the trial as mitigating factors. In 2004, the New York Court of Appeals held that the death penalty was unconstitutional. Federal authorities also were not invoking the death penalty. It became apparent that the services of the Society's capital division were no longer needed so the unit was disbanded. During the last federal administration, the Supreme Court granted the Justice Department's request to revive the death penalty in federal cases after seventeen years of nonuse. President-Elect Biden promised to end federal death sentences by legislation. A number of states have abolished the death penalty in recent years. Nevertheless, death penalties and executions by states will continue and the Supreme Court will be involved.

Justice Brennan's concern in the Lowenfield case, with the Supreme Court's denial of the opportunity to be heard and listened to when his execution was scheduled, has proven to be prescient in light of recent events. Despite raising legitimate constitutional issues, which often have led lower courts to grant stays, obstacles have been placed to block being heard on mental competency and other constitutional issues.

First is the limitation on the right to seek habeas corpus in federal court after having been denied relief in state courts. In the *Genovese* case, which I argued as Chief Appellate Attorney, the relief sought by Edward Bennett Williams was by way of a petition for a writ of habeas corpus. Habeas corpus enables a prisoner who was convicted of a crime to ask a court to listen to an argument that the conviction was unlawful. I recall that as a judge's law clerk, I was frequently called on to review handwritten petitions, which were sometimes difficult to read, that prisoners had submitted. While this was a burdensome task, it was important to the right to be heard. In a 1977 opinion authored by Justice Thurgood Marshall, the U.S. Supreme Court recognized the "fundamental constitutional right of access to the courts" which included the right of prisoners to have access to law libraries and other tools needed to prepare such petitions. *Bounds* v. *Smith.*

Habeas corpus is frequently employed to contest convictions of capital offenses while the defendant is on death row. In 1996, President Clinton signed the Anti-terrorism and Effective Death Penalty Act (AEDPA). Under this Act, prisoners have a deadline of one year to file petitions for habeas corpus and can only do so once. In addition, federal courts are required to give deference to state court rulings even if they disagree with the result. Thus, the AEDPA's severe limitations on habeas corpus led to a sharp reduction in federal decisions overturning the death penalty. These provisions enhanced the need to expeditiously enlist attorneys to seek relief from death penalty convictions and sentencing. Kaye Scholer and other large New York law firms answered the call. But the limitation constrained the avenues for relief by death row prisoners.

Next is the use of the "shadow docket," which was utilized in the Lowenfield case, and has become popular in death penalty cases. The term refers to emergency orders and summary decisions that are outside the high court's main docket of argued cases and decisions. The term was coined in a 2015 law review article by William Baude, a University of Chicago Law School professor and former law clerk to Chief Justice Roberts. Baude expressed concern about the lack of transparency in such orders, which are often *per curiam* (meaning by the court as a whole and without identifying the justice who wrote it) and unsigned. Often there is a divide between the conservative and liberal justices, but unless there are four dissents, those who joined or not joined in the opinion may not be identified.

In its year-end report for 2020, the American Bar Association (ABA) Death Penalty Representation Project reported increasing concern over the recent increase in shadow docket decisions in death penalty cases. Often late at night and on the eve of executions, the Supreme Court has engaged in a practice of vacating stays issued by lower courts. The stays would have permitted the lower courts to allow litigants to be heard on the merits, particularly relating to the mental competency of the prisoner. Using the shadow docket, without argument or full briefing, the Supreme Court just denied a stay pending appeal of a constitutional challenge to a Texas anti-abortion law. Justice Kagan in dissent wrote, "the majority's decision is emblematic of too much of this court's shadow decision making—which every day becomes more unreasoned, inconsistent and impossible to defend."

Recently, the Supreme Court, with dissents including from Justice Gorsuch, the first appointee of the prior administration, ruled that a prisoner cannot be executed if he lacks a "rational understanding" of why the State wants to execute him. But as the make-up of the court changed, there have been executions where mental incompetency issues were raised, but a stay to consider those issues was denied.

Three federal executions were scheduled for January 2021, before a new president was inaugurated. Among them was the second woman to be executed by federal authorities. The Inter-American Commission on Human Rights has issued opinions in death penalty cases that are not binding but have resulted in stays of execution. The government ignored the Commission's request for a delay so that the Supreme Court could hear and consider the woman's petition. A lower court temporarily stayed her execution because her lawyers contracted COVID-19, but the D.C. Circuit reversed. She had a history of sexual abuse and rape. She was diagnosed with temporal lobe epilepsy, psychosis, traumatic brain injury and fetal alcohol syndrome. An Indiana judge stayed the execution so mental competency tests could be administered. The Supreme Court overturned the stay and she was executed days before the inauguration of a new president who might have commuted the death sentence. Her pleas of insanity were not heard or listened to.

In a recent case, which bears a resemblance to the Lowenfield case, the government executed Wesley Ira Purkey. As described by his attorney, Rebecca E. Woodman of Kansas City, he was so impaired by Alzheimer's disease, schizophrenia, and brain damage that he believed he was being killed in a conspiracy to retaliate for complaining about prison conditions. He had no rational understanding of the government plan to kill him for a crime he committed years ago. On the very day Purkey was scheduled to be executed, a federal district judge issued an injunction based on evidence of his mental incompetence. The court of appeals upheld the injunction. At 2:45 a.m., the Supreme Court vacated the injunction without explanation and Purkey was executed at 8:10 that morning. Four justices dissented. Justice Sotomayor wrote: "[P]roceeding with Purkey's execution now, despite the grave questions and factual findings regarding his mental competency, casts a shroud of constitutional doubt over the most irrevocable of injuries." *Lowenfield* redux!

Mental competency remains an ambiguous element of death penalty jurisprudence. Without the opportunity to hear and decide cases after briefing and argument, the law on this important subject cannot develop or be implemented. States have considered legislation on the issue but to date none has been enacted.

In its 2019 report, the ABA's Death Penalty Project raised a concern that in a series of cases, the Supreme Court decided to consider that setting an execution date is a factor favoring denial of a stay. This in turn has encouraged states, which have the power to set execution dates, to intentionally set execution dates while legal proceedings are pending so as to get an unfair advantage in opposing stays before the Supreme Court. In one case, involving the defendant's request to have clergy of his religion present at the execution, Justice Kagan wrote, for the four dissenting justices, that the majority's decision was made so that the state could "meet its preferred execution date." In another case involving a challenge to the method of execution by legal injection, the Supreme Court held that "last minute stays should be the extreme exception, not the norm." In response, Justice Breyer in dissent urged that ending delays at the expense of constitutional protections would pay "too high a price." Many times, the application for a stay is timely even though an execution date has been set. For example, where innocence is the issue, evidence such as from DNA may have been uncovered late in the game. My application for a stay in the Lowenfield case was timely for the reasons described here, even though an execution date had been set. Lawyers, often functioning pro bono and having been brought into a case late, have an ethical obligation to seek a stay of execution where they have concluded that there has been a denial of constitutional rights. The courts should have an equal obligation to hear such argument.

A decision handed down, as I write, is illustrative of the current Supreme Court's view of the need to be heard in circumstances akin to the death penalty. In *Jones* v. *Mississippi*, a divided Supreme Court upheld a juvenile's sentence to life imprisonment without parole. The dissenting opinion stated: "[L]ife without parole sentences, like capital punishment, may violate the Eighth Amendment when imposed on children." For that reason, precedents—which the majority rejected—require that juvenile offenders "must be given the opportunity to show that their crime did not reflect irreparable corruption." In other words, they have a right to be heard, which the Court denied in this case.

An important issue in regard to the death penalty is innocence. According to a database maintained by The Death Penalty Information Center, since 1973 there have been 185 persons on death row who have been exonerated. According to the Center, the causes are mainly official misconduct, perjury, and wrongful accusation. Racial bias has also been ascribed as a basis for wrongful conviction based on the relative number of executions of minority defendants. The advent of DNA evidence has enhanced lawyers' ability to prove innocence even where the prisoner is on death row.

There are no reliable statistics on how many of those executed have later been proved to be innocent. Courts are reluctant to hear cases seeking to prove innocence after execution. And lawyers' time is better spent in representing those still alive on death row. Nevertheless, it is generally accepted that of the 1,562 persons executed since the Supreme Court reinstated the death penalty in 1976, a number were innocent. The Death Penalty Information Center has put together a list of twenty executed persons who, based on the evidence, were "possibly innocent." There is now a case in the Tennessee courts where the daughter of an executed prisoner is asking a court to clear her father's name by allowing belatedly discovered DNA evidence to be used. Clearly, it would be preferable and humane if the defendant was serving a prison sentence, and still alive to take advantage of late discovered DNA evidence.

Finally, as I learned in the U.S. Attorneys' office in regard to the Rosenberg's death penalty, the finality of the sentence precludes taking advantage of subsequent legal and constitutional decisions that would have supported the vacating of the conviction or sentence.

There has been an increase in the quality and quantity of legal representation. Law firms have established pro bono departments which volunteer to represent those on death row. Moreover, death penalty projects have sprung up locally, as was the case with the New Orleans project with whom I worked in Lowenfield. But the courts and the legislatures need to remove the roadblocks that prevent the lawyers from having a fair opportunity to be heard.

•　•　•

Chapter XII
PRO BONO

Apart from my five years in government service and my first case in private practice "prosecuting" price-fixers, my pro bono representations, particularly arguing two capital cases in the U.S. Supreme Court, were the pinnacle of my personal pursuit of justice.

Legal Aid Society of New York

Shortly after I started working for the law firm, I volunteered at the Legal Aid Society headquarters in Harlem to help people who could not afford a lawyer. The matters were fairly simple such as negotiating lower car payments. Later, I joined the Board of Directors of the Legal Aid Society of New York. This organization, which was largely supported by the private bar, provides legal services for the indigent. This stands in contrast to states where only government-funded public defenders provide legal services to the indigent. Judge Dimock thought that having the government on both sides of the same case was a kind of fascism. My work with the Legal Aid Society not only provided personal satisfaction but also support for an important institution in achieving justice for those who otherwise would not have access to the courts.

With the help of David Wechsler, a full-time Legal Aid employee, I organized a program which we called "Second Act," by which lawyers, who were winding down their private practice or retiring, could work full- or part-time on legal aid matters. One lawyer retired early from his private practice to devote himself to work full-time at Legal Aid representing children in family court proceedings. He was gracious enough to address sessions we held to induce others to join this program. Another attorney specialized in representing tenants in dispossess cases in state court. He carried his office in his briefcase and typed his own briefs. Our informative sessions attracted additional lawyers including Jay Greenfield, a partner in the Paul, Weiss law firm, who joined the program full-time. These lawyers' devotion to this cause far exceeded mine. In 2008, when I moved from being a partner to counsel status, I participated in the program for particular cases.

Judith Kaye, Chief Judge of N.Y. Court of Appeals, Giving Legal Aid Society Award for Outstanding Public Service

In one case, a defendant had been picked out of a lineup as someone who committed a robbery. I showed a photograph of the lineup to my colleagues who consistently identified the accused. I contended that the reason that the accused stood out from others was that the rest of the lineup consisted of policemen out of uniform. I argued that the defendant was wrongly convicted due to a faulty identification procedure. The appellate court in Brooklyn rejected my argument. I then received a phone call from Chief Judge Wachtler of the New York Court of Appeals who asked if this was a serious case that should be accepted by the high court. I explained my argument as best I could, but I did not persuade the judge to recommend taking the appeal.

Challenging Secret Post Release Supervision

I had more success in challenging a practice of the New York Department of Correction Services (DOS). In 1998, New York abolished parole and substituted another procedure, Post Release Supervision (PRS), whereby violent felony offenders, after being released from prison, had to undergo supervision and refrain from certain activities. Any violation resulted in being returned to prison. Defendants typically were not told of this consequence when they agreed to plead guilty or at the time of sentencing after trial. The New York Court of Appeals, the highest state court, had previously held that prison officials are bound to follow the directions in the commitment order that accompanies a prisoner. The Department of Corrections would often have the court clerk add PRS to the commitment order without informing the accused. Thus, there was a question as to whether a released prisoner could be returned to jail for violating the terms of PRS when—even though the commitment order provided for PRS—the Judge did not inform the defendant of that prospect at the time sentence was pronounced.

I agreed to prepare a brief, which would challenge the administration of PRS, on behalf of the Society as a friend of court (*amicus curiae*). The amicus brief would be filed in a series of five cases, each with somewhat different facts. The Society also represented an individual defendant in one of those cases. The Society was concerned about its dual role as *amicus curiae* and representing an individual. A suggestion was that, as *amicus*, I represent an upstate public defender organization. I rejected that idea, as I knew that the New York Legal Aid Society was prestigious and had close relations with the Chief Judge of the Court of Appeals, Judith Kaye. By chance, I was lecturing on antitrust at a New York State Bar meeting when I ran into Chief Judge Kaye, whom I knew from ceremonies where she gave Society awards to me and others. I told Judge Kaye that I could not speak with her because I had a case before her court. She pressed me as to what it was about and I told her. She expressed interest in reading my brief and considering this important issue. I knew at that point that there was no longer any concern about appearing *amicus curiae*.

The Appellate Division, which is the intermediate appellate court in New York, had rejected the objections to the PRS procedure. That court held that by statute, the imposition of PRS was mandatory. Accordingly, the Appellate Division held that the details of whether or how PRS was pronounced by the sentencing judge, or recorded by the court clerk, did not undermine the legitimacy of the sentence.

Adopting the arguments in my amicus brief, the Court of Appeals reversed. The court found that sentencing by a judge was an essential part of criminal procedure. Therefore, the PRS aspect of the sentence should have been pronounced by the judge at the time of sentencing. The high court accepted my argument that it was not sufficient for the court clerk to have inserted a provision for PRS in the commitment order. The Court of Appeals also held that it was error for the State to have entered into a plea bargain with a defendant who had not been informed of PRS. In addition, the court held that its ruling applied to cases where defendants pleaded guilty without a plea bargain as well as where the defendant was sentenced after having been found guilty at a jury trial.

There is a principle that courts avoid deciding constitutional issues where there are alternative grounds to reach the same result. Here, the court did not need to reach the constitutional issues I raised. But as a matter of appellate strategy, making a valid argument that a statute or procedure violates the Constitution can influence a court to try to reach the same result on other grounds. Here, the court stated that it did not need to reach the constitutional issues because it was able to resolve the issue on state statutory grounds. Thus, the court held that the Department of Correctional Services lacked the statutory authority to impose PRS, or to return prisoners to jail for violating PRS, where at the time of sentencing the court failed to mention the prospect of PRS. The Court of Appeals' order prohibited the Department of Corrections from imposing PRS without proper notice to the accused. Thus, we brought an end to the administrative, nonjudicial imposition of postrelease supervision.

Team of Lawyers Who Argued PRS Cases for Legal Aid Society

At its annual award ceremony, the Legal Aid Society reported the result as a "sweeping victory" and honored me and my team at Kaye

Scholer. It should be noted, however, that the Court of Appeals declined to grant the inmates immunity from future imposition of PRS but only granted them a new sentencing procedure. Importantly, those who had been returned to prison for violating PRS got a second chance.

The postscript is that there were numerous prisoners entitled to similar relief who were not parties to these court actions. In order to remedy these injustices, we mobilized the associates in my firm who had worked with me on the appeal, together with lawyers from Paul Weiss and O'Melveny & Myers. We fielded teams of young lawyers to file similar petitions on behalf of other prisoners. Additional petitions were filed on behalf of numerous inmates, which were not contested by the State.

The Oil for Food Scandal

This potential representation was not exactly pro bono, as there was a possibility of a contingent fee if the case materialized and succeeded in obtaining a recovery. Minnesota Senator Norm Coleman, who was leading an investigation into the scandal, described it as "the most extensive fraud in the history of the United Nations." In 1990, in Operation Desert Storm, President Bush pushed Saddam's army back from its invasion of Kuwait. The United Nations then imposed sanctions on Iraq to prevent it from pursuing further military incursions and from creating nuclear weapons. Thus, there was an embargo on Iraq's sale of oil, its principal source of funds. As a result of banning Iraq's biggest export, its economy faltered and its citizens were deprived of food and medicines. In 1996, to alleviate a humanitarian crisis, the U.N. implemented the Oil for Food program. Iraq was allowed to sell oil, provided that the proceeds were used to purchase food and medicines. This in turn led to widespread cheating by Sadaam Hussein in concert with oil companies, banks and others.

Carole Basri was born in the Iraqi city of her last name. She was on the faculty of Fordham Law School and annually ran a forum on corporate compliance. She asked me to lecture at several of the events.

The regulatory requirements defining executives' responsibility for the accuracy of financial statements had changed substantially since the matter I previously handled before the SEC (described later). Ms. Basri had been involved in the transition government of Iraq and made several trips there. She approached me to represent the government of Iraq in seeking to recover funds from companies involved in the Oil for Food scandal. Many billions of dollars were said to be involved. The Miami-based international law firm of Greenberg, Traurig was later brought in as cocounsel.

We made some preliminary inquiries into the facts from public records. Apparently, much of what were supposed to be food and pharmaceutical deliveries, which were to justify the sale of oil, turned out to be empty boxes. It appeared that some domestic U.S. oil companies were involved. Some well-known international banks may also have played a role. Russian operatives also appeared to have been an important part of the scheme, and it was unlikely that they could be reached legally. In consultation with the client, I contacted the U.S. Attorneys' Office in the Southern District of New York, and Robert Morgenthau, who was then District Attorney for New York County, to ask them to consider opening investigations. They were receptive.

It quickly became apparent that merely asking a major accounting firm to investigate the facts and develop evidence was not sufficient. I learned that Paul Volcker, the former chair of the Federal Reserve, was winding up an investigation on behalf of the UN. I was put in touch with one of Volcker's senior investigators. He agreed to meet with me secretly at an out-of-the-way restaurant in New York City. He expressed a willingness to work with us as soon as the U.N. investigation was complete, which would be soon. He told me that no one without access to the evidence that the U.N. had uncovered, could possibly find the ghosts that underlay the scandal. He suggested that he might bring in others from the U.N. investigation to help.

Ms. Basri introduced me to a representative of the client. I met with an Iraqi official who told me that lawyers in Iraq had done considerable work in uncovering aspects of the scandal. Since these lawyers would be risking their lives to provide us with evidence, he suggested that they receive a percentage of any recovery. This was reasonable and ethical, as they would be compensated for legal work done. Then came the surprise. He said that for his troubles, he would have to receive 5 percent of any recovery. That was a nonstarter. I told him that under our ethical rules, lawyers could share fees but only for legal work actually done. He was not a lawyer, and was a government official. We also discussed payment for the investigators, which initially would cost a few hundred thousand dollars—well within the assets of the Iraqi government. He declined, saying that we, the lawyers, would have to fund those services. That was also unacceptable. I relayed these obstacles to Ms. Basri who said she would see what she could do. The result was that neither my firm nor Greenberg Traurig were retained to further pursue the matter. I assume that as a result Iraq never recovered these losses.

The Second Amendment

I volunteered to judge National Moot Court competitions held in the mock courtroom at the City Bar Association. Interestingly, the Ivy League law schools did not win the prizes at this event. The Yale Law students in particular often were too focused on policy to make effective legal arguments. I was one of three judges who heard a moot court argument of the then pending Supreme Court decision on the scope of the Second Amendment. All three mock judges accepted the students' argument that this constitutional provision was not intended to protect individuals' ability to have guns. Rather, it was aimed in part at the formation of state sponsored militias, such as were needed to fight in the American Revolution for independence from Britain. The revolution was over but militias in Southern states were used to put down slave rebellions and the votes of those states were needed to approve the Constitution.

Unfortunately, the real Supreme Court voted the other way, leading to thousands of deaths, including school children. In the wake of seven recent mass shootings and thousands of murders, there is a renewed but probably futile cry for gun safety measures. But there is surprisingly little said about reversing the Supreme Court's 5–4 decision in *District of Columbia v. Heller,* authored by Justice Scalia, holding that the Second Amendment protects individual gun rights. Indeed, President Obama, and others who advocate gun controls, have stated—apparently for political reasons—that they respect Second Amendment rights. All members of the Supreme Court are aware of the principles regarding adherence to precedent absent special circumstances. And the justices often disagree on whether the special circumstances are present in particular cases. These principles are specified in a number of high court opinions most recently by Justice Kavanaugh in a dissenting opinion in *Ramos v. Louisiana.* He explained that constitutional decisions are more easily overruled than statutory decisions. A prime example is *Plessey v. Ferguson*, which upheld separate but equal treatment, and was reversed by *Brown v. Board of Education,* when the consequences of racial segregation in schools were documented for the court.

It is time for politicians, particularly Democrats, to stop saying that they support a so-called Second Amendment right to own guns. Enacting effective gun control legislation is unlikely to occur due to Republican opposition and National Rifle Association influence. Another approach is to overturn the *Heller* decision, recognizing that this might require changes in the make-up of the Supreme Court. Hopefully, at some future time, in an appropriate case, an advocate will file what has come to be known as a Brandeis brief; that is, a brief that relies on a compilation of scientific information and social science. Such a brief would document the physical and psychological impact on society of gun violence. The brief could portray gun violence as a public health danger, as recognized in President Biden's job bill, which allocates $5 billion for prevention over eight years. President Biden has reinstated the federal government's compilation and study of data relating to gun violence, which could provide the evidence for such a brief. The brief could show that the year 2020 was a record year for deaths from gun violence, and that 2021 is trending toward being worse. It could demonstrate the relationship between gun deaths and gun possession, which *Heller* held is a Second Amendment right. Thus, at the same time that deaths from guns are rising, 23 million guns were sold in 2020, a 66 percent increase over the prior year. These facts would inexorably lead to the conclusion that the founders did not intend the Second Amendment to allow weapons designed for war and guns in the hands of those who committed crimes or are mentally incompetent, all of which have led to this uniquely American carnage.

Bar Associations

While some bar associations around the country mainly provide a social outlet for lawyers, the Association of the City of New York afforded many opportunities for learning and teaching. When I returned to New York from D.C., Judge Walsh urged me to join the Law Enforcement Committee of the City Bar Association. We studied the developing case law and published recommendations. Most of the Committee members and I did not agree with some of Judge Walsh's proposals. For example, Walsh encouraged the committee to advocate the abolition of Miranda warnings, which were statements to suspects that they have a right to an attorney and to remain silent. Experience over years demonstrated that these warnings did not materially interfere with law enforcement. The Committee did not adopt this suggestion.

I chaired the Trade Regulation and Antitrust Committee of the City Bar Association. We published an annual review of antitrust case law, which kept us on our toes. We also sponsored speakers including

Professor Handler's Annual Antitrust Review, which he prepared and published with the help of Kaye Scholer lawyers.

I was elected to the American College of Trial Lawyers, which required a certain amount of trial experience and recommendations from opposing counsel. Candidates were not even supposed to know that they were being proposed. The College sponsored coaching for students in mock trial situations in which I participated as an instructor. An annual meeting was held at the Boca Resort in Boca Raton, Florida. Sometimes we attended with one or more of our children. In the elevator, we ran into a gentleman wearing purple Bermuda shorts and colorful socks, who asked our sons, Jordan and Matthew, whether they realized that he was Warren Burger, Chief Justice of the Supreme Court. Over time, I lectured frequently at the American Bar Association's National Institutes on antitrust, nuclear equipment litigation and other subjects. Preparation for these lectures enabled me to keep up with current developments. And sometimes, I was retained on the recommendation of lawyers who had heard my lectures.

Community Activities

Despite a busy litigation schedule and frequent travel, I was able to "give back" by undertaking community activities. I agreed to serve as counsel for our synagogue for which I participated in the redrafting of its governing documents and negotiation of contracts with service providers. Ultimately, I became Vice President and a trustee. I also coached our boys' community baseball teams, and ran an after-school basketball program.

A community concern has been pollution from noise, particularly at odd hours, due to airplanes taking off and landing at a nearby airport in Purchase, New York. In addition to commercial jets, a focus has been on expanding facilities for private planes (which also make noise), such as are being built by a company called "Million Air." In 2017, the Republican County Executive announced plans to sell the airport to a private company. Privatization created a risk of an increase in air traffic. The Purchase Environmental Protective Association (PEPA) asked me to work with Citizens for a Responsible County Airport (CRCA) to oppose privatization. The Executive Director of CRCA, an investment banker with a pilot's license, was knowledgeable on the technical aspects. Earl Doppelt, a PEPA board member and Kaye Scholer client, knew of my advocacy skills, which he thought would contribute to preparation of a White Paper. In addition to pollution from noise, the paper described the runoff of deicing fluid in a nearby reservoir that is a source of drinking water. The White Paper was widely circulated to county legislators and at public rallies. The result was that a Democrat won the next election and privatization was avoided. PEPA honored me at the next annual meeting. Having had one environmental case, described later, on the wrong side of green, this was a rewarding opportunity.

•   •   •

Chapter XIII
CONGRESSIONAL TESTIMONY

In 1975, I testified before the House Judiciary Committee, Subcommittee on Antitrust, in regard to proposed antitrust legislation. Gerald Ford, who had been vice president before Nixon resigned, was president. Thomas Kauper was the Assistant Attorney General in charge of the Antitrust Division of the Justice Department. A Democratic Congress was focused on enhancing antitrust enforcement and proposed what became the Antitrust Improvement Act of 1976. My only knowledge of Congressional hearings had been while I was in college watching hearings at which the Senate accused Senator McCarthy of wrongdoing. These hearings were contentious so I was not quite sure what to expect. As it turned out, the hearing at which I testified was collegial.

At the outset, I summarized the written statement that I had provided to the Committee. I answered questions from congressmen who had different perspectives on antitrust enforcement. The prospective questioners consisted of eight committee members and two counsel—more than the three judges I was accustomed to appearing before on federal circuit courts. This was five years before my first Supreme Court argument. Congressmen from both sides of the aisle were cordial and complimented me for being well-prepared, informative and helpful. I was impressed with the members' depth of knowledge of the antitrust case law and issues that they presented in their questions. There was no sign of the divisive and obstructive tactics that mark Congressional hearings today.

The subject of my appearance was a proposal that was intended to enact into law the doctrine of *parens patriae*. The term literally means "father of our country." In a legal sense, the doctrine implies that the government needs to take action to protect its citizens when they are unable to protect themselves. As applied to antitrust, the concept had been the subject of a number of conflicting court decisions. The proposed bill authorized State attorneys general to bring antitrust suits on behalf of injured consumers. The issue of whether *parens patriae* suits by the States are useful is complex. Centralized antitrust enforcement by the well-staffed and expert lawyers in the Justice Department's Antitrust Division is obviously more efficient than having numerous state attorneys general bring lawsuits. However, certain presidents may not favor vigorous enforcement so the states can provide a counterbalance. In any event, my task was not to favor or disfavor the draft legislation. Rather, I was focused on ways it could be improved and avoid constitutional infirmities.

Parens Patriae lawsuits resemble class actions in the sense that the state acts like the class plaintiff and sues on behalf of its citizens. However, the proposed bill lacked the protections in the class action rule. I induced the committee to add such requirements. One problem was that under the bill as drafted, there was no requirement that consumers be notified and given the opportunity to opt out of the state's lawsuit and bring their own suit. If some consumers simply filed their own suits, this could result in a double recovery. Or a court might bar consumers' individual suits because of the pendency of the states' lawsuit. Moreover, consumers might not file their own suits because they were unaware of the potential claim. A court might find that the statute implicitly barred suits by citizens who did not want to be part of the *parens patriae* suit.

Assistant Attorney General Kauper had testified earlier that a solution was simply to bar individual consumer actions. I told the Subcommittee:

"Now, it seems strange indeed in a bill designed to liberalize private anti-trust recovery and strengthen enforcement, for the Assistant Attorney General to suggest taking away the consumer's long-standing right to pursue treble damages on his own behalf." Kauper's suggestion was not adopted in the final bill.

I pointed out that after Kauper testified, the Supreme Court rendered a decision in a class action case holding that notice to the public was a constitutional obligation necessary to accord due process. I recommended that the bill be amended to incorporate notice and opt out provisions, which the courts would be required to follow, similar to the class action rule (Rule 23 of the Federal Rules of Civil Procedure). Following my recommendation, such a provision was incorporated into the bill as enacted. The final bill requires that notice be given by publication or otherwise of the pendency of the state's suit. The new statute also allows citizens to opt out of the state's suit and bring their own actions for damages. Double recovery is avoided by a provision that the award of damages in the state's suit must be adjusted so as not to duplicate individual citizens' actual or potential recovery.

Chairman Rodino asked me about a purported comment in my prepared statement that the bill would "terrorize" businesses. I had used the term *"in terrorem"* which is a Latin word meaning, "in fear," "as a threat or warning." He said the purpose of the bill was to strike terror into prospective violators of the antitrust laws. I explained that I did not intend to say that the basic idea of allowing states to file *parens patriae* suits would terrorize business owners. Rather, I had referred to the *in terrorem* impact of the bill as it related to the prospects for double recovery, which would be troubling.

The final bill adopted a suggestion, which I made at the hearing, that the suit must be brought on behalf of "natural citizens." I pointed out that allowing suits by companies in the chain of distribution could also create double recovery problems. This potential could only be avoided by complex and impractical tracing of whether overcharges were passed on by the original buyer to wholesalers and then to the manufacturer.

Another area of contention was the draft bill's provision for recovery of "aggregate damages." That concept might be difficult to apply in cases other than those involving price-fixing charges. To address this issue, the bill as enacted limited aggregate damages to cases involving price fixing. In closing, I noted that most states had their own so-called "little" antitrust statutes some of which provided for penalties more severe than the federal statutes. I hoped that this bill would not detract from state attorneys general efforts to utilize their state antitrust statutes where appropriate.

•   •   •

Chapter XIV
BANANAS

After four years as an associate, I was elected to the firm's partnership. As a predicate to that process, those of us who were up for consideration were invited to the summer homes of each of the managing partners, supposedly to check out our social skills and to meet our families. Handler was fastidious about his home and swimming pool in Yorktown Heights, New York. But that did not stop our three-year-old son from rubbing a watermelon slice against an iron-grated chair around the pool. Another candidate, Josh Greenberg, asked his three-year-old daughter to be sure to pee before leaving. In response, she loudly proclaimed that she had already done so in the pool. Despite these gaffes, we all were elected to the partnership.

At this point in time, I decided to make some changes in my relationship with Professor Handler. I was assisting him in court during an argument on a preliminary injunction to block a merger. He was having trouble hearing the judge and answering questions. So, I whispered: "Why don't you let me ask the questions?" I took over and that was the last time I wrote out scripts or was second seat.

One of my colleagues in the U.S. Attorneys' Office was Winthrop Allegaert. Win and his wife were neighbors in Scarsdale, where Fran and I played tennis with them. Win's wife was known as the "rat lady" of Scarsdale because of her work in getting the village to rout out rats coming from the Bronx River where they bred. While working at Davis Polk & Wardwell, Win was in charge of a case brought against United Brands. He left Davis Polk, took the case with him, and recommended to the client that it retain us for trial.

There were two unusual aspects to this trial. First, during the trial, the CEO of our client, United Brands, knocked his attaché case through a window of his office in the Pan Am Building in New York (now the MetLife Building), and jumped to his death. We were concerned that this had something to do with the possible results of the trial. But later inquiry revealed no evidence of that.

Another unique aspect of this trial was that it was conducted by Judge Murray Gurfein, a United States District Judge in the Southern District of New York. The judge was a brilliant lawyer, having worked for Thomas Dewey when he was New York District Attorney, prosecuting organized crime figures. Judge Gurfein had been a prosecutor at the Nuremberg trials of Nazis after World War II. Fran and I observed his cross-examination at those trials on a video at the Holocaust Museum in D.C. He also was a cousin of Fran's mother, Sylvia Morganstern, nee Gurfein. When Fran's grandparents emigrated to this country, their sponsor was Judge Gurfein's father. Handler knew Judge Gurfein professionally and from charitable work. Judge Gurfein was active in HIAS, which provided refugee aid and relocation of Holocaust survivors after World War II. At a pretrial hearing, Handler disclosed the relationship between the judge and Fran's mother. Plaintiff's lawyer did not object.

International Railways of Central America (IRCA) sued United Brands for monopolization in violation of the antitrust laws and for breach of contract. United Fruit (UF) was the predecessor to United Brands. UF had been the subject of a consent decree entered into with the U.S. Department of Justice in 1958, which required that it divest various holdings including IRCA. IRCA operated a railroad that transported UF's bananas grown on the west coast of Guatemala to a port on the east coast, from which the bananas were shipped to the United States and elsewhere. UF decided to close its west coast plantation, known as Tiquisate. As a result, IRCA lost most of its business.

I was to try the case. Handler arranged to have the courtroom wired for sound so he could sit in the jury box and listen to the trial, which was before the judge without a jury. On the first day of trial, as I made my opening statement, my voice reverberated with an echo that was intolerable. So, Handler bowed out and I kept him informed as the case proceeded. My second seat who examined a number of the witnesses was Fred Yerman. While over the years I was gratified to hear former colleagues thank me for what they learned from me, I was amused by Fred's reminder that during that trial, I cautioned him to button his suit jacket when rising to address the court or examine witnesses. Fred later became a skilled litigating partner and preceded me as chair of the firm's executive committee.

During pretrial discovery we found an opinion letter written by Davis Polk, which concluded that there was no defense to the breach of contract claim. We sought to exclude this and other documents from production based on attorney-client privilege. Plaintiff challenged the claims of privilege. We asked that the documents that we wanted to exclude be reviewed by a special master, particularly because many documents were written in Spanish. The judge advised that he could read Spanish, and so would review the documents himself. We presumed that while he upheld the privilege, he had read the Davis Polk opinion. This was worrisome.

The trial, before Judge Gurfein without a jury, consumed fourteen days and more than two thousand pages of transcript. In preparation for trial, we learned about the banana business. Next to strawberries, bananas are one of the most perishable foods. The bananas grown at Tiquisate were subject to destruction by windstorms. UF developed another type of banana called the Valery, which could withstand storms, but because of its thinner skin would be damaged by a long rail trip. The Valery also required less land to grow.

IRCA claimed that UF violated Section 2 of the Sherman Antitrust Act. This statute does not make it a violation of the antitrust laws to have a monopoly. Rather, the Act proscribes monopolization. That requires proof that a company with monopoly power willfully used that power to restrain competition and, in a private suit, to injure the plaintiff. IRCA claimed that UF sold its plantation in a way that precluded any competitor from purchasing it for cultivation of bananas. We contended that UF had not been a monopoly since the consent decree was entered in 1958. But even assuming that UF had monopoly power, we developed other defenses. Thus, through the testimony of the president of UF and other witnesses, we proved that there were legitimate business reasons for closing the plantations. Thomas Sunderland, the president of UF, testified that there were riots and labor strife in the area. There also were guerilla rebels who had killed one the company's managers. A new Communist government discouraged banana growing on the Pacific coast and favored cotton.

We presented an expert witness who testified to financial losses in reports on which Sunderland relied. Experts are often needed at trial, but present a peril if not carefully prepared. Our expert was not scheduled to testify until after lunch. Over my objection, he insisted on having a beer with lunch. I had instructed him not to use the blackboard in the courtroom because it would facilitate cross-examination. Sure enough, early in the direct testimony, he went to the blackboard and proceeded to outline his conclusions. Nevertheless, the key was not the accuracy of his analysis as such but the fact that Sunderland relied on the company reports that the expert explained. Judge Gurfein found Sunderland's testimony to be credible.

In making evidentiary rulings during the trial, Judge Gurfein frequently overruled my objections to admitting plaintiff's documents into evidence. Plaintiff's lawyer, a single practitioner, was disorganized and had numerous papers strewn across counsel's table. He would reach in and grab a document, seemingly without any logic, and offer it in evidence. I would object vigorously. The judge would admonish me to be patient while he read the document. Then the judge would opine: "There is a sense of verisimilitude about the document," and admit it into evidence.

After the trial, we submitted 245 proposed findings of fact, each with support in the record, and 21 conclusions of law, each with case support. The court adopted most of them in a detailed opinion. The judge ruled in favor of UF on the antitrust and the contract claims. Plaintiff's counsel told me that if he knew I was going to try the case, and not Handler, he would have asked the judge to recuse himself. Surely, that made no difference in the result. IRCA appealed. I argued the appeal before Chief Judge Lumbard, and Judges Mulligan and Friendly. Henry Friendly had been a name partner in a large New York law firm, and had a reputation for brilliance. Later, Fran and I met Judge Friendly while vacationing at the Chatham Bars Inn on Cape Cod. He told me that his daughter had arranged for a vacation so he could get over the recent death of his wife. He seemed lonely, spending his days reading a multivolume history of the Supreme Court. So, we kept him company by joining him for breakfast. Unfortunately, he took his own life shortly thereafter.

In a long opinion, the court of appeals affirmed, holding that the trial court's findings were not clearly erroneous and were supported by the evidence. Due to Judge Gurfein having leaned over backward to rule against me on evidentiary issues, there were no possible grounds for plaintiff to argue that there were errors in the trial. At that point, I realized that the Judge's leanings were to avoid legal error as well as to avoid any prejudice from the family relationship.

• • •

Chapter XV
U.S. SUPREME COURT—ANTITRUST

For this, my third Supreme Court argument, I was accompanied by my son, Jordan. After the argument, we had lunch at Duke Ziebert's on K Street where House majority leader Tip O'Neill was dining. Jordan asked for his autograph and he asked where Jordan was from. Upon hearing that he was from Scarsdale, Mr. O'Neill retorted, "I was on your diet"—referring to the popular book by the so-called Scarsdale Diet Doctor, who was murdered by the head mistress of a private girls' school with whom he had a relationship and who thought he also was involved with his nurse.

An association of "mom and pop," meaning small, family-owned drug stores in Alabama, sued some thirty pharmaceutical companies, all of whom I represented. My experience before the Supreme Court in the two pro bono death penalty cases enabled me to land this retainer. The claim was that the pharmaceutical manufacturers charged lower prices to a county hospital pharmacy than to the drug stores. Plaintiffs sought to enjoin discrimination in pricing that violated the Robinson Patman Act. Apart from the legal issues, I thought that the court would be sympathetic to the county hospital's pharmacy as it served the poor. An adverse decision could lead the manufacturers to lower their prices to the association's mom-and-pop drug stores. Or they could raise prices to the county hospital. During argument, Justice Lewis Powell, who wrote the majority opinion, focused on how the court's decision would impact food prices charged to the court's cafeteria as compared with private restaurants.

The Robinson Patman Act was passed in the New Deal era in 1936 when there was more concern with fair pricing than competition. In the years I practiced, this Act was rarely the subject of government enforcement, as discrimination in price is often a means of enhancing competition. Enforcement agencies—the Department of Justice and the Federal Trade Commission—were more concerned with pursuing those who sought to eliminate competition through price fixing and monopolization. In recent times, most of the Robinson Patman cases have been filed by private suitors.

In order to sustain a private claim, the plaintiff must show that there is injury to competition in general and that the plaintiff has suffered damage by reason of the injury to competition. Defenses are that the discrimination in price was the result of cost differences, or that the pricing was justified in order to meet competition from others. There are two kinds of suits. One claims "primary line" injury, that is, where a competitor's discrimination in favor of a customer causes that customer's competitors who paid the higher price to lose business. Another is "secondary line" injury where a customer claims that giving its competitors lower prices causes it injury. I was involved in consultations and litigation involving both types of potential violations.

Congress had previously rejected proposals to subject government purchasers to the Robinson Patman Act. I argued that this fact together with the legislative history of the statute established that purchases by the county hospital pharmacy were not intended to be covered. Plaintiffs relied on an exception to the Robinson Patman Act, enacted in 1936, which included public libraries, purported to be governmental entities, but did not include other governmental entities such as pharmacies. During the course of the argument, I criticized a decision by Justice Brennan in which he had assumed that libraries were usually government entities. My research revealed that most public libraries were open to the public but privately endowed. In fact, Benjamin Franklin established the first privately endowed public library in Philadelphia more than two hundred years ago. Justice Brennan turned his chair around and left the bench. I was concerned that he was angered by my argument. Subsequently, I learned that Justice Brennan's wife was taken to the hospital, and that is why he left the bench. I also observed that Justice O'Connor was nodding during my argument, and I hoped that meant she agreed with my points. I later learned that she had a tic that had nothing to do with her views on the argument.

In a five-four opinion, authored by Justice Powell, the court ruled that the pricing had to be nondiscriminatory even though one party was a government entity. Justice O'Connor wrote a dissenting opinion, as did Justice Stevens who opined that a state government hospital's pharmacy did not compete with ordinary drug stores in the sense that the Robinson Patman Act anticipated. My clients were not perturbed by the court's ruling, as they said they would not lower their prices to the drug stores, but they would raise prices to the county hospital's pharmacy.

• • •

Chapter XVI
ANTITRUST PLUS

Antitrust litigation often is not limited to antitrust issues. As illustrated in this chapter, cases that involve antitrust claims often include issues relating to the law of contracts, patents or the securities laws.

Proxy Fight—Antitrust + Securities Law

I argued on appeal for one of the firm's corporate clients that involved what was described as one of the most bitter and hard-fought corporate takeover fights in history.

The litigation in federal court in the Southern District of New York was assigned to Judge Lloyd MacMahon, who was known to run a tight courtroom. He developed an outstanding reputation for controlling unruly and violent mob defendants in narcotics conspiracy cases. In one case he ordered the U.S. Marshals to shackle, handcuff and gag the defendants who had been interrupting the trial by throwing things and shouting obscenities. In civil cases, Judge MacMahon was viewed as sometimes overly strict. In one case, in which I appeared, Judge MacMahon announced that he had read the briefs and come to a decision so there was no point in my presenting oral argument. I insisted on arguing anyway to no avail. In essence I was denied a realistic opportunity to "be heard."

Curtiss-Wright Corp., my firm's client, was in a proxy fight with Kennecott Copper Corp. Kennecott, the largest copper producer in the United States, acquired Peabody Coal Company, which it divested after the Federal Trade Commission challenged the merger on antitrust grounds. From the sale of Peabody, Kennecott received $807 million in cash and other consideration worth hundreds of thousands of dollars. Kennecott wanted to use the funds to purchase Carborundum Company. Curtiss-Wright, which had a 9 percent interest in Kennecott, wanted the proceeds of the Peabody sale to be distributed to shareholders or used to acquire half of Kennecott's shares at a price favorable to shareholders. For the Kennecott election of directors, Curtiss-Wright named its own slate of directors, who would support its proposal. Kennecott induced the State of Utah to enjoin further activity by Curtiss-Wright. Kennecott also sued Curtiss-Wright in federal court in the Southern District of York. Utah authorities continued to try to restrain Curtiss Wright's takeover activities, so Judge MacMahon enjoined Utah from interfering with the federal case. Paul Curran, who came to Kaye Scholer from the U.S. Attorneys' Office when I did, and who later became U.S. Attorney, handled the trial before Judge MacMahon.

Judge MacMahon ordered an expedited trial, which was needed on the securities law issues in light of the imminent stockholder's meeting. Judge MacMahon rejected Curtiss Wright's request to postpone the trial of the antitrust issues, despite the need to conduct discovery and analyze the complex market definition issues. After a three-day trial, Judge MacMahon held that Curtiss-Wright's proxy solicitation violated the securities laws because Curtiss-Wright did not disclose its failure to have made a "thorough investigation" of the issue before the Kennecott board. The trial court also held that Curtiss-Wright's acquisition of Kennecott stock was in violation of the antitrust laws because one of Curtiss-Wright's subsidiaries competed with Carborundum, which Kennecott was about to purchase. Curtiss-Wright was enjoined from further proxy solicitation and from voting its shares. The Kennecott annual meeting was permitted to proceed.

At the oral argument of the appeal from Judge MacMahon's adverse ruling, my opponent was Marvin Schwartz, head of the litigation department at the law firm of Sullivan & Cromwell (which had turned me down for a summer job after my second year of law school). T. Roland Berner (known as Ted), was the Chairman of Curtiss-Wright. Before the litigation, he announced publicly that the management of Kennecott was incompetent and that he was confident that its shareholders would side with his company's position. When I arrived at the court of appeals for the oral argument, Berner was there waiting for me. He told me that if he did not like my argument, he intended to march up to the podium and take over (he was an attorney). Nothing like some pressure before an argument! There turned out to be no need for Berner to take over. Rather, Mr. Berner emerged from the courtroom with a smile.

I began the argument by asserting that under the trial court's decision, "the securities laws have been used to deprive shareholders of their right to vote." I took the position that Curtiss-Wright had not violated the securities laws by misleading the Kennecott shareholders because its proxy materials stated that it had *not* made a "detailed study" of the consequences of Kennecott's program. In what it described as the "hurly burly" of a proxy fight, the court of appeals accepted my argument and held that Judge MacMahon should not have second-guessed the precise wording of Curtiss-Wright's proxy solicitation. Moreover, Kennecott itself made no effort in its proxy materials to clarify the language. One of the appellate court judges asked what relief I was seeking. I responded that the court should order "Kennecott's votes voided and a new solicitation ordered." The court agreed and decided that the Kennecott annual meeting should be voided and there should be a new election of directors.

I also convinced the court of appeals that Judge MacMahon should not have summarily rejected Curtiss-Wright's request for more time to prepare its defense to the antitrust claim. In particular, there were outstanding issues relating to the definition of the product and geographic markets that required discovery and analysis. In order to assess the competitive effect of Curtiss-Wright's acquisition of Kennecott' shares, more time was needed to develop evidence of the structure, history and probable future of the relevant markets. At trial, Kennecott's expert was recorded as describing his "mythology" of market share calculations. The court of appeals noted that this may have been a typo, but that "mythology" was a more accurate description of his expert testimony as compared with "methodology."

After the appellate decision, the parties entered into a settlement agreement, the terms of which attested to the victory on appeal. Curtiss-Wright was allowed to increase its interest in Kennecott; Kennecott agreed to pay substantial attorneys' fees to Curtiss-Wright; Curtiss-Wright achieved representation on the Kennecott board of directors; and Kennecott agreed to consider Curtiss-Wright's proposal for use of the funds from the Peabody sale.

Generic Drugs—Antitrust + Patent and Trademark law

In 1975, I was asked to come to the office of Fred Livingston, the chair of Kaye Scholer's labor department. Fred had been an advisor to seven Secretaries of Labor and founded the firm's extensive labor law practice in 1947. Jay Waks, another attorney in that department, was a prolific lecturer and author, which enhanced his business development capabilities. His articles came to be known in the firm as "Waks Paper."

Fred told me that he had a phone call from Paul Miller, who had been an associate in Livingston's department, and had left to join the in-house legal staff of Pfizer Inc., the pharmaceutical company. Fred asked me to respond to a request for an antitrust lawyer to come to Pfizer and discuss a new matter. I put on my best three-piece Paul Stewart, navy blue, pinstriped suit and a conservative tie; I polished my black wingtip shoes and off I went. I was greeted by the CEO, Ed Pratt, who was wearing an orange plaid suit with a wide loud tie, and loafers with buckles like the Pilgrims wore. Several in-house attorneys including Paul Miller also were present. Pratt told me that the company was dissatisfied with the results in litigation handled by their regular counsel, Dewey, Ballantine. The firm was one of the staid Wall Street firms. Recently, in its attempt to compete by signing laterals and guaranteeing huge draws, that firm declared bankruptcy.

As an associate at Kaye Scholer, Miller learned and informed Pratt that our firm represented plaintiffs in antitrust litigation. Pratt suggested that as plaintiffs' lawyers, we might be more effective in defending such cases. Of course, I told them that I was one of the plaintiffs' antitrust lawyers in the firm. Jesse Heiges, the General Counsel, was a member of the Forest Hills Tennis Club where the U.S. Open was played, so we had a common interest.

The matter involved generic drugs, which are unbranded drugs whose patents have expired. Today, generic drugs play an important role in enabling patients to get drugs with the same chemical composition as branded drugs, but at lower cost. Even large pharmaceutical corporations now sell generic drugs alongside their higher-priced branded versions. The Food and Drug Administration (FDA) tries to ensure consistent quality. In the early days, however, many of the generic drug firms were upstarts without quality control. For example, I represented Dow Chemical in a case against a seller of generic Novahistine, a cough medicine that we gave to our children. The plant in Brooklyn, which we got to inspect, was dirty and odorous. We settled the case by shutting them down.

Pfizer's concern related to a patented diabetes drug called Diabinese. An individually owned company in New Jersey threatened to sell an identically shaped and similarly named version before the Pfizer patent expired. Pfizer asked me to investigate the facts, and—working with their patent counsel—to provide an opinion as to whether the patent could withstand an antitrust attack and a challenge to its validity. I put together a team including Gerry Sobel, a partner who was a licensed patent attorney, and Randy Sherman, who became one of the firm's top litigators. On my next visit, I carried a thick volume of analysis. Miller advised me to jump to the last page with the conclusion that we could successfully defend whatever the generic company threw at us in litigation.

We filed suit in federal district court in New Jersey alleging trademark, trade dress and patent infringement. During the hearings in Newark, New Jersey, our local counsel advised us not to step out of our hotel rooms in the evening, as Newark was a dangerous city. In response to our motion for a preliminary injunction, the judge made it clear that we would likely prevail at trial. The defendant acceded to an injunction, which the judge personally typed out and got the defendant to sign. Soon thereafter, we learned that the defendant had its infringing product back on the market. We moved to hold him in contempt of court. On threat of jail, he agreed once again to cease sales. His company ultimately declared bankruptcy. Pfizer was delighted and this was the beginning of a relationship of our law firm and Pfizer that continues to this day.

After working as cocounsel with patent lawyers from other law firms, whose practice was limited to patents, I soon realized that while such firms were expert in substantive patent law, they were not always adept at trying cases. As a result, we established a patent department in our firm. Gerry Sobel, who was admitted to the patent bar and trained in litigation at our firm, headed up the unit. Steve Glassman and Milton Sherman had science degrees as well as litigation experience in the Civil Division of the U.S. Attorneys' office. Gerry and I regularly counseled on antitrust issues relating to patents.

Managed Care—Antitrust + Contract Law

Eli Lilly made the antidepressant, Prozac. Lilly acquired a pharmacy benefit manager (PBM). That is a company that manages prescription drugs by establishing a formulary—a list of drugs—which health insurance companies use as a guide for whether to reimburse its insured customers for the cost of prescription drugs. If a drug is not on the formulary, the physicians will likely look for alternative medications so patients' purchases will be covered by insurance. The Federal Trade Commission (FTC), which regulates pharmaceutical acquisitions under the antitrust laws, imposed a condition on Lilly's acquisition of the PBM to prevent it from using its new subsidiary to eliminate competition.

Soon after acquiring the pharmacy benefits manager, Lilly removed Pfizer's antidepressant drug, Zoloft, from the manager's formulary so it could not effectively compete with Lilly's Prozac. I was retained by Pfizer. I put together a team that included a young partner, Tom Smart, and Lori Leskin, an associate who was adept at using computerized information at trial and became a talented litigating partner. We took a two-pronged approach: with the FTC on antitrust grounds and the court where we filed suit against Lilly for breach of contract. Pfizer's in-house antitrust lawyer, Kent Bernard, and I visited the FTC in Washington. We argued to the FTC that Lilly had violated the order that gave antitrust approval to Lilly's acquisition of the Pharmacy Benefits Manager. Accordingly, we urged that Lilly should have to divest the PBM.

New York courts have a special part for complex commercial litigation. We filed suit in New York's Supreme Court (in New York that is the trial court level). Tom appeared before Justice Ira Gammerman, who was assigned to the case. We had moved for a temporary restraining order to get back on the formulary while the case proceeded. Rather than rule on our motion for a temporary restraining order, the judge set the case for a trial in a few weeks, leaving us a brief time for discovery.

I tried the case before Justice Gammerman without a jury. We sought an order specifically enforcing the contract with the PBM, which is a form of equitable relief that is tried before a court only. Justice Gammerman was known to inject some humor into trials. Thus, during the course of the trial, he asked me how many patients were prescribed Zoloft. When I told him the number, he laughed and said, "There must be a lot of happy people out there." He also was a prolific user of his laptop during trials. His former clerk worked in our firm and I told him how pleased I was that the judge took copious notes on his laptop. The former clerk told me that the judge was probably playing computer games and not taking notes. No matter what he was doing with his computer, Justice Gammerman followed the testimony with precision. The judge was also known to interrupt cross-examination with his own questions. Normally, that would be annoying, but he was able to anticipate my questions and in response to questions from the judge, the witnesses were more likely to give responsive answers.

Lilly retained the law firm of Dewey Ballantine. Lilly's lawyer argued that specific performance was not warranted because that relief was only allowed as a remedy for breach of contract when performance was so unique that money damages could not compensate for the loss. To counter this, I retained National Economic Research Associates to calculate the loss. Our expert testified that the past losses alone would exceed $400 million. Lilly then abandoned its legal objection to specific performance and argued that there was no breach of contract.

Lori had uploaded all of the deposition transcripts onto her laptop. When a Lilly witness testified inconsistently with his deposition testimony, she immediately found the Q & A on the computer and I was able to impeach the witness without delay. This was a new tool, which—with the help of Lori—we used in subsequent trials.

Justice Gammerman granted our demand for specific performance to put Zoloft back on the formulary. Lilly appealed and the Dewey law firm assigned the oral argument to one of its experienced litigators, who had not been at the trial. At the argument before the Appellate Division, I pointed out numerous instances where the Dewey lawyer misstated the evidence at trial, with which I was more familiar, having tried the case. The Appellate Division affirmed the judgment. Eventually, Lilly divested the PBM. I am not sure if that was due to FTC action, or—as a result of our trial—Lilly's inability to eliminate competitors' products from the PBM's formulary, or both.

Textiles - Antitrust + Patent Law

A violation of the antitrust laws in connection with application of a patent could result in a finding of patent misuse, which would preclude enforcement of the patent. We were retained to represent companies in the textile industry known as throwsters. Kayser-Roth, Burlington Mills and others manufactured what was known as double knit, which was a synthetic textured yarn used in various clothing items including men's so-called "leisure jackets" and slacks. Some fifty lawsuits were filed by throwsters to declare patents developed by Leesona Corporation to be unenforceable because of patent-related antitrust violations. In so doing, the throwsters repudiated the patents under which they had been licensed. We alleged that Leesona entered into agreements with competing manufacturers who were licensed under these patents, which amounted to price fixing. Leesona counterclaimed for patent infringement.

Cases had been filed in two federal districts so the Multidistrict Panel transferred them to federal court in Miami, Florida. The result was the longest litigation in my career—ten years. Judge Clyde Atkins, who was reputed to have ambitions to be nominated to the court of appeals, may have been passed over due to the length of these proceedings. He was known as "Hard Luck Clyde" because of the difficult cases he was assigned by chance. It was a pleasure to appear before Judge Atkins as he would start by providing his tentative views gained from reading the briefs, and then pose the questions he had in mind. This made it much easier to frame an effective argument—to be heard and to be listened to. Many of the lawyers on our side were patent lawyers. I was the lead antitrust lawyer for all of the alleged patent infringers.

During the hearings and trial in Miami, we stayed at the Key Biscayne Resort, and of course we played tennis during the breaks. At breakfast, one of the patent lawyers told us that he met an attractive woman at the bar the night before. He told us that the woman was talented as well— she had her own plane, which she flew on business between Miami and Colombia. The patent lawyer had apparently not realized what commodity was frequently transported on that route. After we returned home from the trial, the lawyers were asked to provide affidavits attesting to the character of the patent lawyer. Being a supposedly wealthy lawyer, he was accused by the FBI of financing his new girlfriend's cocaine operation. We explained his reason for being in Miami, and he was fortunate to have avoided the criminal charges.

I conducted the deposition of the retired CEO of Leesona at Boca Grande on Gasparilla Island off the Gulf Coast of Florida. This was a haven for the super-rich. Many mansions were surrounded by high walls including one owned by the De Beers diamond family. We stayed at a boatel, which was frequented during tarpon fishing tournaments for which Boca Grande was famous. And we played more tennis.

After extensive pretrial discovery including depositions, Judge Atkins granted my motion for summary judgment on our claim of patent misuse from a violation of the antitrust laws. Price fixing is what is called a *per se* violation, meaning that if proven, there is no need to prove injury to competition. The court found that Leesona entered into agreements with competing manufacturers of the patented equipment. Under the agreements, Leesona would receive one-third of the royalties collected by other manufacturers from the throwsters who were using the machines of that manufacturer. In this way, Leesona set the level of compensation for itself and for its competing machinery manufacturers. The sales price of the machinery consisted of two parts—the initial price of the machine and the royalty payments. Leesona's agreement to share the royalties resulted in a guaranty of income to its competing manufacturers and effectively fixed the portion of the price attributable to royalties. In this way, Leesona was able to limit negotiation between throwsters and individual machinery manufacturers.

The court rejected as irrelevant Leesona's contention that this arrangement was procompetitive because it allegedly made entry into the machinery manufacturing business more attractive by guaranteeing a specified compensation. In a way, these pricing arrangements resembled the GE and Westinghouse post-conspiracy pricing mechanisms that we challenged at the Justice Department.

The Fifth Circuit Court of Appeals affirmed the grant of summary judgment. The next step was a trial to consider whether Leesona had purged its misuse and could resume enforcing the patents and collecting royalties. While on the plane to Florida for the trial, I asked the associate who was assigned to the case for the trial prep materials. He had three-hole notebooks labeled with the name of each witness neatly printed on the covers. But when I opened the notebooks, the pages were blank. When we landed, I arranged for my secretary to fly to Florida. We spent the next day preparing the witness examination materials.

The trial before Judge Atkins without a jury ended in a judgment that in effect cut the baby in half, holding that our clients were excused from paying back royalties, which were substantial, but going forward the misuse was purged. The remainder of the proceedings involved patent validity and damages issues, which I left to the patent lawyers and one our bright young associates, Stuart Freedman.

◆ ◆ ◆

Chapter XVII

NUCLEAR POWER—OYSTER CREEK
AND THREE MILE ISLAND

Suing General Electric

The Oyster Creek nuclear power plant in Toms River, New Jersey, was one of the first commercial nuclear plants. New Jersey Power & Light, a subsidiary of General Public Utilities (GPU), which we had represented in the price-fixing cases, purchased the plant from GE. The sale was a turnkey operation, meaning GE would do all the work needed not only to supply the nuclear equipment, but also to get it up and running. Completion of the plant was delayed for some three years during which the utility lost significant income.

We sued for breach of contract. Judge Milton Pollack, of the Southern District of New York, was assigned to the case. He was a no-nonsense judge who did not brook delays in bringing a case to trial. GE was represented by the firm of Donavan Leisure, known for its litigation prowess. George Leisure, who had preceded me in the U.S. Attorney's Office, was in charge of the defense. The facts were complicated. GE blamed the delays on events allegedly beyond its control including changes in regulations by the federal Atomic Energy Commission, which was the predecessor agency to the Nuclear Regulatory Commission. GE also pointed to unanticipated labor disputes. We alleged that the delay was mainly due to cracks in the containment vessel, which were the result of GE's negligence. In order to repair and inspect the cracks it was necessary to find a short and slightly built engineer who could crawl into the vessel.

Each side retained a battery of technical experts. Judge Pollack told us that experts normally do not lie, so instead of time-consuming depositions the experts should sit across a table, question each other, and try to reach an accord as to the facts. This was a groundbreaking and successful effort. I later described this innovative procedure in an article on how to make litigation more efficient.

The Donavan Leisure lawyers asked the court to allow them to inspect the plant. We arrived at the plant and were given yellow hazmat suits, like the ones in the movie *The China Syndrome*, starring Jack Lemmon and Jane Fonda. We were also given dosimeters to measure our radiation exposure. We were told that the exposure was no more than would result from a dental X-ray. The president of the American Cancer Society recently advised avoiding the radiation exposure from dental X-rays unless the patient is symptomatic. GE's plants, as compared with others, were said to be "dirty." That meant that when the plant was shut down for maintenance, there would be radioactive material around. While we were putting on our hazmat suits, alarm bells went off and we all jumped to attention. We asked our minders: "What was that?" One of the workmen replied that he had put his shoes into a device to test whether it had radioactive material on it. We asked what he was going to do. He calmly replied that he was going to wash the material off his shoes. The GE lawyers became anxious to make this a very brief tour, which we were glad to facilitate.

Partway through the pretrial proceedings, George Leisure asked me to lunch. He told me that he found the case impossible to deal with because it was so complicated. He said he consulted with a corporate lawyer in his firm who was responsible for the GE relationship. He was told to imagine this was a lawsuit over construction of a two-family home. In the meantime, we got permission from the court, over GE's strenuous objection, to review documents at the GE nuclear library in California. Richard Seltzer of our firm, who later became a successful real estate litigation partner, returned from his review of the library with an astounding document. It showed that GE was concerned about the China syndrome. As explained in the movie of that name, the China syndrome was a colorful description of a concern that if the coolant system for the reactor pressure vessel was breached, there could be a meltdown that would be very serious and hypothetically could make a hole in the earth in the direction of China. This had nothing to do with our claim. But the next morning I received a call from GE's in-house counsel inviting me to lunch. He made a generous settlement offer, which our client accepted, and that ended the case favorably.

Suing Babcock & Wilcox

Walter Cronkite, the renowned CBS newscaster, began his nightly newscast: "Good evening. The world has never known a day quite like today. It faced considerable uncertainties and dangers of the worst nuclear power plant accident of the atomic age." On March 28, 1979, the Three Mile Island nuclear power plant No.2 (TMI 2) experienced a partial meltdown of its nuclear core due to a loss of coolant accident. The TMI 2 nuclear accident remains to this day, (in the words of the Nuclear Regulatory Commission (NRC), "the most serious accident in U.S. commercial nuclear power plant operating history."

Put simply, in a nuclear reactor there is a hot core that must be cooled by water. If there is a leak due to a malfunction, the loss of coolant could result in a meltdown of the core and the release of radioactive material. Ironically, the TMI accident occurred twelve days after the opening of the movie, *The China Syndrome*. Fortunately, there was no China syndrome effect. According to the NRC, the small radioactive releases from TMI 2 had no detectable health effects on plant workers or the public. After the accident one of the company engineers had to be dropped down into the unit to inspect the core and assess the damage. I asked him if he was concerned about exposure to radiation. He boldly replied that he grew up in Florida and believed that he had more radiation exposure from working in the orange groves than he would get inspecting the core. I took this as an attempt at humor.

The most complex and difficult case of my career was representing General Public Utilities (GPU) and its subsidiary Metropolitan Edison Company in a suit against Babcock & Wilcox (B&W), the manufacturer and seller of the two Three Mile Island (TMI) plants. In early 1980, I was retained by Jim Liberman of Berlack Israels & Liberman, the general counsel of General Public Utilities (GPU), to file suit against the manufacturer, Babcock & Wilcox. I knew Jim and GPU officers from the price-fixing cases we filed against their equipment suppliers and the Oyster Creek nuclear litigation. Jim was a Yale Law graduate who favored Yale Law attorneys. This was the same law firm that had offered me a job when I was a judge's law clerk to work as a corporate lawyer.

There were two units at the site. Three Mile Island 1 (TMI 1) was out for servicing. TMI 2 was in operation when the accident occurred in that plant. In our complaint, we alleged that B&W failed to warn GPU of known safety hazards in the nuclear steam supply system that GPU purchased from B&W. B&W disputed these allegations, and contended that the accident was caused by GPU's negligence in improperly maintaining the equipment, in failing to adequately train its operators, and not following its own procedures.

We knew from prior investigations by a president's commission (and others) that there was at least some fault on both sides. Under Pennsylvania law, which was applicable, the court would have to weigh the comparative negligence of each party. In order to recover all of its damages, a plaintiff must prove that the defendant's negligence was 51 percent responsible. If plaintiff's negligence was 25 percent responsible, it could recover only 75 percent of its damages. Our client's interest was not merely financial recovery. While the outcome of the trial was not predictable, our client was anxious to get B&W's culpability into the public debate, which up to then was focused on the actions of the utility's operators.

We learned that there would be press coverage of the trial. Public perception was important. I contacted the *New York Times* reporter assigned to the case, not to influence him but to make sure that he understood the technicalities. The *Times* assigned Frank Prial, its wine reporter. In 1981, when it was reported that Israel bombed an Iraqi nuclear reactor, Prial happened to be in Paris. He was sent to the Middle East to cover the story. Hence, a wine reporter was assigned to cover a nuclear accident trial. I invited him to lunch at which he ordered and drank a bottle of wine, and listened to my technical lecture. He wrote an excellent lead article before the trial began, setting forth the position we were taking and the technical aspects of the accident. However, he only lasted a few days at the trial and someone else was assigned. At the end of each trial day, I would spend a few minutes with the *Times* reporter explaining the testimony of the day.

I assembled a team of lawyers. For the technical aspects of the case, I brought in Richard Seltzer, who had worked on the Oyster Creek case and Steve Glassman, a graduate of MIT and former Assistant U.S. Attorney. Our deposition takers and defenders included Andy MacDonald, a tough litigator. For the difficult legal issues to be briefed, we enlisted Myron Kirschbaum and Joel Katcoff. We also needed outside expert help. I retained Dr. Richard Lahey, the chair of the Nuclear Engineering & Science Department at RPI, as a trial expert. Dr. Lahey tutored me on the technical aspects of the accident, as I had no science courses in college. After intensive instruction by Dr. Lahey, I reached a point where I thought I knew more about the operation of a nuclear plant than some of the young operators, who had been trained by Admiral

THE NEW YORK TIMES, TUESDAY, NOVEMBER 2, 1982

3 Mile Island Owners and Builder Fault Each Other for '79 Accident

By FRANK J. PRIAL

Attorneys for the builder of the reactor damaged in the accident in 1979 at the Three Mile Island nuclear plant in Pennsylvania and the plant's operator traded strong accusations yesterday about which was to blame for the nation's worst commercial nuclear accident.

Robert B. Fiske Jr., an attorney for Babcock & Wilcox, which built the reactor accused the plant's operator, the General Public Utilities Corporation, of "indulging in recklessness" and of "deliberate and willful misconduct."

He made the remarks as a trial opened in Federal District court here to determine responsibility for the billion-dollar accident. The suit was filed by the utility company, which contends that Babcock & Wilcox is to blame and is seeking $4 billion in damages.

The nonjury trial, which is expected to last several months, is being heard by Judge Richard Owen.

Babcock 'Misconduct' Charged

David Klingsberg, representing General Public Utilities, said the manufacturer had failed to update emergency operational procedures for its reactors nationwide, which he called "a frightening episode of corporate misconduct."

In his response Mr. Fiske described what he called a "pervasive pattern of appalling indifference on the part of General Public Utilities management," and accused the company of falsifying reports about steam leakage in the reactor system for several weeks before the accident because it feared losing money if the reactor was shut down.

He also said that the company's reactor operators "didn't have even a fundamental understanding of how a nuclear reactor works" and that for a while the utility's official in charge of training new operators did not himself have an operator's license because he had failed the Nuclear Regulatory Commission test.

The official finally obtained a license, Mr. Fiske said, only after having someone else take half of the required examination for him.

"The company said later that they didn't consider that cheating," he said.

Both Sides Charge Cover-Up

Each side accused the other of having made or covered up serious errors related to the accident in an effort to save money.

Mr. Fiske said the utility should have shut down the No. 2 reactor that was later destroyed in the accident to repair the leaking valves, but did not do so because the reactor's twin was closed for repairs and shutting both would have cost the company as much as $500,000 a day.

A key contention by Mr. Klingsberg is that the accident at Three Mile Island, which involved a partial uncovering of the reactor core, releasing dangerous amounts of radioactivity, was almost identical to a problem that Babcock's own engineers had encountered a year and a half earlier and had devised ways to prevent.

He said memorandums were written after the 1977 incident at the Davis-Besse generating plant in Ohio, owned by the Toledo Edison Company, recommending safety procedure changes for all reactors, but that Babcock officials never informed clients nationwide of the problem because "it would have hurt their marketing image."

The Babcock & Wilcox attorney said the utility had all the information it needed to avert the accident but was too inept to use it.

Rickover on nuclear-powered submarines but were not graduate nuclear engineers. I even had dreams in nuclear engineering terms. We also retained David Taylor, an engineer who moved into our offices to advise us on a daily basis.

B&W retained Robert Fiske, a partner in the Davis Polk law firm. Bob and I had been colleagues in the U.S. Attorneys' office where he headed an organized crime unit. Bob had also represented Allis-Chalmers in the price-fixing cases. Later, he was named as U.S. Attorney by President Ford. In view of our prior relationship, we conducted extensive depositions and document discovery in a cooperative manner without the need for court intervention. The assigned judge, Richard Owen, commended us for that.

We decided to sue in federal court in the Southern District of New York. We were concerned that in Harrisburg, people might be prejudiced against the local utility, which some may have perceived was responsible for endangering the population. There were pending lawsuits against the utility by neighbors in regard to the possible effects of radioactive leaks. We concluded that the case would be very technical and possibly beyond the ken of lay jurors who might have gripes with their local power provider. In return for waiving a jury, B&W's lawyers agreed to a speedy trial before Judge Richard Owen.

Before the trial was scheduled, B&W filed a motion for summary judgment to dismiss the damage claims based on the law without the need to resolve issues of fact. Only claims for repair or replacement would remain if the motion was granted. B&W relied on strict "limitation of liability" clauses in the contract of sale. In anticipation of this defense, I consulted with Richard Epstein, a professor at the University of Chicago Law School and an expert in tort law. We decided that in order to avoid the bar imposed by the limitation of liability clauses, we would not include claims for relief based on breach of contract. Rather, we enumerated five claims under tort law theory. Thus, we alleged that

B&W is liable under the Pennsylvania law of strict liability, ordinary negligence, gross negligence, and reckless misconduct. The court dismissed the strict liability claim on the ground that strict liability does not apply to a suit between parties of equal size and capability. Judge Owen denied B&W's motion to dismiss the remaining tort claims. With this favorable decision, the path to trial was cleared.

Shortly after the accident, a Special Inquiry Group was appointed by President Carter to report on the causes of the accident. Within weeks, in March 1979, the Group issued the *Report of the President's Commission of the Accident at Three Mile Island* (The Report). Much has been written in this Report as well as in books expressing theories on the possible causes of the accident. It is not possible, nor is it my purpose, to explore all of these details. Rather, with the help of Dr. Lahey, I only summarize the highlights of the trial.

The Report presented serious hurdles that we would have to overcome to succeed at trial. It contained a minute-by-minute description of what occurred and how the utility as well as B&W personnel and the NRC responded. At 4:00 a.m. there was a reactor trip. This was indicated by an alarm sounding and a thunderous noise. According to the Report, there was a problem in a feedwater loop, which kept the reactor from overheating. A relief valve at the top of the system's pressurizer opened automatically to relieve the pressure in the reactor. But it stuck in the open position when the pressure dropped, and this was undetected due to the available instrumentation. This allowed reactor coolant to escape through the open valve at a rate equivalent to 220 gallons of water per minute. A phenomenon—known as flooding—prevented the water in the pressurizer from draining back into the core. Thus, using the instrumentation available to them, the TMI 2 operators thought that the reactor system was still full of water. This resulted in a "loss of coolant accident" (LOCA)—a term used throughout the trial. The events described so far took about twelve seconds. What followed was less awful because the valve eventually closed, and the emergency core cooling systems were activated, which prevented a total meltdown of the radioactive nuclear core. That would have been far more serious.

The *Report* concluded that the operators had not been trained to deal with this situation; nor had their written emergency procedures described the problem. But that was understandable considering that this type of accident scenario was not generally known in the industry at the time. An issue presented at trial was who was responsible for the lack of preparation—the utility, the NRC, B&W, or all three.

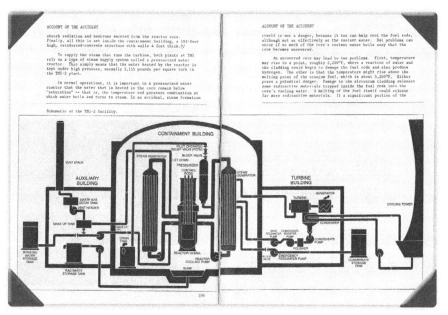

Schematic of TMI-2 Machinery

In September, 1977, a similar accident involving a loss of coolant occurred in a B&W reactor at a plant known as Davis-Besse in Toledo, Ohio. Fortunately, the Davis-Besse plant had been operating at low power, and the operators were able to contain the loss of coolant before any serious damage was done. The Davis-Besse operators realized early on that the valve was stuck open, and they closed it before further damage ensued. During the TMI 2 accident, the two B&W engineers who had analyzed the Davis-Besse failure were sent to TMI, but no one at B&W realized that the occurrence at TMI was the same as the accident that had occurred earlier at Davis-Besse.

The heart of our case was that B&W should have warned GPU and other utilities with plants of the same design that they need to be alert to an accident similar to that in Toledo. Thus, in an internal memorandum, which we obtained in document discovery, B&W recognized that such an accident could occur in plants with the same equipment, but it failed to warn other utilities that had plants of the same design so they could prepare for that eventuality.

After the Davis-Besse accident, B&W sent a team of engineers to Ohio to investigate the cause and come up with a plan to avoid a similar accident elsewhere. The head of the safety division, Bert Dunn, wrote a memo to eleven B&W personnel advising them to warn other B&W reactor owners to revise emergency instructions to prevent a recurrence. The memo provided instructions on how to avoid damage from such an event. Dunne wrote, "Had this event [at Davis-Besse] occurred at full power . . . it is quite possible, perhaps probable, that core uncovery and possible fuel damage would have occurred." He proceeded to implicate B&W's negligent omission: "The incident points out that we have not supplied sufficient information to reactor operators in the area of recovery from LOCA [loss of coolant accident]. I, therefore, recommended that operating procedures be written to allow for termination of high-pressure injection . . ." Dunn went on to warn that the danger of another accident "deserves our prompt attention and correction" and was "very serious." No such instructions were sent before the accident.

My opening statement to the court emphasized the Dunn memorandum. I told the court that Dunn's memorandum was the "smoking gun" in the case. I summed up my opening argument stating that, "It is a frightening episode because of the horrendous damage which Babcock's misconduct caused and the unthinkable risks to human life which it created."

B&W was headquartered in Virginia. We did not want to sue in their hometown for obvious reasons. But because of that fact, the B&W employees were beyond the subpoena power of the court in New York. Fiske refused to produce Dunn and other B&W employees during the presentation of our case. We were able to sustain our burden of proof from the Dunn document, and the testimony of GPU engineers that they did not receive any warning or instruction from B&W regarding the Davis-Besse accident. We also knew that Dunn likely would be called during the defense case when I would be able to cross-examine him.

We presented our case through the testimony of the plant operators and executives as well as the expert testimony of Dr. Lahey. During the testimony of GPU's operators and executives, Fiske cross-examined in an effort to show that the operators made critical errors. Fiske contended that the utility had manipulated leak rates to avoid a maintenance shutdown, which—if the plant was shut down—there might not have been an accident. Nothing about that is mentioned in the Report, presumably because it had nothing to do with the cause of the accident. B&W's lawyers claimed that there were problems with condensate polishers, which had not been repaired in accordance with recommendations. Finally, Fiske sought to prove that deficiencies in operator training set forth in the Report led to the failure to diagnose the cause of the accident early enough to avoid the damage. Of course, if the Dunn recommendation had been pursued, knowing the potential consequences of the Davis-Besse accident, training would have focused on dealing with such an event. Nevertheless, Fiske's cross-examination of the GPU witnesses had a worrisome impact on the trial judge.

For his trial testimony, Dr. Lahey created several mock-ups of how the accident occurred and the implications of the flooding phenomena. He explained the inability of the pressurizer to drain due to how it connected to the reactor system—an undesirable feature, which was unique to B&W designs. He used a pail of water to catch the liquid being discharged, which happened to spill during his testimony. Judge Owen jokingly commented, "Another loss of coolant accident!"

During some of the arguments over evidentiary issues, Judge Owen seemed deferential to Fiske whom he respected as a former U.S. Attorney in the Southern District. On the Wednesday before Thanksgiving, the court adjourned for a long lunch hour so we could all attend the annual Federal Bar Association luncheon at the Waldorf Astoria Hotel. At this affair Judge Walsh, my old boss at the Justice Department, bestowed the Learned Hand Servant of Justice award on Leon Silverman. In so doing, he mentioned me and the others who worked with him and Leon at the Justice Department. When we returned to court, Judge Owen leaned over the bench and said that he did not realize that I had worked with Judge Walsh at the Justice Department. From then on, I received the same respect as Fiske.

A key point in the trial was the argument of the defendant's motion to dismiss at the end of plaintiff's case. Once again B&W relied on the contractual limitations in the contract of sale. B&W also took the position that the accident would not have occurred unless there had been operator negligence. I argued that if B&W had duly warned GPU about the Davis-Besse incident, there would have been no occasion for operators to function in an emergency situation. We overcame a major hurdle when Judge Owen denied the motion to dismiss at the end of our case.

Some three months into the trial, while Dunn was on the witness stand, the parties decided to settle the case for $37 million to be paid in discounts on the purchase of future equipment, much of which was expected to be used for the clean-up and restart effort. GPU's view was that it accomplished much of its goal in making a prima facie case of Babcock's liability and revealing to the public its serious omissions set forth in Dunn's memos. We had proven that B&W failed to warn of the possibility of an accident similar to that at the Davis-Besse plant in Ohio. Babcock & Wilcox was concerned about the impact of continuing the trial on future nuclear facility projects. A concern of both parties was the impact of the trial on upcoming hearings on whether TMI 1, a sister unit to TMI 2, would be allowed to restart. At subsequent hearings at the NRC on the reopening of TMI 1, the parties cooperated.

Suing The Nuclear Regulatory Commission

We sued the Nuclear Regulatory Commission in federal court in Harrisburg, Pennsylvania, under the Federal Torts Claims Act (FTCA). As in the B&W suit, our complaint alleged a failure to warn based on the Davis-Besse accident. We developed information that NRC officials investigated the cause of the Davis-Besse accident but did not warn other utilities with B&W units of the same design. The Report stated that the agency knew that "similar pieces of equipment with comparable probabilities of similar failure modes were installed in other B&W plants." Internal NRC memos described what the agency called precursors that "should have produced guidance that, if it had been used, would have prevented the extensive core damage that occurred at TMI." We located an NRC employee who could provide valuable information as to the agency's failure to warn. In addition, an internal NRC memo expressed concern about an indication from the pressurizer that would mislead the plant operators to turn off the injection of coolant. This in turn could cause uncovering of the radioactive nuclear core with its concomitant dangers.

It is impractical for individual utilities to investigate the failures in particular plants around the country. For that reason, regulations required the NRC to warn licensees of defects and hazardous conditions. The NRC admittedly followed a practice of undertaking inspections and investigations of adverse events in nuclear plants and disclosing information about such events that potentially posed a threat to public safety. The NRC was the central warning system for the entire country. But the agency failed to warn GPU in this instance.

The complaint also alleged that the NRC failed to require Babcock & Wilcox to analyze small breaks in a coolant system like the one that was caused by the faulty valve at TMI. Specifically, we claimed that the NRC was negligent when it approved the Babcock & Wilcox design because the agency "should have known that it was necessary to require manufacturers . . . to analyze small breaks in the reactor coolant system such as a stuck-open, pilot-operated relief valve." The complaint alleged that the safety analyses submitted by Babcock & Wilcox addressed small breaks of about five square inches whereas the valve that malfunctioned at TMI had an aperture of about one square inch.

Nor was the NRC of help while the accident was in progress. According to the Report, the NRC personnel's attitude was that "this is the licensee's (Metropolitan Edison, a subsidiary of GPU) accident not ours. We are not here to take charge." And they did not. The Report also concluded that during the course of the event, an NRC official was concerned about symptoms of an uncovered core, but he failed to so advise the operators in the TMI Unit 2 control room.

Thus, it appears that we had an open-and-shut case on the facts. The remaining obstacle was the law. Based on the doctrine of sovereign immunity, the government cannot be sued except as allowed by the Federal Torts Claims Act (FTCA). This statute does not permit suits against the government for acts that are within the discretion of the regulatory agency. Relying on that provision, the government moved to dismiss the case. I argued against the motion in federal court in Harrisburg. The closest I got to TMI was to see the cooling towers out of the window of our local attorneys' second floor office.

In a twenty-four-page opinion, the district court denied the Government's motion to dismiss. The district judge rejected the government's argument that the utility's claim was barred by the discretionary function exemption in the FTCA. The court ruled that the record fails to reveal whether NRC scientists actually made a discretionary decision not to warn of Davis-Besse. Rather, the court concluded that "through default or caprice, they [the NRC] simply abdicated their responsibility." The court held that the "governing standards are not so vague or inexact as to call for unfettered scientific 'discretion.'" Rather, the court concluded that "equally broad exercises of judgment have survived similar challenges" in other cases. The district court relied on a precedent in its circuit, which held that "the judgments which Government scientists may permissibly make are circumscribed by applicable regulations; where decision-makers exceed that scope, liability may properly be imposed." The same opinion cautioned that the discretionary function exception only applied to agency decisions involving the resolution of political, social or economic policy. The district court concluded that this governing precedent should not allow the government to portray as a discretionary function an engineering decision to refrain from warning utilities of defects leading to accidents that could cause great harm to other nuclear plants and public safety.

The Government appealed to the Third Circuit Court of Appeals. I argued that appeal in Philadelphia. This was an example of losing a case that I thought was a sure winner. It is also an example of—to quote Justice Oliver Wendell Holmes—how "hard cases make bad law." The hard case was not our case. Rather it was a U.S. Supreme Court decision regarding an airplane crash that was handed down after I had briefed and argued our case against the NRC in the Third Circuit Court of Appeals.

While the appeal in our case was pending decision, the U.S. Supreme Court dismissed a case under the FTCA. We were allowed to file further briefs commenting on this case. The suit was filed against the Federal Aviation Agency (FAA) on behalf of passengers on the Brazilian airline, Varig, who died in a Boeing plane crash over the Atlantic Ocean. The only FAA involvement was approving the plane for safety. The Supreme Court held that approval by FAA was a discretionary act that was exempt from legal claims under the FTCA. Clearly, for the plaintiffs suing the

FAA, this was an unattractive case on the facts. The plane was owned and operated by a Brazilian airline, had no American passengers and was flying from Brazil to Africa. The timing was unfortunate. Citing this recent Supreme Court decision, the Third Circuit dismissed our case against the NRC on the ground that the NRC's regulatory actions and its decision not to warn other utilities were within the exception in the FTCA for discretionary acts. The Third Circuit narrowed the precedential effect of the case on which we principally relied. Thus, the Third Circuit ruled that its 1974 opinion "must be read cautiously because in the Varig case the discretionary exception covered an agency decision that rested on highly technical information." The court held that the NRC exercised discretion in making a judgment on public health and safety after evaluating the happening of an out of the ordinary event at a nuclear power facility. The Third Circuit also ruled that it was legally irrelevant that the NRC was negligent in failing to warn or to take the design defects into account in the regulatory process. In dismissing the case, the court blocked a remedy for inaction specified in the Report, which concluded, "We have found in the Nuclear Regulatory Commission an organization that is not so much badly managed as it is not managed at all."

Postscript on Nuclear Safety

According to the World Nuclear Association: 'Nuclear developments in the USA suffered a major setback after the Three Mile Island accident . . ." A number of orders and projects were put on hold or canceled. For more than thirty years, starting in 1977, before the TMI accident, until 2013, there were no new nuclear power construction starts. This was due in part to more economical gas-fired generation. Today, nuclear power provides about 20 percent of the nation's electric power generation, slightly more than coal-fired plants. Significantly, nuclear power provides 55 percent of the nation's carbon-free generation. More construction is needed to maintain or improve this ratio. That requires overcoming opposition based on safety concerns. Following the accident in Japan's Fukushima plant in 2011, the U.S. nuclear industry established sixty-one local centers and two national centers to respond to nuclear plant accidents within twenty-four hours. But in some cases an earlier response may be necessary. If a qualified nuclear engineer is on-site, and there is a more reliable warning system, a response in far less than twenty-four hours is possible. Safety performance reportedly has improved since TMI. There is, however, room for further improvement.

The Report made a number of recommendations to avoid future accidents, which I will not detail here. Rather, here are some lessons that I deduced from discussions with our trial expert, Dr. Lahey. For several reasons French nuclear operations were safer than those in the U.S. First, France designed and built their own nuclear reactors. They had only one design for operators to learn about. America had four manufacturers, Combustion Engineering, GE, Westinghouse, and Babcock & Wilcox, each with a different design. GE's units were said to be the Cadillac because of their reliability. In contrast, Babcock's unit was the Porsche because after maintenance shut down, it could start up much faster than other units. But this design carried risks. In Europe, nuclear plants were built in clusters so the owners could afford to have a qualified nuclear engineer on-site at all times. As allowed by NRC regulations, American nuclear power plants do not have to staff plants with graduate engineers. Moreover, American plants were usually built far from other plants, and often to avoid local opposition, in out of the way locations. This made it uneconomical to staff each unit with someone who has a doctorate in nuclear engineering.

I was later consulted by Florida Power & Light, which had a Babcock & Wilcox nuclear plant of the same design as TMI. It was remotely located in farmland in northern Florida. I explained how GPU had not been warned by B&W or the NRC of the implications of the Davis-Besse accident. I advised that they make sure that FP&L engineers and operators were up to speed on how to deal with such an accident should it occur at its plant.

Dr. Lahey admired the work habits of our legal team who labored diligently seven days and nights a week to prepare for trial. In reviewing this chapter for accuracy, he complimented Kaye Scholer for its "professional job" in litigating the TMI case. He opined that our attention to detail was not always the case at sites where nuclear power plants are constructed. He opined that those in key manufacturing positions are sometimes more interested in having a beer and watching sports on TV than tending to their jobs. As a result, accidents happen.

♦   ♦   ♦

Chapter XVIII

LECTURING AND PUBLISHING

Antitrust Centennial—Twilight or Resurrection

It is widely recognized that, in the 1980s, President Ronald Reagan was responsible for the decline in antitrust enforcement. I knew this at the time from the drop-off in my antitrust practice. Toward the end of Reagan's second term, Professor Handler sought to give antitrust an injection by celebrating the forthcoming hundredth anniversary of the Sherman Antitrust Act which was enacted in 1890. In my capacity as chair of the Antitrust and Trade Regulation Committee of the Bar Association of the City of New York, Handler asked me to organize a lecture program. Many of the speakers, including myself, called for a renaissance of antitrust enforcement, not merely to rebuild our law practices, but for the good of the nation.

The centennial program provided an opportunity not only to review the academic literature and recent case law, but also to reflect on my own experience in antitrust litigation. My role in the Electrical Equipment price-fixing cases led to an understanding of how joint efforts by the government and private attorneys could strengthen competition through antitrust enforcement. Other speakers commented on mergers and acquisitions, tie-ins and other aspects of antitrust law.

My lecture, which was published in the Cardozo Law Review, was entitled, *Balancing the Benefits and Detriments of Private Antitrust Enforcement.* I began by quoting from the 1890 debates over the Sherman Antitrust law. Senator George predicted that because of the obstacles that plaintiffs would face in litigation, the private right of action would not be an effective method of enforcement. He must have anticipated that Justice Scalia and other conservative justices would dominate the Supreme Court, and render private actions difficult to pursue to a judgment on the merits. I quoted Senator Sherman, the sponsor of the Sherman Act, who opined that, "the cases that will be brought will be by men of spirit, who will contest against these combinations." In the sixties, when I was pursuing the electric equipment suppliers for price fixing, my colleagues and I had that spirit. But effective private enforcement could not survive the eighties without government taking the lead.

The twilight of antitrust was not merely caused by political inaction. New jurisprudence also was a contributing factor. Scholars developed what was called the neoclassical efficiency model for antitrust enforcement. The focus was on whether the alleged unlawful conduct had an adverse impact on consumers by keeping prices high. Preservation of competition was no longer the goal. That goal was said to protect weaker firms from more efficient companies who might lower prices to consumers. The theory originated with professors at the University of Chicago and became known as the Chicago School. Judges and scholars, including Robert Bork (who was rejected by the Senate for the U.S. Supreme Court as being too extreme) and Richard Posner of the Seventh Circuit (who heard appeals in the Brand Name Prescription Drug cases, which I litigated), as well as Ward Bowman, the economist who cotaught my antitrust course at Yale, were all influential disciples of the Chicago school. As a counterpoint, in my article I quoted my old friend from clerkship days, the venerable Judge Learned Hand who wrote in his decision in the *Alcoa* monopolization case:

"Many people believe that possession of unchallenged economic power deadens initiative, discourages thrift and depresses energy; that immunity from competition is a narcotic and rivalry a stimulant, to industrial progress; that the spur of constant stress is necessary to counteract an inevitable disposition to let well enough alone."

At the same time, I recognized that, as Chief Justice Hughes of the U.S. Supreme Court stated, "As a charter of freedom, the [Sherman] Act has a generality and adaptability comparable to that found to be desirable in constitutional provisions." (*Appalachian Coals, Inc. v. U.S.* (1933). Ironically, some of the judges who—in their antitrust decisions—veered from the legislative intent when the Sherman Act was enacted are the same judges who interpret the U.S. Constitution as originalists.

As I write, President Biden has issued an Executive Order directing a return to the antitrust policies of the two Roosevelt presidents of the prior century. This order portends a return to the enforcement of the antitrust laws based on restoring competition for social and economic purposes. The order thus steers a course away from the Chicago school concern that antitrust enforcement could threaten the efficiency of businesses and lead to higher consumer prices.

In my article, the thesis was that without private actions only the government would decide on the best approach to enforcement, which in essence leaves antitrust enforcement at the whim of whoever is president. Private enforcement brings litigants and the judiciary into the mix as judges decide, after considering lawyers' arguments, what activity violates the antitrust law. I debunked suggestions by the Chicago School judges and scholars who recommended eliminating the treble damage incentive to bring private suits and to require a losing plaintiff to pay the costs and attorneys' fees of the defendant. I noted that while the Chicago School was deemed "the new learning," there was emerging a "new, new learning" that did not necessarily accept the principle that claims based on exclusionary conduct are usually without foundation. My lecture concluded that private actions not only provide deterrence against violations, but also ensure a cauldron of cases and controversies that produce a continually evolving brew of developing antitrust doctrine.

Perhaps that wish will be achieved at the antitrust millennium, but it is not consonant with my own experience since the electric equipment prosecutions and with current antitrust case law. The liberal interpretation of the pretrial discovery rules has posed a substantial disincentive to bringing private antitrust actions. Busy executives and managers do not like having their day-to-day work interrupted by sitting through depositions, or having to produce all of their files going back years, irrespective of the prospect of improving their competitive position if the case is won.

Moreover, significant obstacles to private enforcement continue to be imposed by the judiciary. In my article, I traced the burdens that a private plaintiff must sustain not merely to win at trial, but to get to trial—and be heard on the merits. The first was to establish standing to sue, the subject of an earlier published article that I authored, entitled "Bullseyes and Carom Shots: Complications and Conflicts on Standing to Sue and Causation Under Section 4 of the Clayton Act." These phrases, which were taken from the case law, illustrate the courts' struggle to define the standard for satisfying the predicate of standing to sue in a private antitrust action.

In my centennial article I also discussed a further obstacle to sustain a private action. Zenith Radio, an American seller of consumer electronic products, sued thirty Japanese exporters of those products. The Third Circuit Court of Appeals found sufficient proof of collusive meetings resulting in predatory (lower) pricing in the U.S., which injured Zenith. In a five-four decision, the Supreme Court reversed. The holding was based on the lack of "plausibility" of the plaintiff's claims. Justice White in dissent termed this a new concept that replaced the standard rule for allowing a case to be heard at a trial, which was whether there was a genuine issue of fact to be tried. Unlike today, the justices did not split along party or doctrinal lines. Justice Marshall, a liberal, voted with the majority. The dissenters included Justices Stevens and Blackmun, Republicans appointed by Nixon (and called "The Minnesota Twins," after the baseball team).

The pinnacle of the adverse impact of the plausibility doctrine on antitrust enforcement came with another Supreme Court decision, *Cargill v. Montfort of Colorado, Inc.* The court reversed decisions of the district court and court of appeals, which had allowed a suit that was seeking an injunction against a merger of the plaintiff's larger competitors in the meat packing industry. The lower courts had not decided the merits; they merely were allowing the case *to be heard.* The Supreme Court reiterated its view regarding the implausibility of claims of threatened injury from predatory pricing. I wrote:

> "Let us harken back to the 'humble man' whom Senator Sherman said that he sought to protect against a combination of its competitors to sell their product at a loss and drive him out of business. Imagine him faced not only with a combination of the number two and three competitors in his market, but also the burden of overcoming with substantial evidence and sophisticated economic analysis, the combined intellectual doubts of Judges Bork and Posner, cited approvingly by the Supreme Court.
>
> And if the humble man's economic expert gets too sophisticated and his evidence too massive, he may run into judicial manageability problems which affect standing. The question one might ask is: Are we indeed approaching the ultimate in antitrust rationality, or is the going now so rough that the private plaintiff should be put on the endangered species list?"

Justice Stevens in his dissent put the impact of the court's decision starkly:

"It would be a strange antitrust statute indeed, which defined a violation enforceable by no private party. Effective enforcement of the antitrust laws has always depended largely on the work of private attorney generals, for whom Congress made special provision in the Clayton Act itself."

The Reagan administration's Justice Department position in this case was that private plaintiffs' actions alleging predatory pricing should be rejected *per se*, that is without any need for legal or factual analysis. The Court did not adopt this harsh recommendation. Its position in this case does, however, reflect the Reagan administration's attitude toward private antitrust enforcement.

In the curriculum of my course in complex litigation at the University of Miami Law School, I included one of the most significant bars to private antitrust enforcement. In 2013, the Supreme Court reversed a decision allowing a class antitrust action to proceed against the cable company, Comcast. The suit was brought by subscribers of cable services and alleged that Comcast had engaged in monopolistic practices in the Philadelphia area, which enabled it to dominate the market and raise prices. The decision was written by Justice Scalia and joined by the four conservative justices. The court ruled that the class action could not proceed because the economic model proposed by the plaintiffs did not show an impact on individual customers. A strong dissent was written by Justice Ginsburg and joined by the three other liberal justices. The dissent pointed out that the majority opinion ruled—contrary to precedent—that impact had to be proven at the outset before trial and that common impact, that is a showing that prices as a whole had increased, was insufficient. This ruling put an almost impossible burden on consumers seeking relief under the antitrust laws for their payment of increased prices resulting from monopolistic practices. This case was significant as it solidified a line-up of conservative versus liberal justices, which was reflected in cases barring plaintiffs' securities and employment discrimination actions. In my teaching, I subtly endorsed Justice Ginsburg's dissenting opinion.

The latest antitrust battleground involves the high-tech industry. A district judge in D.C. just dismissed a suit which the FTC had filed against Facebook on the ground that the complaint failed to define the relevant market and show that Facebook had a monopolistic share of the market. The resulting outcry in Congress is that the courts have become too conservative and therefore new legislation specifically targeting big tech is needed. But the judge who rendered the decision was appointed by Obama. More important, the elements missing from the complaint have been a fundamental requirement of antitrust for more than a hundred years.

One Democratic Congressman has called for a massive overhaul of the antitrust laws to police the largest tech companies. Republican congresspersons have expressed similar views. Supporters of the legislation say that the Sherman Act was designed to regulate oil companies. But over many years, antitrust cases have been filed involving numerous industries and large corporations including IBM and Microsoft. Among the policy issues presented by proposals to rein in big tech is whether it is more important to protect consumers' ability to continue to obtain the free services or to aid smaller competitors who want to provide such services for a price. As noted, the courts have long recognized the constitution-like flexibility of the antitrust laws which can be adapted to a variety of industry settings. Concomitantly, over the years, antitrust jurisprudence has emerged from a mix of evidence, arguments and judicial decisions in litigations. This process might produce superior long-term results as compared with Congressional decree that is influenced by the politics of the moment.

• • •

Chapter XIX
SEARCHING
FOR NEW HORIZONS

As a result of the government's lack of interest in antitrust enforcement during the Reagan administration in the eighties, my plaintiffs' antitrust practice dried up. Without the tools of grand juries, subpoenas and the threat of jailing participants who did not cooperate, private parties lacked the resources to pursue private antitrust cases. I was not without clients. Actually, a client under my nose was the firm's own corporate department. Sidney Silberman, the chair of the firm's executive committee and the corporate department, supplied clients involved in litigation. Despite his positions in the firm, he told me that he had not realized the skills and work ethic of our litigation lawyers. The Curtis-Wright case, which I have described, is an example of a client referred from another department of the firm.

Based on the relationship established with the utilities in the price-fixing cases, we were retained to file legal actions that involved claims other than for antitrust violations. One of American Electric Power's large steam turbine generators experienced a fault that required extensive repairs, during which the plant was out of service. We sued Westinghouse, the manufacturer, for providing defective equipment. After initial discovery, Westinghouse moved for summary judgment to dismiss AEP's claim without trial on the ground that there was no genuine issue of fact regarding its liability. The case had been assigned to Judge Robert Carter, whom I had met when I was researching my Law Journal comment on the NAACP's lawsuit against Alabama.

In the AEP case, we learned from the law clerk that the judge was on vacation in Greece. Accordingly, we moved for more time to respond to the motion. When he returned, he was angry that we had not responded and put us on a very tight schedule. I called in our team of lawyers and instructed them to prepare affidavits, documentary exhibits and briefs that would be at least four feet high. I argued against the motion on the ground that there were genuine issues of fact to be tried. The court denied the motion. As a result, we were able to settle the case for a fair portion of the damages incurred by our client.

In considering the development of an additional specialty, I focused on the growing volume of litigation involving product liability. I had no experience with claims of personal injury from allegedly defective products. However, there was the AEP case against Westinghouse and other suits where I represented electric utilities that sought financial damages in cases filed against manufacturers of defective products. There also were the Three Mile Island litigation and the Oyster Creek case, described earlier. I concluded that I might be able to parlay this experience into litigation regarding defective products that allegedly injured individuals.

Lesson learned: Be flexible. Don't be afraid to shift gear in your career: Adapt to the times.

Rhizopus

I set up a lecture tour in Frankfurt, Germany, where we had an office, and where I could portray myself simply as an American litigator. I delivered a talk, which was published in German and English, before the German arbitration association on alternative dispute resolution. To counterbalance the European lawyer's fear of American litigation, the article described ways to resolve claims without the expense and time of court proceedings. Retired judges were available for a fee to hear and decide cases without the delays of pretrial activity or backlogged dockets.

I also lectured on American product liability law, with particular reference to our jury system. My audience was an association of lawyers in the pharmaceutical, chemical, and oil industries. I included commentary on punitive damages, which is a concept peculiar to our jurisprudence. In addition to compensating plaintiffs for losses incurred from a defendant's wrongdoing, American juries and courts can impose additional damages where the wrong is willful or malicious. My foreign audience was particularly concerned with "runaway" juries who, out of sympathy for plaintiffs, might impose punitive damages that are out of proportion to the plaintiff's actual loss. Depending on the circumstances, judges may reduce a punitive damages award. The award of punitive damages may also be challenged on appeal. Nevertheless, the risk of a jury verdict with punitive damages struck fear in the lawyers in the audience.

One lawyer who heard my lecture was counsel to a German company that was the subject of a jury verdict in Missouri for a large sum of punitive damages. As a result, I came away with a client, Beiersdorf, known in America for Nivea skin care products. Beiersdorf was sued in Missouri state court by a plaintiff who had back surgery after an injury from a bicycle accident. A surgeon applied a sterile dressing over an open wound. On top of the sterile dressing, the surgeon applied elasticized bandages made by Beiersdorf. The bandages are known for their elasticity, which made them popular with football players. The labeling stated that the bandages were not sterile. For that reason, physicians did not use them in direct contact with open wounds. Surgeons commonly applied the elasticized bandages over sterile dressings. Plaintiff developed a fungal infection called Rhizopus, which led to further surgeries and pain and suffering. The surgeon was sued because he allegedly left the dressing on too long, enabling the wound to leak through the sterile bandage onto the elastic tape. There was evidence that Beiersdorf personnel were aware of the fungus in certain batches of the bandages, but did not order a recall. Plaintiff argued that the company was aware of the common use of its bandages to cover sterile dressings on open wounds. A jury awarded punitive damages of over a million dollars.

I mentioned the Beiersdorf retainer to Paul Miller, who was assistant general counsel of Pfizer Inc., the pharmaceutical company for whom I had handled antitrust litigation and counseling. Miller warned that I would lose badly in the local courts, and for that reason his company relied only on local lawyers for product liability cases. We did lose badly after an appeal to the intermediate appellate court. We then appealed to the Missouri Supreme Court. The oral argument was held in Columbia, Missouri, the state capital. The chief judge was a professor at the local law school and asked me perceptive questions. The court reversed the punitive damages award on the ground, which I had argued, that the warning label clearly stated that the bandages were not sterile. The court concluded that the company's conduct was not willful or reckless.

Beiersdorf then sued its insurance company in Connecticut because the insurer refused to reimburse it for my fees. The insurance company was represented by a lawyer, whom I knew from law school, with offices in Stamford, Connecticut. I suggested that, as he was located in Connecticut, he must be able to hire Yale Law School graduates. He replied that, "We don't get them and we don't want them." YLS graduates, he said, don't like to do the drudgework often involved in preparation for litigation. He told me that his firm preferred lawyers from the University of Maryland, or similar lesser-known law schools, because they are more willing to work hard, no matter what the assignment.

In this trial, the insurance company complained that my fees were higher than those ordinarily charged in Missouri. I testified that the reason for my higher fees was that I won, and the local lawyer lost. I explained that my practice was nationwide and that clients paid my higher fees because I provided superior legal representation. I tried cases and argued motions and appeals in almost every state in the Union. The travel involved was burdensome to me and my family, but I could not have had the same level of practice if I had limited my practice to New York City. Beiersdorf recovered my fees from the insurance company.

Fracture-phobia

After the victory on appeal before the Missouri Supreme Court, I received a call from Paul Miller at Pfizer asking me if I would accept a retainer as National Coordinating Counsel in the artificial heart valve cases. Pfizer had acquired Shiley Laboratories, located in Irvine, California. The company was founded by Donald Shiley, a space engineer. Mr. Shiley invented a metal artificial heart valve to be implanted in patients with defective aortic or mitral heart valves. Before the invention of artificial heart valves, patients had no choice but to experience a slow death. Combined with the development of open-heart surgery, this invention provided hope for patients with diseased natural heart valves. A small percentage of the Shiley valves fractured at the point of a weld. When that occurred, if the patients did not get to a hospital and have open-heart surgery within a short time, they would die. For those relatively few patients who suffered from a fractured valve, the company paid an appropriate settlement. Some eighty thousand Shiley valves had been implanted. My challenge was to obtain dismissal of lawsuits filed by people with the implants who sued for emotional distress damages they allegedly suffered from anxiety that their valves might fracture.

In defending the lawsuits, we were plagued with adverse publicity. The *Los Angeles Times* was running a string of articles critical of Shiley for having kept the valve available for implant. One of the most vocal critics was Sidney Wolfe, of Public Citizen, a watchdog group that was part of Ralph Nader's organization. The group published a list of pharmaceutical drug and devices that in its view, despite FDA approval, should not be used. Wolfe was quoted as saying that if each of the patients implanted with the valve were paid one hundred thousand dollars to settle clams they might file, the company would be cleaned out. This prediction never came close to fruition, but the mere allegation added to my burden.

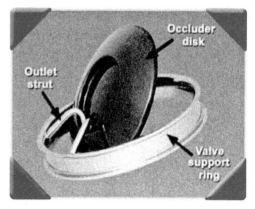

Artificial Heart Valve

The client also was ordered to appear before the House Oversight Committee chaired by Congressman John Dingell of Michigan. Our cocounsel, Arnold & Porter, took the lead in dealing with the Committee. I prepared our expert cardio-surgeons for their testimony. These surgeons were also prepared to testify at trials. In other types of cases, expert witnesses were subject to attack as "guns for hire," who were paid for their favorable testimony. But here, these surgeons not only testified that the benefits of the valve outweighed the risks, they actually were implanting the valves in patients who were desperately ill with no alternative to treat their heart disease.

Our client's witnesses were preceded by testimony by Sidney Wolfe. After he completed his testimony, Wolfe refused to relinquish his seat to me. I needed to sit next to our expert witnesses so they could conveniently consult with me as their counsel. The Committee issued a report that simply chastised the FDA and Shiley for not withdrawing the valve from use quickly enough.

I was briefed by Bob Ross, the in-house Pfizer attorney in charge of managing the Shiley litigation, as well as the Shiley's lawyers from California and other states, who were all product liability specialists. They pointed out that in asbestos cases, plaintiffs had been allowed to pursue lawsuits claiming "cancer phobia" out of fear that their exposure to asbestos would lead to lung cancer, which often occurred over time. They reasoned that "fracture-phobia" might be accepted by courts as an equally valid ground for claims.

I put together a team and instructed them to search for case law where plaintiffs whose products had no visible defect sued because others with the same product had malfunctions. They found, for example, a case where some Firestone tires had hidden defects that caused accidents, and the court denied relief to those whose tires performed satisfactorily. I developed a policy argument based on the fact that few, if any, pharmaceutical products were 100 percent effective or without side effects. During my arguments of motions to dismiss in these cases, I used as an example the fact that there are five hundred to one thousand deaths per year due to penicillin-induced anaphylaxis in patients allergic to the drug. Today, there are numerous ads on TV for pharmaceutical products with a frightening list of side effects, some of which can be fatal. In support of motions to dismiss, I argued that if damage claims were allowed to all patients whose product worked well, but who claimed that they were upset because they heard that some other patients experienced adverse side effects, that would wreak havoc in the industry as well as flood the courts with baseless law suits. I argued motions to dismiss and won in thirty-six state and federal courts. I also sustained these rulings in appellate arguments.

A case in California, argued by a local attorney, held that there was one exception to the law I had developed that a claim could not be allowed unless the valve failed. The exception was if plaintiff could prove fraud by the seller. The company had complied with FDA requirements on its warning label, so fraud would raise difficult hurdles for plaintiffs to overcome. A trial of a fracture claim was scheduled in Irvine, California, where Shiley was located. At the time, I was arguing motions in different jurisdictions. I assigned the trial to my Los Angeles office partner, Pierce

O'Donnell, who was a colorful and skilled trial lawyer. As cocounsel in this trial, I assigned Jack Urquhart, a lawyer from Houston, Texas, who was very persuasive with juries.

I spent considerable time in Irvine working with Jack and Pierce organizing and strategizing. The trial went well. Pierce told the jury that the Shiley valve was like the Eveready Bunny in the TV commercials—it just kept on running. As a favorable verdict loomed, we were able to reach a modest settlement with the plaintiff. But the California case exception for fraud cases foretold the prospect of further trials, expense and the chance of losing before one or more juries. A class action, filed in federal court in Cincinnati, Ohio, provided a potential path out of the litigation.

• • •

Chapter XX
NEW SPECIALTIES COME TO YOU

Newly minted lawyers often ask, "What specialty shall I pursue in my future career?" Professor Handler once suggested that I might find a specialty in trademark and copyright law. I declined in favor of chancing a career in whatever litigation came along, which would be more interesting and challenging. Young lawyers can develop a specialty in certain areas of the law, such as patents or taxation. Patent lawyers need a background in science. Tax lawyers will be helped by getting a master's degree in Taxation, as my son Jordan did. Specialties can be enhanced by working with a lawyer who has expertise in the field. For me, and most others, an area of specialization may be chosen for you depending on the needs of a client who walks in the door. You handle the first case in the field and succeed. You are retained again. By then, you have acquired the knowledge needed to specialize. You can lecture and write in the field. More clients will come. That was the basis of my entry into the field of class action law.

Class Actions
By way of background, the class action concept derives from English common law. The modern rule was incorporated as an amendment to Rule 23 of the Federal Rules of Civil Procedure in 1966. Under this rule, a person could file a lawsuit on behalf of many others. The goal was to

provide a vehicle for claims that were too small for any one person to sue. The individual might not be able to fund a lawsuit that involved retaining expert witnesses and taking extensive pretrial depositions and document discovery. The class action device enabled one or more persons to file suit on behalf of all those who incurred similar injury or financial loss.

The amended rule requires that the plaintiff show that the claims involve common issues of law and fact, and that the common issues predominate. In addition, the plaintiff would have to demonstrate that she has a claim that was typical of those in the class, and that she was capable of adequately representing the rest of the class. Pursuant to the rule, the court must decide whether to certify a class. If the court certifies the class, plaintiff sends notice to the class members by mail, or publication in newspapers or trade press. The notice informs potential class members as to the nature and basis for the claim. Recipients can file a paper opting out of the class if they want to pursue their claim individually. If they do not opt out, they are in the class and bound by the results of the litigation. If the class plaintiffs recover damages by way of a judgment or settlement, the court awards attorneys' fees and costs to the class plaintiff's attorney.

From the defendant's point of view, a class action might provide an opportunity to settle many actual and potential lawsuits in one fell swoop. In that way, a defendant could save the burdens and costs of litigating many claims in different jurisdictions. The downside for defendants is that class certification could enlarge the number of plaintiffs to a point where there is pressure to settle irrespective of the merits of the cases. The presence of a class action lawsuit might also alert others to file individual claims and opt out of the class action.

Several state court jurisdictions, as well as some federal district courts, had a reputation for being class action friendly venues. These courts would certify classes and force settlements without a careful analysis of whether the requirements of the rule were satisfied. These state and federal venues came to be known as "judicial hellholes" and were listed on a website with that name. To address this abuse, Congress enacted the Class Action Fairness Act of 2005. This legislation made it easier to remove state class actions to federal court. It also allowed appeals from district court class action decisions under certain conditions. With a bright young lawyer, Alan Rothman, I published an article in the *New York Law Journal* discussing the case law that developed under this statute.

As a rapidly developing field of law, the requirements for class certification were defined and refined by court decisions. I was fortunate to have entered the field on the ground floor and to have participated in court proceedings that shaped class action law. Class action lawsuits often involved antitrust claims, consumer fraud claims, and product liability claims. I was counsel in class action litigation in each of these areas.

International Class Action Settlement

Stanley Chesley filed a class action on behalf of Shiley valve implantees in federal court in Cincinnati, Ohio. He was a plaintiff's class action lawyer known as "the master of disaster." Most personal injury lawyers preferred to file suit on behalf of individual clients on a contingency basis, taking a third or so of any recovery as a fee for legal services. Chesley was not popular with these lawyers because his specialty was to file a class action on behalf of all potential claimants. He made his name with a class suit on behalf of those injured or killed in a Kentucky nightclub fire. Chesley drove me to the airport after a hearing in Cincinnati. Rather than park in a public lot, he pulled his Rolls Royce up to the gate and told one of the guards to watch it, to which the guard responded, "Of course, Mr. Chesley." He was later disbarred in Kentucky for misappropriating funds in the settlement of a fen-phen diet drug class action suit.

The federal court in the Southern District of Ohio and the judge to whom Chesley's case was assigned were known to be favorable to class certification. Chesley had a long-standing relationship with the judge.

My first reaction was to move to dismiss based on the cases I had won. But the judge indicated that he would not decide such motions until after a class was certified. In consultation with Paul Miller, who was then cogeneral counsel of Pfizer, we decided to attempt to use this class suit as an opportunity to resolve the vast bulk of the litigation that remained and might be filed in the future. Under the supervision of the court, we engaged in settlement negotiations.

We added to our team Kenneth Feinberg who was then a partner in our D.C. office, and later opened his own practice achieving success in high-profile compensation matters including the distribution of funds for 9/11, Hurricane Katrina and BP oil spill victims. The Netflix show "Worth" depicts Ken's heroic efforts, working without fee, for the 9/11 Victims' Compensation Fund, Just before the deadline, he secured sufficient participation to avoid an economic disaster from class actions while compensating the victims' families without their having to undergo the burdens and uncertainty of litigation. Ken had been the special master, appointed by Judge Jack Weinstein, a district judge in the Eastern District of New York, to mediate a class action settlement in the Agent Orange litigation. Agent Orange was a defoliant sprayed in the Vietnam War. A class action lawsuit was filed on behalf of retired military personnel against Dow Chemical Company claiming injury from exposure to the defoliant. This was the first nationwide class action settlement of its kind. The Shiley heart valve class action was the second.

Our local counsel was Jim Adams of Frost & Jacobs. He gave me as a memento a red wooden baseball bat signed by all of the Cincinnati Reds team with a note saying, "We know how to play baseball in Ohio as well as you in New York." They also knew how to play class actions in Ohio, as illustrated by the Shiley valve case and the penile prosthesis case I describe in the next section.

Feinberg, Miller and I met with Chesley at the courthouse in Cincinnati. Judge Spiegel said he would not let us out of the room until we reached a settlement. This was disturbing, as I was anxious to get home. Feinberg's experience as a mediator led him to push Miller and me toward making concessions. While we sometimes resented his encouragement to accede to some of plaintiffs' demands, in the end Ken's mediation skills helped to bring the parties together. Chesley's mantra was "Let's get it done!"

Other plaintiffs' lawyers filed individual cases and threatened to undermine a class settlement by opting out of the class suit. Chesley gave them titles and assignments to represent various subclasses—those injured, those who had reoperations to remove the Shiley valve and substitute a different brand (a life-threatening procedure), and those who died from a fracture. We also included foreign patients in the class. We provided notice of the settlement to the health ministries of countries where the Shiley valve was implanted. Poland sent a representative to the class action hearing.

The final agreement provided for a fund of $75 million, which could be replenished if needed to satisfy conditions of the settlement. A supervisory panel of experts was appointed to administer the fund. Each valve recipient would receive $4,000 for psychiatric help in dealing with emotional distress. Spouses could also receive such payments. Centers were set up at various locations around the country where recipients could have their valves examined by a super-X-ray machine imported from Germany. If a potential fracture was observed, they could have a reoperation and receive compensation. If a valve fractured, the injured person or her estate would receive compensation, without the need to file a lawsuit in court, based on a grid with a $500,000 minimum payment. Based on his experience with Agent Orange, Feinberg advised us "to hide in the weeds" when it came to compensation for the plaintiffs' lawyers. To avoid any semblance of collusion, we left that decision entirely to the court. Alan Goott, a partner in our firm who worked with me on these cases, was responsible over the long run, for reviewing and acting on the periodic reports of the supervisory panel set up under the settlement agreement.

At the class action hearing, I presented the evidence and legal argument in support of the settlement. I pointed out that prior to the invention of the artificial heart valve, patients who had diseased natural valves became disabled and soon died. There was no perfect risk-free artificial heart valve available. The Shiley valve reduced the risk of clotting, which was a problem with other artificial valves. The fracture risk was about 0.025 percent. I called David Rosenberg, a Harvard Law School professor, as an expert witness in mass torts to testify to the superiority of the class action procedure, which was an element in the rule that we had to establish. I also called Dr. Anthony Moulton, a cardio-surgeon, to testify to the absence of any risk-free valve, and the reasons why he and other surgeons implanted the Shiley valve knowing of its risks. Chesley called as his expert Professor Arthur Miller of Harvard Law, who was the author of a treatise on federal civil procedure, and a television personality.

In my argument, I responded to questions regarding the judge's and Public Citizen's concerns about the prospect of reoperations. Valve recipients had the option of taking advantage of an FDA-approved procedure for acoustical testing as well as X-ray procedures to ascertain if their valve had a potential fracture. I made it clear that we did not want to encourage reoperations where the risk of mortality was 5 percent as compared with the much smaller chance of fracture of the original implant.

In his opinion finding the settlement to be fair, Judge Spiegel cited the cases in which I had obtained summary judgment dismissing claims where the valve had not failed. We had to deal with objections filed by a Philadelphia law firm who represented certain class members. The court rejected the objections. The Sixth Circuit Court of Appeals upheld the trial court's approval of the settlement as fair. The Philadelphia lawyers, who had participated in the hearings in the Cincinnati trial court and the Sixth Circuit Court of Appeals, filed another suit in state court in Pennsylvania, which challenged the class settlement. Harkening back to the Lincoln Center case, for which I drafted an opinion signed by Judge Dimock, I argued successfully that this state claim was barred under the doctrine of *res judicata* because it had been litigated and rejected in federal court.

Shiley developed a new valve, called a "monostrut," which did not have welds and could not fracture. This valve was said to be the safest on the market. It was widely used in Europe. Because of the adverse publicity from the fractures of the earlier valve, the monostrut was not used in the U.S. Subsequently, Miller was appointed sole general counsel. Sheila Birnbaum, a partner in the Skadden Arps law firm, was brought in to deal with the insurance companies, who reimbursed the company for much of the settlement cost. And I became Pfizer's go-to product liability lawyer in nationwide litigations.

The Judicial Panel for Multidistrict Litigation

Certain federal cases that are similar and have been filed in two or more federal courts may be transferred by the Multidistrict Panel of judges to a single district judge for pretrial proceedings. This procedure was based on legislation that was an outgrowth of the procedure used in the Electrical Equipment litigation. The Panel published a handbook on multidistrict litigation which contained sample interrogatories, court orders and other documents we had filed in the Electrical Equipment cases. The transfers of cases to a single district court avoided repetitious and unnecessarily burdensome duplication of depositions, interrogatories and document production. Again, following the practice of the Electrical Equipment cases, a document depository would be set up for use by all the plaintiffs. And, as we did in the earlier cases, the coordinating judge would appoint lead counsel to conduct depositions, prepare and serve discovery requests, and argue motions. The multidistrict judge, to whom the cases were transferred, decided all pretrial motions. If the cases were not settled or dismissed on motion, the cases would be transferred for trial back to the district where they were originally filed. There was a downside for defendants in some cases. A ruling that cases were subject to multidistrict procedures would be publicized and could result in more cases than might otherwise have been filed.

The Breast Implant cases, in which my firm was not involved, had been transferred to a single court by the Multidistrict Panel. After settlement of the Breast Implant cases, the product liability plaintiffs' lawyers cast about for another litigation to pursue. Plaintiffs' lawyers filed class action lawsuits in different districts seeking damages for men who had penile prostheses. The plaintiffs' attorneys named the devices "penile implants" to identify with breast implants. These devices were designed to address male impotence. The defendant was American Medical Systems (AMS), a subsidiary of Pfizer. The Pfizer chairman told a story, which was probably apocryphal, about his embarrassment when a staid member of the Board of Directors asked, "What are penile implants?" He responded that "penal" implants were something done in prisons.

I appeared before the Multidistrict Panel to argue against applying this procedure to the cases involving penile prostheses. I argued that plaintiffs' lawyers had tried to stack the deck by purposely filing similar class actions in different districts. Moreover, there were only a few cases each year claiming that the device malfunctioned. The company readily settled those cases if they had merit, and tried those which did not. Judge Merhige from Virginia, who had been the coordinating judge in cases involving women's IUD devices, and whom I knew from the Reynolds Metals case (described later), asked, "Isn't this a defective product deserving of multidistrict treatment?" I replied:

"Your honor, the product is similar to the organ that it replaces. It sometimes does not inflate when you want it to. It sometimes deflates prematurely. But it doesn't explode. And when the patient has a problem, he sees his urologist who can usually fix it."

The audience of lawyers, who were waiting to argue their cases, burst into laughter. The motion for multidistrict treatment of penile prostheses cases was denied in an opinion that later was cited by the Sixth Circuit Court of Appeals in support of the denial of class certification in these cases.

The Phantom Court Order

A class action was filed in federal court in Ohio by a patient on behalf of all patients with these prostheses. I arrived at the offices of our local counsel who informed me that he was a physician as well as a lawyer, and that he had defended the Breast Implant cases. He advised me that the judge to whom our case was assigned had never met a class action lawsuit that he would not certify. He also reminded me that there was no appeal from the grant of class certification. He warned that this judge would certify a class; and we would have no alternative but to settle. Stan Chesley, the "master of disaster" from the heart valve litigation, was representing the plaintiff.

At the first court hearing, the judge began by telling me that he was inclined to grant class certification unless I convinced him otherwise (which was the reverse of what the rule required). I argued that class certification was inappropriate because of the absence of common issues. Alleged problems with the prostheses were varied and specific to individual patients. Thus, the issues of causation and injury could not be determined on a common basis. In this case, the named plaintiff had a unique ailment. He had Peyronie's disease, which is a curvature of the penis. He also was receiving permanent disability payments from Ohio for psychiatric problems. I reasoned that this plaintiff was not a typical or adequate class representative. If, as was likely, the jury rejected his claim, that adverse judgment would disadvantage all of the other class members who were patients with this device. The judge reserved decision. At the judge's suggestion, Chesley filed an amended complaint adding additional class representatives.

After the arguments on whether to allow plaintiffs to sue as a class action, the judge was hospitalized. Strangely, an unsigned opinion, which granted class certification, emerged from the hospital and was filed in the court. I concluded that the unsigned order failed to meet the fundamental requirements of the class action rule and due process. It was apparent that the district judge had an illegal bias in favor of class certification. But I was faced with the fact that appeals from class action order were not permitted at this time. The only avenue of relief was to file a petition for mandamus. This procedure imposed a heavier burden than an appeal. We had to show that the trial judge had committed serious error beyond his judicial powers. One way or the other, we needed "to be heard."

For the oral argument in the Sixth Circuit Court of Appeals, Chesley retained Professor Arthur Miller of Harvard Law School, who had been his expert in the Shiley valve class action hearing. Professor Miller and Chesley decided to split the argument. Chesley told the court that he was arguing the facts and Miller would present the law. But during Miller's argument the court asked about the facts, which he got wrong. During Chesley's argument the judges asked about the law, which Chesley was at a loss to explain. I argued the facts, which I knew from having argued in the district court, and the law, which I had briefed.

Mandamus was not generally available as a remedy to appeal from a decision certifying a class. In this case the Sixth Circuit held that based on "the extraordinary facts of this case we find that the district judge's disregard of class action procedures was of such severity and frequency so as to warrant its issuance here." Accordingly, the court granted the petition for mandamus. We were heard on the merits of whether the unsigned order properly certified a class action.

There were two aspects to the court decision. First, the court of appeals excoriated the district judge for his order. The court held that the district court judge's order, which merely parroted the requirements stated in Rule 23, was insufficient. The district judge did not follow the Supreme Court's direction to engage in a "rigorous analysis." Indeed, the Sixth Circuit observed that the district judge's order was a carbon copy of his order in the Breast Implant litigation, which involved very different facts.

The unsigned order still included the original plaintiff as a class representative despite his physical and mental infirmities. The court of appeals rejected plaintiffs' contention that the rule, which required the named plaintiff to be an adequate representative, could be satisfied by recognizing Chesley as competent counsel. Rather, the named plaintiffs had to show that they are personally capable of overseeing the litigation. The Sixth Circuit found that the newly named plaintiffs, which Chesley added to the complaint, did not satisfy the requirement for typicality. Each of the newly added named plaintiffs had different models of the device and different medical or functional complaints. For the same reason, the court of appeals concluded that plaintiffs had not established that there was a predominance of common factual issues. Finally, the Sixth Circuit admonished the district court for ignoring the finding of the Multidistrict Panel that consolidated treatment was not "a just and efficient" means of managing these cases. Accordingly, the rule's requirement that a class action was superior to other means was not satisfied.

The Sixth Circuit also looked at the larger picture in which this same district judge had recently certified three similar class actions. The appellate court found a need to avoid future repeated errors. Accordingly, the court of appeals rendered what became a landmark decision that set the boundaries of class certification. In this regard, the court's opinion was cited by me and others in future cases. Thus, the court explained the difference between "mass torts" and product liability cases, such as the claims against AMS in this case. For example, a mass tort may involve a toxic chemical spill or similar disaster. In that instance there is often a common issue as to whether the event was caused by defendant's negligence. Moreover, the injuries from a mass tort are often similar. In contrast, medical devices and drugs can have physical effects that differ among patients. Patients may have relied on different advice from each of their prescribing physicians. In conclusion, the Sixth Circuit found that we had met our "heavy burden" to be heard by way of mandamus. The Court of Appeals ordered the district judge to decertify the class.

Medical Monitoring

Medical monitoring is a provision that I included in class action settlements to benefit those who were exposed to potential injury or illness that needed to be promptly diagnosed. I was consulted by the Swiss-based chemical and pharmaceutical company, Novartis, which was sued in class actions in state courts in Louisiana and other southern states. The complaints alleged that the plaintiffs contracted bladder cancer from a pesticide called Galecron. This pesticide had been approved in the 1960s by the Environmental Protection Administration (EPA) for spraying on tomatoes and vegetables. When the agency discovered that the product caused tumors in mice, it was taken off the market. Novartis then got approval from EPA for use on cotton on the condition that farm workers must be required to wear long-sleeve shirts, gloves and other protective clothing. As it turned out, in Louisiana and Alabama the farm workers were not about to wear such clothing in the summer heat when cotton was picked. A number of farm workers, workers in the factory that produced Galecron, and the pilots of the planes that sprayed Galecron developed bladder cancer.

My partner, Steve Glickstein, and I had to report our recommendations to the Board of Directors at company headquarters in Basil,

Switzerland. In view of the fact that we had worked nights and weekends to get up to speed on the claims, we got permission from the general counsel of Novartis USA to fly first class on Swiss Air. After the meeting, I enjoyed a tour of the art museum in the city of Basil, which had an extensive impressionist collection. We then headed to the airport where we encountered the president of Novartis U.S.A. The U.S. general counsel was red-faced and offered his first-class seat to his superior who calmly replied that he observed company rules and would travel in economy class.

My advice to the Board was that I should contact the law firm that represented plaintiffs in the tobacco cases, who were experienced class action lawyers. We could negotiate a class action settlement that included medical monitoring to those exposed to the pesticide and compensation to those who contracted bladder cancer. We would file a motion in court to schedule a hearing at which we would seek certification of a class and—when the class was certified—approval of the settlement. This federal case would supersede the state class action suits that were pending. The directors expressed concern that bringing in eminent plaintiffs' product liability lawyers, as compared with the small firms that had sued them in state courts, might create risks. I explained that these tobacco lawyers, like anyone else, would be glad to take the case, as it would be profitable. They would know how to settle on grounds that a court would approve. They also would know how to cooperate with the small-time lawyers who had filed the existing state court actions by giving them responsible positions, as Chesley had done in the heart valve cases.

The new class action lawyers filed suit in federal court in Mobile, Alabama. We then negotiated a settlement that provided a grid that would award fair compensation to those who contracted bladder cancer, compensation for those who died from exposure, and a medical monitoring program for those exposed but not ill. We cleared the settlement informally with the district judge, who then held a hearing certifying the class and finding that the settlement was fair and reasonable. Apart from the satisfactory conclusion of the disparate state litigations, I was pleased that we had done something meaningful to help the victims of this exposure.

Incidentally, this experience alerted me to the dangers of herbicides and pesticides—even those approved by EPA. I forbade our landscapers from spraying these products even though we had weeds on our lawn. And I recently convinced the manager of the homes in our community to retain an expert to provide a report on what sprays are unsafe for application. I read the EPA reports, which found that almost all pesticides and herbicides are "possibly carcinogenic." For that reason, they should not be used at all on lawns and trees.

Federal Jurisdiction Over Class Actions

A class action was filed in state court in South Carolina by a patient who died after taking the antibiotic Trovan developed by Pfizer. After being on the market briefly, some patients exhibited side effects, so the FDA limited its use to serious cases of hospital pneumonia that could not be cured by existing antibiotics.

Federal courts can only have jurisdiction over cases where the plaintiff and defendant are of diverse citizenship and the claim is for more than $75,000. Congress passed a law called the Supplemental Jurisdiction Act, which allowed federal courts to have jurisdiction over additional claims that do not meet the jurisdictional dollar requirement if the claims are related to the basic claim. This statute was designed to avoid having to litigate before some state courts that were reputed to certify class actions without regard to whether they satisfied the requirements of the federal class action rules. Here, the plaintiff claimed more than $75,000 in damages, which—if filed alone as an individual case—would have been sufficient to remove the case to federal court.

But some absent class members would have claims for less. We removed the case to federal court. Plaintiff moved to dismiss for lack of federal jurisdiction. The federal district court held that it had jurisdiction and plaintiff appealed.

I argued the appeal to the Fourth Circuit in Richmond, Virginia. The other circuits were split as to how to interpret the new statute's jurisdictional standards. This was the most complex appellate argument I experienced. A young associate of the firm, Robert Grass, helped me through the maze of analysis. The statements in the legislative history of the statute were squarely contrary to our position on federal jurisdiction.

During my argument, Judge Motz, a Clinton appointee from the district court in Maryland, sitting by designation as an appellate judge for this argument, asked me about the legislative history. As I was about to give my prepared answer, Chief Judge Wilkinson interrupted. The judge had clerked for Supreme Court Justice Powell and intellectually was aligned with Justice Scalia. He asked me whether the language of the statute itself was clear on its face. I responded that it was clear and favored my position. The judge said there was no reason to discuss the legislative history. At this point I knew that one judge would rule my way and another judge had a contrary view. The third judge was visiting from the Ninth Circuit in California and did not say a word during oral argument. But in the end, she joined in Judge Wilkinson's opinion. The majority opinion held that if the named plaintiff had a sufficient claim for the jurisdictional amount, then—under the new statute—the federal court had supplemental jurisdiction over all the other class members, even though some of them would have smaller claims. Judge Motz dissented.

In view of the split among the circuit courts on this issue, a case deciding it would surely make its way to the Supreme Court. I urged my client to see it through. But the company was concerned with the potential class action liability if we lost and so we settled the case. Subsequently, in a case involving the Alaska oil spill by the *Exxon Valdez* tanker, the

Supreme Court in a 5–4 decision ruled consistently with the Fourth Circuit's decision in the case I argued.

Postscript on Class Actions

When I taught class action law at the University of Miami Law School, I was critical of Supreme Court decisions, often written by Justice Scalia with Justice Ginsburg dissenting. These decisions put roadblocks in the way of legitimate class actions. Thus, in a series of opinions, the Court put a federal policy favoring arbitration above the benefits of class actions. This enabled corporations to insert arbitration provisions, which were often written in small print, into consumer and employment contracts, which expressly provided for arbitration of disputes and—as Justice Scalia held—precluded the filing of class actions. Even if they read the small print, consumers and employees were not in a position to challenge these provisions. The majority opinion rejected an argument that such clauses should not override the right to file a class action where there was a disparity in bargaining power between a large corporation and its employees or customers. In the event that persons unwittingly entered into such consumer and employment contracts, they forfeited their right to be heard by a court and jury in a class action (which might be all they could afford) in the event of a dispute.

◆   ◆   ◆

Chapter XXI
UNCHARTED TERRITORY

Previously, I discussed the lesson learned during my judicial clerkship—that if a judge could render a decision in a previously unknown area of the law, a lawyer, who had more time to spend on a particular case, could address a subject that was not learned in a law school class. What follows are cases on subjects I did not study in law school, and with which I had no prior experience.

Libel and the First Amendment

A publisher of a report similar to *Consumer Reports*, but for industry, was about to publish an article warning of toxic ozone fumes emanating from a photocopier made by American Photocopy Equipment Corporation (APECO). APECO sued in federal court in Chicago and filed a motion for a temporary injunction against the publication. I flew to Chicago expecting a one-day hearing. The two principals of my client insisted on coming along. APECO was represented by Bert Jenner of Jenner & Block, who had been counsel to the Republicans during the Watergate hearings and was known as one of Chicago's best trial attorneys. Jenner told the court that he wanted to call some witnesses and the judge said his docket was free. Jenner then called each of the two officers of our client to the stand. Lesson learned: Do not bring clients to a hearing of this kind.

What followed was a two-week trial. I had not brought clothes, so each day I had to purchase a shirt, socks, and underwear on my way from court to the hotel. There was a blizzard in Chicago. We had to move to another hotel as a convention was booked at our hotel. I asked Jenner when the trial was going to end because I wanted to get home. He replied that his wife had been in the hospital for a month and he had only seen her twice. That was his problem. We heard that Jenner's modus operandi was to go out for dinner and drinks until the wee hours while his staff prepared him for the next day of trial. He was adept at cross-examining on complex scientific issues, without a note, while drawing pictures in the air with his hands.

The Illinois law of libel was unique and complex, so I retained a lawyer I knew from the electrical equipment cases as cocounsel. Dick Powell was a partner in Isham, Lincoln & Beale, which represented a Chicago newspaper. The firm provided expert advice on Illinois libel law. President Lincoln had supposedly been a name partner in the firm.

I argued that irrespective of whether a publication was true or not, the First Amendment precluded a prior restraint of speech. The plaintiff's remedy was for damages after the fact if it could prove that the publication wrongfully injured it. In final argument, the issue was whether the First Amendment rule against a prior restraint of speech applied to commercial speech. Jenner relied on an old article in the *Harvard Review* (not the *Law Review*), written by Dean Roscoe Pound, an eminent jurist. I relied on a dictum, meaning not a holding but a statement, in a U.S. Supreme Court opinion in which Bear Bryant, the coach of the Alabama football team, sued the *Saturday Evening Post* for accusing him of fixing games. I urged the court to follow the dictum of the U.S. Supreme Court over the *Harvard Review*. The judge ruled my way and denied the injunction. Subsequently our client issued a retraction. Its testing was flawed as it ran the copiers continuously, which was not done in practice. We learned that the judge chastised

Jenner for not having elicited that fact in his cross-examination. Of course, I was also unaware of this flaw in the client's testing procedure.

The Maritime Commission

In 1973, I appeared at a hearing before the U.S. Maritime Commission in D.C. I represented American Export Isbrandsten Lines (AEIL), a shipping company. Jakob Isbrandsten was an imposing figure, who inherited Isbrandsten Lines from its founder, his father, Hans Isbrandsten. Jacob merged his company with American Export Lines.

Maritime law, with which I had no experience, is a field different from Admiralty law. As I had never been before the Maritime Commission, I retained Richard (Dick) Kurrus, a Washington lawyer specializing in this field, as co-counsel. Kurrus was a wheeler-dealer who frequently took time away from our case to work with Congressional committees. He belonged to a club where we regularly had lunch during the hearings. Other Washington wheeler-dealers would often come by our table to chat with Dick. I asked him how he had become a maritime lawyer. He explained that his first job was with one of the largest firms in Boston. An early assignment was to assist a partner at a trial in Maine. As their train arrived in Portland, the partner asked Dick to get the suitcases down from the rack and take them off the train. Dick replied that his mother did not sacrifice to send him to the Harvard Law School to carry suitcases. That is how he became a maritime lawyer.

AEIL, together with other shipping companies and the Antitrust Division of the Justice Department, were challenging a merger between U.S. Lines and Sealand, the first and second largest companies in the container shipping industry. The issue was whether a merger agreement should be approved under the Shipping Act of 1916, which authorized the Commission to approve all shipping agreements. The hearing focused on competitive issues that were related to traditional antitrust analysis with which I was familiar. I had to learn about the container shipping industry. Container shipping was an efficient way to transport goods by sea. Large containers were preloaded, sent by truck or rail to the pier and automatically lifted onto the vessels. This was more efficient than the old method of loading merchandise into the hold of a ship without first being in a container. U.S. Lines was the number one competitor with over 20 percent of the market. Sealand was number two with 15 percent of the market and owned by R.J. Reynolds, the tobacco company. I was lead counsel for AEIL at the hearings before an Administrative Law Judge. I worked closely with Don Flexner, the Justice Department attorney, who later joined David Boies' firm.

The hearings were a circus. There were no rules of procedure or evidence and little decorum. Lawyers would jump up at their whim and make objections and arguments. It was difficult "to be heard." Our position was that the merger would create a new entity that could exercise its monopoly power to take business from AEIL. AEIL currently handled shipping from the East Coast of the U.S. on the Atlantic route to Europe. The merger would allow the enhanced Sealand to divert this traffic through Halifax, Nova Scotia.

After the hearing, the hearing examiner recommended that the Commission should disapprove the merger agreement. At this point, AEIL and I were out of the case. Later, Reynolds offered to operate the two companies independently. As a result, the Commission approved the deal holding that it was not a merger but a cooperation agreement. In its opinion, the Commission chastised the Justice Department for not challenging anticompetitive activity of foreign shipping companies with whom the American companies had to compete. The D.C. Circuit court of appeals reversed the Commission's decision. It held that because the deal was in fact a merger, the Commission had no jurisdiction to consider its legality. Rather the merger was to be reviewed by the courts under the antitrust laws. The Department of Justice had filed suit in federal court in New Jersey to enjoin the merger under the antitrust laws. By the time the case came up for trial in federal court in New Jersey, the five-year period for consummation of the agreement had expired and the case was held to be moot. AEIL went bankrupt in 1977 and was sold to another shipping company. In 1982, U.S. Lines declared bankruptcy as its slow-moving container ships were overrun by other companies' speedier, more modern ships, which took over much of its business.

Delaware Chancery Court

Another venue that was new to me was the Delaware Chancery Court located in Dover, Delaware. The courtroom was in a colonial-style cottage with quaint chintz curtains on the windows, in sharp contrast to the majestic marble courtrooms in other states and federal buildings. The stated purpose of the Chancery Court is to resolve disputes about the internal affairs of companies that are incorporated in Delaware. In old England, courts were divided between law and equity. Courts of law would apply the common law (prior case law) and could provide relief by way of monetary damages. Courts of equity were considered more flexible and would provide relief such as injunctions and specific performance of contracts. In the late eighteenth century, most states were moving away from the division of their courts between law and equity. In contrast, Delaware established its Chancery Court (court of equity) in 1792, and it remained as such over the ensuing years. On the court's website, the reason for creating a Chancery Court is explained: " . . . [T]here arose controversies and contests growing out of business, and the necessities for the redress of injuries which resulted from the breach of duties or the nonperformance of obligations that called for the use of the means to enforce observance through ancient remedies." That precisely defines the relief I sought on behalf of my client.

I represented Newco (short for "New Company"), which was the name given to a subsidiary established by The Equitable Life Assurance Company to be the party to a takeover of the Beauty Division of Revlon, the cosmetics company. Newco entered into a contract with Revlon to effectuate the acquisition. The contract contained a "breakup" clause pursuant to which the party canceling or not abiding by the contract would have to pay damages in a fixed amount. In 1985, Ronald Perelman, through MacAndrew's & Forbes, a holding company, acquired Revlon for $2.8 billion. Perelman refused to honor Newco's contract to purchase Revlon's Beauty Division. I filed suit in the Delaware Chancery Court to enforce the contract.

At the first hearing, we appeared before the chancellor assigned to hear the case. Whether due to poor eyesight or a shy personality, the chancellor kept his head buried in the documents in front of him. As a result, I had no idea if my argument was penetrating—whether he was really "listening" and absorbing what I had to say. We faced a serious problem in seeking specific performance of the contract. Revlon's Beauty Division was not a cohesive body with headquarters and manufacturing facilities in some designated location. Rather, it was a loose-knit series of factories and sales offices spread across the globe including Asia Pacific nations. It would have been almost impossible for a chancellor to oversee the transfer of those assets to Equitable. So, I had to come up with some other approach.

I conducted the deposition of a savvy attorney who ran Perelman's empire through MacAndrews, and who had been a partner in a large Philadelphia law firm. In pretrial discovery, we obtained financial statements created by MacAndrews. It turned out that there were substantial differences between the financial statements given to banks to obtain financial support, and the financial statements used in the acquisition of Revlon. The witness had no good explanation for these discrepancies. As a result, we were able to settle the case for twice the breakup fee in the contract. The client was overjoyed with this result. This was an example of how a misrepresentation, which might not be directly relevant to the litigation issues, can turn a case around.

Intellectual Property and New Technology

In the early days of my law practice, there were no word processors, only typewriters. There were no copying machines, as we know them today—only what were called wet copiers. If you wanted copies of what you were typing, you put carbon paper between sheets of paper and the typing went through to create a copy. In court, lawyers did not—as they do now—distribute numerous copies of documentary exhibits to opposing counsel, the court, the clerk and the jury. Instead, there was an original document that was shown to opposing counsel, handed to the clerk to mark as an exhibit, shown to the court, and then to the jurors, who passed it around.

Legal research was done by going to the office library or, if necessary, the bar association's more extensive library. There, we consulted indexes to find cases in published volumes that were pertinent. There were volumes for district court cases in what was called "the Federal Supplement." Circuit court of appeals opinions were reported in volumes named "Federal 2d" and later "3d." The "U.S. Reports" contained Supreme Court opinions. If you found a helpful case, you needed to use another volume called "Shepard's Citation Service" to trace whether it was still good law or had been overruled. I was asked at one point to check out a service called Lexis, which had reproduced all reported cases on computer. Key words could be used to find the cases that were pertinent. I took an issue and researched it in the conventional way, which took several hours. Then I tried Lexis and found the answer in fifteen minutes. The firm ordered the service. Today, firm libraries are obsolete. Everyone uses Lexis from his or her desk computers.

Before the advent of word processing on computers, stenographers had to use typewriters for briefs and memoranda. The law firms had steno pools to do the typing that individual secretaries could not handle. The steno pools had night staff that would stay up all night and type. It appeared that some of the night workers suffered early mortality. I would dictate a brief or argument. During the day, my secretary would take dictation on a stenotype machine of the kind used by court reporters. I would mark up the typewritten version. If time was of the essence, the night staff would retype it and send it to my home in Scarsdale, New York, a suburban village. I might mark up the draft further by hand and send it back to the office for final typing. The transportation was by a local taxi service, which would take the packages on their runs with passengers.

In the early eighties a new technology enabled messages to be sent electronically among lawyers in the law firm. With it, you could type memoranda on a word processor and send them to others in the firm. Peter Weill, a Kaye Scholer partner in the Banking and Finance Department, adapted the technology to the firm's internal communications, which he called "Kmail." Later, the system known as "Email" could be used to communicate with clients and others outside of the firm. I became a prolific user of this technique, which I was told by our IT Department set an annual firm record. The partners at Kaye Scholer took turns inviting associates and other partners to our homes for dinner parties and summer swim outings. One of the associates asked if he could come upstairs and see what he called command central, from which email ideas, edits, and instructions emanated, sometimes at 3:00 a.m.

Another invention that lawyers came to use was the FAX machine. Before the development of the FAX, Xerox Corporation began marketing what it called a Telefax. This was a machine that could send documents wirelessly from one location to another. I litigated a trademark case involving the Telefax. Although I did not study trademark law in law school, one of our partners, Fred Freund, who represented PepsiCo, would regularly circulate the published results of trademark cases. Without looking at the court's holdings, we would guess whether particular marks were sufficiently similar to be infringing. This exercise developed a sense of what courts are likely to find in trademark cases.

The early marketing conundrum for commercial use of Xerox's Telefax was that a buyer would not find it useful if a company to whom it wanted to transmit a document lacked a Telefax machine to receive it. One answer was for a company to purchase the machines and provide them to centers in different cities. Customers could go to a center in their town and "telefax" a document to a center in another town. The designated recipient could go to the center and pick up the copy.

In this case, a buyer of the machines franchised others who set up offices to send and receive Telefax documents. He sold the rights to franchisees for $5,000 per machine. But instead of locating in major cities around the country, this buyer chose to limit his scope to cities in the state of Florida. He then took the money from the franchisees and lost it gambling. Customers complained to Xerox. I filed suit for trademark infringement and fraud. The court issued an injunction against the defendant's further use of the Telefax trademark. Soon, Xerox lost out to AT&T, which marketed the "FAX" machine that transmitted documents over telephone lines directly from the sender to the recipient.

Security and Exchange Commission

Roy Ash was one of the so-called whiz kids (including President Kennedy's defense secretary Robert McNamara) who, during World War II, were sent by the military to Harvard Business School to learn to handle the logistics of supplying the armed forces. Upon graduation from high school, Ash got a job with a bank in California. He enlisted in the army where a colonel, who observed his talents, included him in the Harvard program. After the war, Ash founded the high-tech company Litton Industries based in Boston. Later, he was named head of the federal Office of Management & Budget by President Nixon who wanted to bring business expertise into the federal government.

Thereafter, Ash became CEO of Addressograph-Multigraph (AMC). AMC used metal plates to automatically address labels based on a nineteenth-century patent. Ash's goal was to develop its computer technology. That did not work out. Stockholders complained to the Securities and Exchange Commission, which undertook an investigation into whether the financial statements showed inadequate reserves. The Chief Financial Officer and other company officials retained Washington lawyers who specialized in dealing with the SEC. Ash hired me, based on a referral by one of the attorneys I worked with in the Electrical Equipment litigation. I defended Ash at a deposition conducted by the SEC in Washington. During the lunch break, we ate at Roy Rogers (Ash was a down-to-earth guy), where Ash engaged in detailed conversation with the cashier regarding the machine used for billing at checkout.

Each of the potential defendants had to prepare and file with the SEC a document called a "Wells Submission," which explained why the client should not be the subject of a civil complaint seeking penalties. The Washington lawyers presented analyses by accountants as to why the reserves were adequate. I took a different tack. I researched the *Harvard Business Review* to find articles on the responsibilities of Board Chairmen. I retained a Harvard Business School professor who had written that CEOs do not have responsibility for the details of financial statements but can rely on others for their accuracy. As one of the "whiz kids" from Harvard Business School, I assumed that Ash knew the ins and outs of financial statements. But, as I argued, the company's reserves were the legal responsibility of the Chief Financial officer, not the CEO. Later, after the 2008 recession, the CEO's responsibilities and liabilities were changed by legislation and regulation. I lectured on the subject at corporate compliance programs, run by Carole Basri, who had retained me for the Iraqi Oil for Food scandal matter. But the Ash case occurred at an earlier time.

The Washington lawyers mocked my presentation, which they said was too long, employed the wrong strategy, and would probably not be read by the SEC staff. The result was that Ash was the only officer who was not named in the civil complaint. I also had landed another client.

Gold Mine

Sure enough, some months later I received a call from Mr. Ash asking if anyone in our firm knew anything about gold mining. I found an associate who graduated from Texas U. Law School where he had taken a course in oil and gas law. Close enough! We called Ash back and he told us a tale of his gold mine. Ash and Charles "Tex" Thornton, his partner at Litton Industries, lived in California and purchased a ranch in Elko, Nevada, where they could spend time with their families between commutes to Litton in Boston. Out west, when a neighbor wants to sell property and the cost is reasonable, the custom is to purchase it rather than risk an unfriendly new neighbor. Roy and Tex purchased the T Lazy Ranch for five figures. The property had an abandoned gold mine called the Gold Quarry Property, which—upon examination by experts—turned out to be one of the richest gold mines in North America.

Roy and Tex entered into a lease with Newmont Gold Co., related to Newmont Mining, an international mining company. Under the terms of the lease, Newmont was to mine and process the gold and pay royalties to the owners. The royalties were expected to set up Ash and his family for life. Ash believed that Newmont was violating the terms of the contract. In particular, it appeared that Newmont was withholding its efforts to develop the mine because it preferred to sell gold that was mined on its own properties, which were not burdened with royalty payments. Newmont put the mining and selling of the gold on Ash's property on the back burner. The dispute came to a head when Newmont filed suit in federal court in Reno, Nevada, in which it sought a declaratory judgment that certain of its facilities need no longer be dedicated to the Gold Quarry mine.

On the phone, I asked Ash to tell me the details of the dispute. In preparation for a quick trip to Los Angeles to meet with him, I did a computer search of all the technical terms he had mentioned, which at the time were incomprehensible to me. In those days, printers would produce pages in a roll like paper toweling. I stuffed all the pages into my attaché case and headed to the airport with the Texas U. associate. When we arrived at Ash's California office, I found that Tex was also present and he had invited the Chicago firm of Latham & Watkins, with whom I was to compete for the case. We discussed the facts and the potential strategy. At that point the Latham lawyer turned to me and asked, "You are from New York City. How do you know so much about gold mines?" I did not say that I had just read about it on the plane. I was retained.

I engaged local counsel in Las Vegas who warned that I was up against a lawyer from Salt Lake City, Utah, who was one of the nation's leading experts on gold mining law. He predicted that I would be buried. I met with plaintiff's counsel for lunch in a hotel in Salt Lake City to try to resolve the dispute. Salt Lake City was "dry" in the sense that restaurants were not allowed to sell alcoholic drinks. But just outside the entrance to the hotel restaurant, you could order a small bottle of liquor like the ones distributed on airplanes. Then the waiter would bring the bottle to your table to enjoy with your meal. The Salt Lake City lawyer informed us that he was a fallen Mormon. So, we enjoyed our drinks and lunch, but failed to settle the case.

We filed our answer to Newmont's complaint. I sought discovery of documents and took depositions of Newmont's executives. The lease and related documents established that Newmont had agreed to develop the Gold Quarry property in a diligent and miner-like manner. We filed a cross-motion for summary judgment declaring that the facilities in question were dedicated to Gold Quarry. I flew to Reno for a hearing. We stayed at Harrah's, which was then the only major hotel in Reno. In order to get to an elevator, you had to pass through what seemed like miles of slot machines. It was sad to see elderly people, some of whom were hooked up to oxygen, playing the slots for what looked like their last quarter.

We appeared before a U.S. magistrate judge who would recommend a decision to the district court. I had a three-hole notebook with my argument and detailed references to the record of discovery we had developed. During the argument, the magistrate, who was a nice elderly woman, asked the Newmont lawyer for the support in the record for several of his points. She asked, "Why, when I ask Mr. Klingsberg for the support for his assertions, he cites chapter and verse in the record, and you are unable to do that?" She indicated that she was going to rule in our favor, which she did. And then, since it was near Christmas time, she invited the lawyers into chambers for some holiday cookies. My opponent declined the invitation and left in a huff. The magistrate's report and recommendation were adopted by the district court after further briefing. The district judge concluded that there was no issue of fact and that the documents supported our position that the facilities listed in the lease had to be dedicated to Gold Quarry.

I argued the appeal to the Ninth Circuit Court of Appeals in California. As was my practice, I arrived the day before the argument and sat in on arguments before the same panel of judges as I would have the next day. In that way, I got familiar with the practices and attitudes of the court, which was far from my home court. Newmont contended that the district court erred in ignoring legal rules of construction in interpreting a contract. I argued—and the court of appeals agreed—that no rules of construction were needed when the documents in question were clear on their face. The Ninth Circuit affirmed the decision below in our favor. By careful and well-prepared argument, we defeated one of the world's biggest gold mining companies and their lawyer, who was reputed to be one of the leading gold mining attorneys in the country. As demonstrated in this case and the tax appeal discussed here, possessing litigation skills is at least as important as having knowledge of the technical aspects of the case, which a good litigator can absorb in preparation, much as the court must do to decide the case.

The Littoral Tide

I had no experience with environmental litigation. If one came along, I would have preferred to be on the "green" side. But defendants are entitled to legal representation and to be heard as well. I was retained by Curtiss-Wright Corporation, which I had represented in a proxy fight lawsuit, to argue an appeal in New York State. Curtiss-Wright was hired to construct a port on the North Shore of Long Island where there are picturesque cliffs overlooking Long Island Sound. In so doing, it built a jetty into the Sound, which interrupted the littoral tide. The littoral tide is in an area from the high-water mark to shoreline areas that are permanently submerged. The littoral tide was necessary to wash fresh sand onto the beach. As a result of building the jetty and interrupting the tide, the cliffs started to crumble and homes had to be moved back to avoid falling into the Sound. A number of home-owners sued. After trial, in which I was not involved, the jury taxed compensatory damages and a imposed a multimillion-dollar punitive damage award. On appeal, I argued successfully that the punitive damages award should be overturned because Curtiss-Wright had construction permits from the Army Corps of Engineers. While we were right on the law, I was unhappy not to have been on the green side of an environmental claim.

Tax Court Appeal

While I argued many appeals from a decision on a motion I had argued or a case that I had tried, I was sometimes retained just to brief and argue an appeal. One such case was an appeal in 1975 from an adverse Tax Court opinion. My friend, Norman Sinrich, was a senior partner in the firm's tax department and an adjunct professor in the NYU Law School graduate tax department. But he did not have litigation experience. He asked me to argue an appeal in the Third Circuit. I had no substantive tax experience, apart from the criminal cases that I had prosecuted. Based on my law clerk experience, I knew that the judges who would hear the argument were probably just as lacking as I was in their knowledge of the tax law issues. So, with study I mastered the tax law at issue and proceeded to the Third Circuit Court of Appeals in Philadelphia.

Our client was a predecessor to the oil company, Hess, which sold its farm equipment business. The purchaser of that business was a predecessor to White Motor Company. Since White lacked funds to pay for the acquisition, the parties agreed that White would pay in stock shares in its company. For tax purposes, the Internal Revenue Service had to calculate the fair market value of these shares. Hess contended that the value was based on the published stock market price. White's position was that the value should be what the parties agreed to in their merger contract. The Tax Court ruled that White's position was correct. Hess appealed.

White was represented by the large international law firm of Baker & McKenzie. Unlike me, White's attorney was a tax expert. We all arrived at the courthouse at about 8:30 a.m. when the court listed the names of the three judges who would be hearing the case. Several young attorneys, who accompanied the Baker partner, were dispatched to the court's library to find tax cases decided by the three judges who were to hear our appeal. The Baker attorney then framed his argument around the appellate judges' prior tax rulings. The only problem was that those cases had little if any relevance to the case at hand.

During my argument, one of the judges asked whether my client's position violated the principle of freedom of contract. I responded by saying, "Your Honor, the parties may agree to whatever they want in their contract. But when the tax man comes knocking on the door, they must abide by the tax law rule that required reliance on the publicly stated value listed by the stock exchange." One of the tax lawyers on our team pulled on my coattail and whispered that you can't say that. To this day, I don't know why he did that. I thought it was useful to make my point colorfully in addition to the dull tax law precedents on which we relied. The Court of Appeals ruled in my client's favor and reversed the Tax Court opinion.

"Going to Hell in a Basket"

Delta Holdings Inc., a Bermuda based reinsurance company, sought investments of about a million dollars each from middle management executives at a number of major corporations including Scott Paper, Kellogg's, and others. Reinsurance is a way to spread losses among insurance companies. Primary insurers underwrite policies and take risks. Reinsurance involves pooling those risks among other insurance companies. The investors were enticed by the prospect of easy profits combined with annual meetings in Bermuda where they could relax and drink mai-tai cocktails. It turned out that the reinsurance company was vastly underreserved and unable to pay for the losses it insured. As a result, the managers lost their companies' investments. I filed suit on their behalf in the Southern District of New York. The case was assigned to Judge John Keenan. The subject was so complex that both parties agreed to try the case before the judge without a jury.

My main witness was an actuary, Mary Hennessy, a partner in the firm of Tower, Perrin. My partner, Paul Curran, advised me that when qualifying our expert actuary, I should start with where she went to high school. I protested that this was irrelevant to her actuarial training but Paul persisted. Sure enough, as soon as she identified the parochial Catholic school that she attended, the judge lit up and said with glee: "You really went to that school!"

There is a saying that actuaries are like accountants but with no personality. Her analysis was competent, but in preparation the testimony seemed dull. I told her that she had to portray the company vividly as "going to hell in a basket," although I cautioned her not to use that precise term. But at trial under cross-examination, she loudly proclaimed that the company was indeed "going to hell in a basket."

The case proceeded throughout the summer and we were concerned that the judge would be disappointed if he could not spend his traditional Labor Day at the trotter races in Saratoga, New York. The defense rested just before Labor Day. I announced that the plaintiffs had no rebuttal testimony and we rested as well. Judge Keenan thanked me for "bringing this trial to a blessed ending."

In a long and scholarly opinion, Judge Keenan held that the defendant violated federal securities law, committed common law fraud, and breached express warranties. The district court awarded my clients $24.3 million in damages plus pre-judgment interest and ordered rescission of the entire transaction. The verdict would have restored my clients' lost investment.

Delta appealed to the Second Circuit Court of Appeals. I argued the appeal before Circuit Judge Ralph K. Winter Jr. and two other judges. Judge Winter was a Yale Law Professor who—together with Robert H. Bork and Ward S. Bowman—was part of the East Coast outpost of the law and economics movement that adhered to conservative theory originating at the University of Chicago. As a Yale Law professor, Judge Winter argued a case in the Supreme Court that loosened restrictions on corporate political contributions, which led to the *Citizens United* case. In his academic writings he favored loosening state regulation of corporations. With these preconceived notions, it was not a surprise that he reversed the verdict. Two other respected judges joined Judge Winter's opinion: Judge Irving Kaufman and Judge Jon Newman, whom I knew from law school. Apparently these two judges, who were not involved with the Chicago School of economics, chose not to challenge Judge Winter's long and complex opinion, which analyzed in great detail the ins and outs of actuarial practice as related to the intricate facts of this case.

While we had proved that the reinsurance company was vastly underreserved leading to insolvency, Judge Winter concluded that this was a business matter and was not illegal. The district court accepted the testimony of Ms. Hennessy that the defendants' actuarial methods and conclusions were contrary to general accepted accounting principles (GAAP) as well as actuarial standards. Judge Winter held this conclusion to be clearly erroneous. He ruled that "Informed guesswork is an accepted basis for determining such reserves," and that the books in issue "were based on such guesswork." In my view, allowing the calculation of insurance reserves to be legally valid when based on "guesswork" would endanger the public who rely on such information.

Judge Winter also gave credence to the fact that Peat Marwick, the large accounting firm, had certified the financial records. After the loss in the Second Circuit, I filed suit against Peat Marwick. In deposition, I examined the young accountant who had done the audit, particularly regarding the adequacy of reserves. She knew nothing about actuarial principles and had merely checked the addition for accuracy. We settled with Peat for a modest sum, which did not adequately compensate the clients.

This was one of the few losses in my appellate career. It proves that while you can win some cases you thought you might lose, you can also lose cases you thought were sure winners. When coming up against a judge with doctrinaire views, you are at a disadvantage in assuming he will listen to your argument with an open mind.

Arbitration

I represented Equitable Life Assurance Company in a dispute with a subsidiary of Tokyo Marine, a large Japanese insurance firm. Equitable had sold Tokyo's subsidiary its liability insurance business in the early eighties. Subsequently, there were liabilities relating to asbestos and other product liability litigation, which resulted in huge, unanticipated insurance claims. Tokyo claimed that it did not purchase that end of the business and was not responsible for these claims. We filed for arbitration, as the contract of sale allowed. The arbitration was held in Fort Worth, Texas. Each side picked an arbitrator and the two arbitrators selected a third whose vote would probably decide the case.

A key witness was the president of Tokyo Marine USA. Even though he had held that job for ten years, he insisted on testifying in Japanese through an interpreter. So, I would ask a question; our translator would translate it into Japanese. The Japanese interpreter retained by Tokyo Marine would challenge the translation. When he translated a question asked by Tokyo's attorney into Japanese, our translator would challenge his translation. Needless to say, this was time consuming and interfered with my ability to conduct effective cross-examination. At the outset of my cross-examination, two muscular Japanese men appeared in the hearing room. They crossed their arms and stared at the president. Apparently in fear of these two fellows, the president blatantly lied.

But we had the documents and were on the side of right. The third arbitrator and our arbitrator decided the case in favor of Equitable. The case was important to Equitable because it was involved in negotiations for an impending merger that likely would have aborted if we had lost the case and Equitable had to absorb the liabilities.

Derivatives

I was asked to attend a meeting at Lehman Brothers to discuss a retainer to represent that firm in a dispute with Salomon Brothers. All that I was told is that the issue involved a financial instrument called a derivative. As I lacked knowledge or experience on this subject I took to the meeting another partner, Alan Kezbom, and a bright associate, Al Fenster, who later became a top partner in the firm's finance department. We sat around a large conference table. The general counsel was sitting next to me, explaining the matter. I was asking questions when a gruffy individual with his tie pulled down to his chest and chewing on a cigar butt sat down at the table. I paid no attention to him. Then, the general counsel whispered that this new participant was Lew Glucksman, who runs the company from the floor of the New York Stock Exchange. After the meeting ended, we sent Fenster to the back room with instructions to find out what derivatives were, and not to return to our office until he had a full understanding of the technicalities. Based on what he learned, we wrote a letter threatening suit. The matter was then settled.

As we learned, derivatives are financial instruments, the value of which is dependent on the value of an underlying asset such as stocks, mortgages, credit card debt and auto loans. Kaye Scholer's finance department was expert in creating derivative instruments, which before the 2008 market crash formed a significant part of its business. Al Bianco, a smart partner who worked on these matters, told me that this was a "house of cards" and would some day collapse. Sure enough, in 2008 derivatives were identified as having created an artificial demand for the underlying assets, particularly mortgages. As such, these instruments were said to be a major cause of the financial crisis. As a result of that crisis, Lehman Brothers went into bankruptcy.

•   •   •

Chapter XXII
WEIRD CLAIMS

Among my litigation experiences were a number of unusual and baseless lawsuits. Such claims unnecessarily burden the courts. There are rules designed to prevent such claims. Rule 11 of the Federal Rules of Civil Procedure requires the attorney who signs a complaint to certify that it is not frivolous. If on motion of the opposing party the court determines that the rule was violated, the court may impose sanctions sufficient to deter future conduct including, where appropriate, paying the fees of the moving party. But the rule has not been totally successful in deterring frivolous claims. Opposing attorneys are often satisfied that they have gotten the case against their client dismissed. Spending time to prepare and file a motion in the uncertain hope that attorneys' fees will be awarded may not be worth the effort. What follows are some examples of unusual claims that I induced the court to quickly dismiss but where I did not move under Rule 11 or seek attorneys' fees.

Testicular Disease

The antitrust laws provide that a successful private plaintiff can obtain treble damages and attorneys' fees. These damages are typically lost profits from injury to competition. In one unusual case, a Rhode Island gas station owner sued Texaco. He claimed that he developed an illness leading to removal of his testicles. He attributed his illness to aggravation caused by the oil company's insistence on his purchasing tires, batteries and accessories as a condition of its selling him gasoline (known in antitrust law as a "tie-in"). Alleging this strange injury claim, as distinguished from a traditional claim for financial loss, suggests that the plaintiff was hoping to focus the jury on his unfortunate illness rather than the legal issue of whether there was injury to competition and that injury caused him financial loss.

I was asked to work with Texaco's in-house lawyers to defend this antitrust action, which had been filed in federal court in Providence, Rhode Island. At the outset of the trial, seeking to further prejudice the jury, the plaintiff's lawyer in his opening statement proclaimed in a thick New England accent that he was from *"Prawvidence,"* his partner was from *"Wawr-wick,"* and the gentlemen at the other table were from *"New Yawk."* With that, the Texaco counsel removed me to the back of the courtroom and brought in local counsel to sit at counsel table. In view of plaintiff's attempt to prejudice the jury, it was important to focus the court on the legal inadequacy of the underlying antitrust claim. At the hotel, I wrote an argument on a yellow pad in support of a motion to dismiss based on the lack of proof of impact on competition. The Texaco lawyer was not convinced but I urged him to just read it to the court. The court dismissed the case. After that I told Handler that I would go anywhere to try a case, but I would not sit in the back of the courtroom.

The Hula-Hula Dance

In the next case for Texaco, I was the only attorney assigned. Louis Lefkowitz, the Attorney General of New York, was running for reelection as a Republican. In July, he obtained an indictment against the leading gasoline producers for price fixing in violation of New York's antitrust law. He had the indictment sealed and opened it on the day after Labor Day when serious political campaigning began. Retail gas prices of the various gasoline suppliers were similar because these prices were published at the pump. Competition drove prices down to the lowest level that was publicly posted by any one of the leading gasoline sellers. We knew of no evidence of illicit meetings or collusive communications. We asked the Assistant Attorney General in charge of the case for his evidence. He replied, "We know what you were doing! You were doing the 'hula-hula dance.'" Needless to say, this response did not sound like the State had evidence to support the charges. In the meantime, Lefkowitz was loudly proclaiming in his campaign speeches that, "I am the candidate who indicted the oil companies."

This was my first appearance in state criminal court. The assigned judge was Bert Roberts, a former Bronx DA and brother of my friend and colleague in the U.S. Attorney's Office, George Roberts. We all knew Judge Roberts to be a bit eccentric but fair. I arrived fifteen minutes early, as had been my habit. The door was locked and the courtroom was dark. About a half hour later a bailiff appeared and opened the courtroom. We waited another half hour for Judge Roberts to appear. He arrived with his hair wet, and—according to the bailiff—straight from the gym. The clerk proceeded to call the pending cases. One lawyer after another gave an excuse for seeking a delay in the trial. All the applications for adjournment were granted. Our case was called at the end of the calendar.

The day before our appearance, King Ibn Saud of Saudi Arabia died. Judge Roberts called all the oil company lawyers to the bench. He told us that the maximum fine was $50,000 per violation, and he would impose a fine for only a single violation if our clients pleaded guilty. He urged that this fine would be a drop in the bucket for these giant corporations so why not dispose of the case. A young in-house lawyer for Gulf Oil from Pittsburgh, Pennsylvania, piped up and berated the judge for his remarks. Roberts asked if he was "sitting *shivah*" (mourning) for King Saud. After the session the Gulf lawyer asked the rest of us, who were all New York attorneys, if we would join him in a motion to recuse Judge Roberts for prejudice. We all knew Roberts to be a kibitzer and that we might have to appear before him in future cases. So, we declined.

Texaco and a number of other companies decided to plead *nolo contendre*, meaning they would pay the fine but not admit guilt. Mobil Oil and some others went to trial. The lawyer relying on the hula-hula dance charge apparently was not a trial lawyer capable of following up on the prosecution. Lefkowitz brought in an assistant DA from Suffolk County to try the case. Recognizing the lack of evidence, that lawyer showed up in court under the influence of alcohol. Judge Roberts declared a mistrial and that was the end of the case. The experience diminished my faith in the criminal justice system as administered by the then Republican New York State Attorney General.

Brokers and Heart Attacks?

Hayden Stone was a well-known brokerage firm but it was in financial trouble. It sold out to another firm, leaving its general counsel and a small number of employees to wind up the business. One of its customers was informed that his margin account was overdrawn by several hundred thousand dollars. The advice turned out to be a clerical mistake. But upon receiving the erroneous advice, the customer had a heart attack and died. Instead of retaining an attorney who specialized in securities law, the plaintiff decedent hired a personal injury lawyer who filed suit for wrongful death. The case was assigned to Judge Carmen Zavatt in the Eastern District of New York (covering Brooklyn and Long Island). Zavatt had been the chief judge and took senior status at the Mineola branch in Long Island. He was a respected jurist who wrote a landmark opinion bringing desegregation to local schools. The judge immediately grasped the legal deficiency of plaintiff's odd claim and granted my motion to dismiss the case.

In another case for Hayden Stone, a plaintiff, who had suffered losses in options trading, sued in federal court in Boston to enjoin the public from trading the securities in his account. I was not familiar with the technicalities of option trading. One of the brokers briefed me but I was still somewhat shaky on the ins and outs of option trading. I was hoping to be able to turn to the broker to help me out if any technical questions arose during argument. When we arrived in court, I invited the Hayden broker to sit beside me at counsel table. The judge asked if he was an attorney, which he was not. The judge sternly instructed that anyone who was not a lawyer must sit on the benches before the bar that separated the audience from the trial court.

I explained to the court that the injunction sought in this case was unlike the typical injunction claim. The usual illustration in support of an injunction is that if the court does not enjoin tearing a house down, further litigation regarding that house would be moot. In this case, stocks go up and down and the general public of buyers and sellers would be impacted by a demand by one stockholder to enjoin all trading in a particular security that happened to be in his option trading account. In view of the fluid nature of the transactions, I argued that an injunction was impractical. I muddled through the options procedures without the broker's advice. The injunction was denied.

Flashing Blue Lights

Viagra pills succeeded penile prostheses as a treatment for erectile dysfunction. Lawsuits followed and I was retained to defend. Some of the claims were unusual. One man claimed that after taking Viagra, he was found hanging from a balcony outside his room at a Las Vegas hotel. Another claimed that he took Viagra, went on a date, did not have sex, and was injured in an automobile accident when blue lights began flashing from his car radio. He claimed that the distraction led to the accident.

While these plaintiffs' claims were plainly frivolous, other lawsuits were supported by a physician's "expert" opinion. A complaint was filed on behalf of a man who had a complete physical examination including an electro-cardiogram and a stress test. He was prescribed Viagra, which he took that evening and had fun. The next morning, he died of a heart attack. I had retained the chief of cardiology at Einstein Medical Center in Bronx, New York. I asked him for his opinion. He opined that people can suffer heart attacks while putting on their shirts in the morning, but that does not establish causation. Our expert explained that exercise, such as walking vigorously on a treadmill, or the sexual activity that this poor man engaged in the night before, could cause fatty cells in an artery to break loose, travel to the heart and cause a fatal heart attack. I asked what could be done to avoid that result since exercise was regarded as healthy. He replied that this could be predicted from an angiogram but that procedure involved risks. He suggested taking a daily aspirin. I asked if that would not cause stomach ailments. He replied, "That, we can cure."

In particular, the impetus for heart attack claims was an opinion by a lone cardiologist at a Veterans' Administration hospital in Stony Brook, New York, named Dr. Mallis. He devised a theory that there was "cross-talk" between the heart and the penis, which led to heart attacks induced by ingesting Viagra pills. He touted his expertise as a coauthor of a study published in a medical journal. We visited the principal author of the study at Columbia Medical School. He explained that anyone who had patients in clinical trials could be listed as a coauthor. But Dr. Mallis has no part in the conclusions expressed in the article. And his theory that cross-talk from Viagra caused heart attacks was baseless.

We filed a motion in a case in New York state court under the *Daubert* standard, based on a U.S. Supreme Court decision holding that expert opinions cannot be submitted to a jury if they are not reliably based on testing and publications in peer-reviewed medical journals. The judge applied this rule and rejected Dr. Mallis's opinion. The case was dismissed due to the absence of scientific causation evidence. That was the end of the Viagra litigations. We had a little victory party for the staff at the office. Bert Slonim, a talented lawyer on our product liability team, was adept at dealing with experts. He passed out T-shirts saying "–Absence of Mallis"—a take-off on the movie *Absence of Malice*.

• • •

Chapter XXIII
SETTLEMENT

During the course of a litigation, I defended the deposition of Bill Steere, when he was CEO of Pfizer. He wanted to prepare in the early morning hours so as not to be absent from his duties. I left at the crack of dawn for my commute into New York City to arrive at the company offices on 42nd Street at 6:00 a.m. While defending Mr. Steere at his deposition later that day, he looked down at my feet and asked if I wore a brown shoe on one foot and black on the other for good luck. I explained that it was a consequence of dressing in the dark.

We regularly attended the annual gala to raise funds for the New York Botanical Gardens, which involved a tour of the spring blooms. Mr. Steere's father had been the chief botanist at the Gardens. Over drinks at the affair, Mr. Steere told me that what he liked about my legal representation was that I did not always win, but I rarely lose. Translated, that means knowing when to settle. I regularly reported to Mr. Steere on the status of litigations and he always asked, "What are the odds of winning or losing, and don't tell me 50–50?"

An important part of being a trial lawyer is to know when to advise a client to settle a case. If the odds of winning are favorable, but the consequence of losing is serious, then consider settling. If the odds of winning are fair, the client is in the right as a matter of law and fact, and the consequences of losing are not significant, then consider advising the client to stay the course—provided that the litigation costs and burdens do not outweigh the results of winning.

Judge Learned Hand wrote, "I should dread a lawsuit beyond almost anything short of sickness and death." While lawsuits may be won or lost after years of litigation, a way to cut short the "dread" is to settle. Apart from the cost of litigation, the burdens of having company personnel sit through depositions and dig through files to respond to document requests, are a distraction from daily business operations. And the tension of contemplating a potential loss may create an emotional drain.

There are important considerations for the trial lawyer and the client to consider, apart from the cold calculation of the odds of winning or losing. There may be instances where despite the prospect of winning at the end of the case, the client can afford to settle and will be benefited by having peace of mind and avoiding the distraction of litigation. There may be times when despite having the law on your side, settlement is the right thing to do. That is illustrated in class action product liability cases where medical monitoring of those using the product can achieve a humanitarian result. These immeasurable considerations are illustrated by some of the cases discussed in this section.

Trying cases and arguing appeals require special skills. Settling cases also requires skill, strategy and patience. To achieve a reasonable settlement various preliminary steps may be taken. Motions *in limine* are motions before trial that may put the case in a favorable position or even dispose of it. For example, the *Daubert* standard can support a motion to keep expert testimony from the jury because the expert opinions are based on junk science, rather than peer-reviewed, published studies and accepted scientific principles. To settle, the advocate needs to convince opposing counsel, and sometimes a mediator, that her case is stronger than her opponent's case. Settlement negotiations require preparation of the same magnitude as a case going to trial. The following are some cases that I settled.

Concrete Pipe

In the *Western Concrete Pipe Price Fixing cases,* we were retained by former Texaco lawyers, who had gone into private practice in San Diego, California. I assessed the evidence of illegal price-fixing, which was irrefutable. The battle would be over whether we could prove that the damages were low enough to enable a reasonable settlement to be reached. At that time, San Diego was basically a U.S. Navy town with few hotels. We stayed at a yacht club where one of the San Diego lawyers was a member. Across the bay was the Coronado Hotel, which had tennis courts. The pro arranged for me to get games during my stay.

On my first trip to the West Coast, I met with an economist who had been retained by the former Texaco lawyers. He was a theoretical economist from Pomona College. Based on my experience in the OVEC case, I decided to fire him and retain econometricians from U.S.C. graduate school. I instructed them to prepare regression analyses, like that prepared by Dr.Adelman in the OVEC case, to compute a non-conspiratorial price to be compared with the actual prices during the conspiracy period. The results could establish whether and how much the collusion caused financial loss to customers who were plaintiffs. The regression analyses could be based on cost indices, utilization of capacity, and any other inputs that the experts concluded could influence prices in a free market.

Numerous cases, which had been filed in the Pacific Coast states, were assigned to Judge Martin Pence of Hawaii. He chose the cities where he held court and preferred San Diego and San Francisco. We neared the date for a hearing on an important motion relating to the damage computations. Fran was carrying our second child. When we visited our obstetrician, he told Fran that if I left for California, she would not need me because she had the doctor. Fran told me that if I was in California when our child was born, I could stay there, and I would never know his or her sex. I asked Gerry Sobel, who was working with me in these cases, to go in my stead. Sure enough, on the morning of the argument, while I was on the telephone at the hospital briefing Gerry, our second child was born. Judge Pence said he understood why I did not attend, and hoped we would name the baby Penny after him. We named him Jordan, after my grandfather.

Gerry Sobel and I divided responsibility, as there were many cases. I took direct charge of the cases in California before Judge Pence. Gerry took on a lone case in Washington State, which went to trial. We worked together with our economic expert to assess the plaintiff's damage calculations. Among other points, we noted that plaintiff's study only relied on averages. I had a book called *How to Lie with Statistics*. From this simplistic book, I decided that the jury could be told the following example of why averages can be misleading: If the average depth of a river is four feet, but at the center is ten feet, a nonswimmer would drown crossing the river. Sometimes an easily understood illustration can be more persuasive to a jury than a complex regression analysis. The jury returned a verdict with modest damages. In the remaining cases, our econometrician's counter damage calculations, and the low verdict in the trial, enabled us to settle for considerably less than the sums that plaintiffs had initially demanded.

The Managed Care Health Insurance System

The cases, which were known as the *In re Brand Name Prescription Drugs Antitrust Litigation,* were transferred by the Multidistrict Panel to Chicago. Together with the electrical equipment cases and a libel case I describe later, I spent much time in Chicago, which being centrally located was a favorite site for transfers by the Multidistrict panel. On one occasion, the Ambassador East Hotel, where the lawyers stayed, turned me away despite a reservation because a convention had stayed over. They referred me to another hotel, which turned out to be a house of ill repute. I returned to the Ambassador and told the desk clerk that

I was standing by to make sure they did not give a room to someone else. They immediately gave me the George Jessel Suite at no extra cost.

One day I was in Irvine, California, for a hearing on a Shiley valve case. I was on my way to the airport to travel to Chicago for a hearing in the Brand Name litigation when I got a phone call saying the hearing was canceled. I flew home to Westchester Airport in New York, arriving at about 11:00 p.m. to learn that the Chicago hearing was back on. The next morning, I made the 6:00 a.m. United flight out of Westchester Airport. By taking the Chicago subway rather than a taxi, I was downtown in court before 10:00 a.m. when court began. Looking back, I probably should have sent another lawyer to Chicago. Or better still, we have learned during the current pandemic of COVID-19, that many legal and business matters can be addressed by Zoom video calls rather than flying in person to a court or meeting. Clients in California would often summon me for in-person meetings as if I just had to take a cab downtown. Apart from the adverse physical effects of frequent flying, it is also a big contributor to carbon emissions and climate change.

Some thirty leading major pharmaceutical companies were sued under the Robinson Patman Act for price discrimination. These cases were an outgrowth of the newly developed health care system, known as managed care, which was introduced to reduce costs. There were hundreds of plaintiffs including mom-and-pop drugstores, supermarkets, and chain pharmacies such as CVS and Walgreens. Plaintiffs claimed that the pharmaceutical manufacturers charged retail pharmacists higher prices than managed care organizations. Managed care companies, such as HMOs, administer health insurance. They publish lists of prescription drugs, called formularies. In order to be reimbursed by insurance companies, the patient must have been prescribed a drug on the formulary. This arrangement gave the managed care firms leverage over the pharmaceutical manufacturers. The managed care companies were able to negotiate what were called rebates, which were a way to achieve price reductions.

Some of the suits were class actions, which the court consolidated. Because of their individual nature, Robinson Patman Act claims are not suitable for class actions. In order to overcome this problem, the class action complaint alleged a conspiracy to violate the Sherman Act, which had weak evidentiary support. Many of the retailers ranging from small drug stores to supermarket chains opted out of the class actions in order to pursue their claims individually. I represented Pfizer.

The judge to whom the cases were transferred was a former assistant U.S. Attorney in the criminal division. He was a novice when it came to antitrust, and at first seemed to identify price discrimination as an offense akin to religious or racial discrimination. We had to educate him as to the necessity for plaintiffs to prove injury to competition. Without the statutory elements of the Robinson Patman Act, price discrimination was procompetitive.

While this was the largest litigation in which I participated since the Electrical Equipment cases, there was no trial to describe. Rather, our firm's role was to contribute to briefs in the district court and the Seventh Circuit Court of Appeals on complex and often obscure antitrust law issues. The Multidistrict Panel described what it called the "labyrinthine history" of the litigation. Initial motions for summary judgment granted by the trial court were rejected by the Court of Appeals in opinions by Judge Richard Posner (a Chicago School judge). The cases were ripe for settlement. We first settled the class action. Others pursued the case further and convinced the judge to reject the injury opinion of the plaintiffs' economic expert (who happened to be a Nobel Prize winner). But weighing the risks and benefits, the client and I did not regret our earlier settlement.

We then had to deal with the retailers who opted out of the class action. The Multidistrict Panel of judges transferred the remaining cases to the Eastern District of New York (Brooklyn and Long Island). These included individual lawsuits by small drug stores that were filed by David

Boies. Boies was a well-known trial lawyer who represented Vice President Gore in the *Bush v. Gore* dispute over the presidential election. By this time, Boies had achieved much success with his new law firm, which he had formed after resigning from Cravath, Swaine & Moore. He was not present at depositions but instead brought in a lawyer from Virginia. I conducted the depositions of his experts. Under cross-examination, the experts were unable to demonstrate that the drugstores they represented were in competition with managed care entities. Nor could they show injury to competition or that such injury impacted their clients. As a result, we were in a good position to settle on modest terms.

When we met to discuss settlement, Boies complained that he had just published a legal memoir and it took much more time and effort than he expected. (Amen to that.) At a meeting in Boies' office with clients present, we failed to reach an accord. I noticed that his wife and law partner, Mary, kept him supplied with Stewart's diet root beer. Next, we arranged to meet at my office. I met Boies downstairs in front of our offices at 425 Park Avenue where he was waiting for his clients. I invited him up alone, pried him with his favorite root beer, and in fifteen minutes we settled the cases. When the clients arrived, we informed them of the accord and they reluctantly agreed. This essentially ended this litigation although there were some opt-out lawsuits that lasted longer without ever reaching trial.

Traffic Jams

An individual client owned a shopping center in Hamden, Connecticut, outside of New Haven. He was a patron of the arts, particularly artists who created sculptures that were in motion. He supported budding sculptors who would provide him with their works, which he displayed in his shopping centers. In the shopping center in question, he had what he called a "ghost parking lot" where the artist literally covered a number of automobiles with a gray metallic substance.

The lawsuit against my client demanded treble damages, attorneys' fees and costs under the antitrust laws. The damage demands, if granted, would have imposed a heavy burden on our client. The plaintiff had filed plans with local zoning authorities that sought permission to build a huge shopping mall near my client's smaller shopping center. My client opposed this construction in the local zoning boards. The mall owners sued him under the antitrust laws, claiming that he was trying to stifle competition. My client contended that the mall would cause traffic jams that would interfere with his center as well as public convenience.

Tom Smart and I tried the case for the defense in Hartford before Judge Jose Cabranes. The judge was savvy in his quest to get the parties to settle. He appointed a former law clerk to a Second Circuit judge to mediate. We would try the case in the morning. Then the judge would declare that he had an emergency case that he had to attend to and we needed to adjourn for a few hours. In the interim we would have settlement discussions with the mediator. I retained National Economic Research Associates to do a traffic study. It showed the congestion that would result from building the new mall. This supported a legitimate reason for our client's opposition to the mall. We also contended that irrespective of our client's motive, his market power was insufficient to be found a monopolist. We convinced the mediator that the facts and the law were on our side. The mediator pressed the plaintiff to agree to a reasonable settlement.

Our client was able to pay the settlement amount by mortgaging the property on which his shopping center lay. After the settlement, the client and his wife invited Fran and me to a chef's table dinner at an upscale French restaurant in New York City. His wife thanked me and said her husband was able to sleep through the night for the first time since the litigation began. That was gratifying.

• • •

Chapter XXIV
LITIGATION AND JUSTICE

Searching for Solutions

Looking back over years of litigation on behalf of plaintiffs and defendants, I have pondered whether our court system facilitates or overwhelms the quest for justice. I summed up this concern during my testimony before the House Antitrust Subcommittee:

> "*Congressman Railsback:* Based on your personal experience, is it costly to defend an antitrust suit whether you win or lose?
>
> *Mr. Klingsberg:* I think it is costly to prosecute or defend. I have done both.
>
> *Mr. Railsback:* Why is that? Why is it so costly?
>
> *Mr. Klingsberg:* I think it is costly because the Federal Rules of Civil Procedure, which were initially designed to avoid surprise, have created a situation where enormous amounts of records are produced most of which are not really needed in the litigation. An enormous number of depositions are conducted some of which are not needed. And the proof of the pudding

is when you get into a situation where you have a motion for preliminary injunction, and you have to go to court with a weekend's preparation, you probably prove 98% of the case that you would prove after five years of preparation."

In 1939, the Supreme Court approved a dramatically different set of rules of civil procedure for federal courts. Many states have adopted similar rules. Charles Clark, a Yale Law professor and later Second Circuit judge, was one of the authors of these new rules. The goal was transparency, which is usually regarded as positive. Surprise and secrecy were no longer to be a hallmark of civil litigation. The rules provided for liberal access to each party's documents, as well as requirements to answer written interrogatories and to testify at depositions. Over time, with the advent of word processing and email, there was a dramatic expansion in the volume of documentation that might be the subject of pretrial discovery. Young lawyers in large law firms would spend the better part of their work days reviewing documents to determine what was responsive to requests, and what can be withheld as protected by attorney-client or work product privileges. Later, documents became digitized, but it was not that much easier to spend a day peering into a machine to read the documents.

As a judge's law clerk, I was assigned to recommend rulings on objections to lengthy interrogatories in private antitrust suits against movie theater chains. Judges lacked the time and interest to undertake this boring and often fruitless task. Later, a new law authorized the appointment of magistrate judges who would assist federal district court judges in overseeing discovery. While relieving judges of these tasks, the burdens on lawyers were not eased by lengthy hearings before magistrates on discovery issues. In a previous chapter I compared our court system with that of Canada. In my lectures in Germany, I observed the European lawyers' fear of the burdens of American civil litigation.

Robert Haig, a partner in the Kelley Drye law firm, edited a New York State Bar Association publication entitled *"Commercial Litigation in New York State Courts,"* which he and his contributing authors updated annually. Bob asked me to author a chapter regarding *"Techniques for Expediting and Streamlining Litigation."* With the help of Jeff Fuisz, a bright young associate, who is now a partner, I made recommendations to address this problem. We endorsed New York State's special Commercial Division where elite judges supervise and expedite pretrial procedures. The Zoloft case described earlier is an example of that system's efficiency. We also endorsed New York's use of technology to equip courts with computerized equipment that allowed the judge and jury to view evidence on screen. I recommended wider use of motions *in limine,* that is, motions that address evidentiary and other issues that could be decided before trial. This would avoid delays in the midst of trial in order to address legal questions that could have been anticipated. I also described the informal sessions between opposing experts which Judge Pollack ordered in the Oyster Creek nuclear plant case. But these and other innovations did not get to the basic issue of whether the burdens imposed by the broad discovery allowed by the civil rules of procedure can be overcome even when there is active judicial supervision of pretrial proceedings.

Here I describe some experiences where clients understandably decided to settle cases despite my advice that they had valid claims or defenses. In those cases, the cost and burdens of litigation outweighed the cost of settlement. A question that the reader might pose in reading about these cases is the extent to which some plaintiffs' attorneys weaponize lawsuits, that is, file suit without a strong factual or legal basis in order to pressure the defendant to pay a large sum by way of settlement or to cease what may be legitimate competitive activity. By the same token, some defendants who are facing legitimate complaints about their activity, or who wrongly inflicted injury on the plaintiff, weaponize the discovery rules in order to pressure the plaintiff to withdraw or settle. Ethical trial lawyers should not sell their skills for such questionable purposes. Trial lawyers pursue justice when they protect their clients from misuse of the judicial system.

Flea Collars

In 1926, Max Stern left Germany. He took with him several thousand canaries, which he and his brother sold in the United States. They developed a pet supply business. In 1959, Milton Handler negotiated the settlement of a dispute between Max and his brother, whereby Max bought out his brother's interest. Hence, the business, Hartz Mountain, named after the Harz Mountains in Germany, became a client of the firm. The company was taken over by Max's son, Leonard, who was an aggressive young businessman. He expanded its pet supplies to include a wide range of products including flea and tick collars. He also entered the real estate business, building homes in what were once undesirable swamp areas in New Jersey. Leonard told me that his motivation to work hard was the prospect of being a restroom attendant if he did not succeed.

Hartz was sued in federal court in Richmond, Virginia, by A.H. Robins, a pharmaceutical firm that owned Sergeants, a competing pet supply company. The complaint alleged a violation of the Robinson Patman Act. The partner in our firm who advised Hartz on antitrust matters, Josh Greenberg, was not a litigator and so he asked me to take over the defense of this case. Robins was represented by the Richmond law firm of McGuire, Woods & Battle. I doubted that the plaintiff could prove the elements and overcome the defenses provided in the Robinson Patman Act. But McGuire was aggressive and there was extensive discovery. I assigned much of the pretrial work to Tom Smart. Tom was born and raised in Kansas and with his blond, straight hair and midwestern accent, was a typical Midwestener. During a break in a deposition, the McGuire Woods partner asked Tom why he associated with a "Jew" law firm. Tom replied that his mother was Jewish and the other lawyer should mind his tongue. Another time, I was in that lawyer's office to discuss possible settlement. He showed me a picture of his graduating class from Virginia Military Institute and pointed to one of the young men whom he described as "a Jewish boy."

McGuire Wood's strategy, in the absence of proof of an antitrust violation, was to bombard our client with requests for documents and endless depositions of its officers and employees. Our Richmond counsel was not optimistic about seeking relief from this onslaught in plaintiff's home court. The interference with the day to day operations of the company began to wear on Leonard Stern. He consulted with his father, Max, who told him to make believe he had made a bad real estate deal and lost the sum that Robins demanded to settle. While I continued to advise that we had valid defenses, the case was settled.

In a subsequent case, filed in Minneapolis, Minnesota, Hartz was concerned about the jury's reaction to me, a Jewish lawyer from New York. We arranged with a jury consultant to have a mock trial. The witnesses were enlisted from the Guthrie theater group in Minneapolis. The questions asked of the mock jurors at the end of the trial exercise revealed that they liked my presentation and harbored no prejudice. The case was settled before trial.

Silver Foil

I represented Reynolds Metals, based in Richmond, Virginia, in an antitrust suit filed by competitors imitating its well-known Reynolds Wrap brand of silver foil. Richmond, the headquarters of General Robert E. Lee, was in some respects still an antebellum town. I met a vice president of Reynolds Metals while waiting for my plane on a Friday afternoon. He said he was going home to Atlanta because Richmond was no place for a newcomer to live. He opined that you could not be admitted to membership in a country club unless your great-grandparents had been members. Prior to 1968, Richmond banned the sale of alcohol in restaurants. To get around this prohibition, the client took us to a two-story house outside the city. Before dinner we were in theory personal guests of the restaurant owner in his home upstairs where we were served cocktails. Then we went downstairs to the "restaurant" for dinner.

I interfaced with the general counsel, a young lawyer named Bill Reynolds, and a member of the family that controlled the company. He explained to me that the Reynolds Tobacco folks were his cousins, some of whom died in their forties from lung cancer due to smoking. Bill was a tennis player, so I would bring my racquet and we played at his club.

Plaintiffs were represented by a well-known plaintiffs' antitrust lawyer, Malcolm Hoffmann, who had written a memoir similar to what I am now writing, and was one of the inspiring books I read prior to law school. He was to conduct the deposition of David Reynolds, the CEO. It was summertime and very hot and humid in Richmond. We offered to make available the company's offices in the suburbs, which were air conditioned. Hoffmann wanted to play by the book and insisted on holding the deposition in a government building, which was an old post office. We were assigned to an airless, un-air-conditioned small room. The Reynolds in-house lawyers decided to light up rum crook cigars, which led Hoffmann to develop a headache and end the deposition prematurely.

Reynolds Wrap and Alcoa's wrap had large shares of the aluminum foil market. The plaintiffs, who were individual entrepreneurs, decided to break into the business with a similar trademark. They sued Reynolds under the antitrust laws for allegedly attempting to exclude them from the market. We countersued for trademark infringement. After much pretrial discovery, I advised the client that I was confident of winning at trial. But Reynolds preferred to settle for what would have been the cost of a trial and appeal.

Hydro Power

John Draghi was the general counsel of New York State Electric & Gas
(NYSEG), a state-owned utility that had created hydroelectric power by
damming lakes in upstate New York. John had heard one of my lectures
at the City Bar Association. He retained me to represent NYSEG in an
antitrust suit. John was a tennis player and while we worked together
on the case, I invited him to play at the New Rochelle Tennis Club. John
said he did not mind losing to me in tennis, but he was unable to bear
that I did not raise a sweat.

Under a new law, the Public Utilities Regulatory Policies Act (PURPA),
utilities were required to sell their hydropower to small companies with
limited capacity as a means of providing cheaper electricity as well as
conserving energy. Hydropower did not pollute the air with emissions
from burning fossil fuels in order to power steam turbine generators.
A countervailing consideration was that damming up the water flow in
lakes and rivers had its own adverse environmental impact. That was
interesting but not the issue in the lawsuit.

The plaintiff, Long Lake, was formed by a group of private investors.
Long Lake was ostensibly formed as a small utility to provide electricity
from hydropower. I suspected that Long Lake's main goal was to seek
antitrust damages by claiming that NYSEG was not selling its hydropower at prices required by PURPA. After discovery, I advised NYSEG
that our analyses showed that its pricing was appropriate under the law.
Therefore, we should win at trial. But the client decided to settle for the
estimated cost of trial and appeal.

◆　◆　◆

Chapter XXV
THE LAST DANCE

Merger-antitrust

Pfizer retained me to seek antitrust approval of the Federal Trade Commission of the acquisition of Warner Lambert, another pharmaceutical firm. The usual issue is whether competition will be unreasonably restrained by the merger. We arrived at the FTC for our first conference and were kept waiting for some time. The FTC lawyers apologized; they were required to don suits and ties when they are meeting visitors who are wearing suits. In our law offices, we also had an informal dress code, but when visiting the government, we wore suits and ties.

The lead FTC lawyer informed us that she was concerned with the overlap in cancer drugs marketed by the two companies. If the companies merged, there was an issue as to whether one or the other's overlapping product could be removed from competition. She was so concerned that we suspected that she had a relative or close friend who had cancer. To gather the facts, we visited Pfizer's vast research complex in Groton, Connecticut, where we met with the oncological scientists who listed all of their products and their applications. The scientists were upset over the prospect of divesting one or more of the drugs that they developed. We could understand their disappointment, as they had worked long and hard to test new cancer drugs only to have them divested by the company as part of the merger approval process. But divestiture of competing products was necessary to secure FTC approval of the merger.

The next step was to fly to Brussels to meet with counsel who specialized in European Union antitrust. On the company plane, the Warner-Lambert attorneys passed out Benadryl anti-allergy pills, made by Warner, so we could get to sleep. The EU had complex and seemingly irrational methods for defining markets and measuring the merging companies' market share, which only the EU lawyers understood. While in Brussels, I was able to spend an afternoon viewing the Bruegel paintings at the city's art museum. In order to get to the Bruegels, the visitor must walk through what seemed to be miles of pedestrian art. But it was worthwhile to get to the end. Upon returning from the EU, we worked with the new CEO, Hank McKinnell, to arrange putting the companies together. In particular, the law required that while preliminary steps were allowed, the companies had to await the completion of FTC and EU review before effectuating the merger. Otherwise, unscrambling would be difficult if the merger was not ultimately approved. The merger was approved.

The Tribulations of Nationwide Litigation

One of the products that Pfizer acquired with the Warner-Lambert merger was a drug for Type 2 diabetes called Rezulin. The drug had a side effect in a small percentage of patients who had an idiosyncratic reaction, something like an allergy to the drug. When that rare side effect occurred, their liver enzymes would elevate to unacceptable levels. In almost all cases, their gastroenterologists would take them off the drug and their enzymes would return to normal. In a small percentage of those patients, there were some who were called "rapid risers," that is, their enzymes rose so quickly that their livers were disabled and they would need transplants or die. Otherwise, Rezulin was effective in regulating the blood sugar of diabetics for almost all patients.

The Rezulin labeling stated in bold that there was a risk of elevated liver enzymes. Nevertheless, the drug was removed from the market by the FDA following a raft of lawsuits, adverse publicity by the *L.A. Times* and attacks by the Public Citizen organization. Rezulin was said to have helped almost two million patients. But sixty-three patients died from liver failure and ten had liver transplants before the withdrawal from the market. The FDA noted that other diabetes drugs, which were recently developed by Smith Klein and Eli Lilly, did not have adverse liver effects. Subsequently, those drugs were withdrawn because of cardiac effects. Diabetes drugs currently on the market and advertised on TV also appear to have serious side effects in some patients. The FDA's risk benefit assessments, which affect human life, are difficult to make and cannot be second-guessed. But the impact of litigation filed by those who were not injured is worth examining.

As we learned from our visit to the Groton research laboratories, the development of a drug to secure FDA approval involves a long and expensive series of tests. First are cell studies in a laboratory; if those are promising, testing on animals follows. Next the FDA must approve testing on people, which involves four phases for safety and efficacy. Much has been written about the trade-off between higher pricing to consumers and the need to fund research and innovation. Legislation has been proposed that would tie the price of prescription drugs to be reimbursed by Medicare to foreign prices and to allow the government to negotiate lower prices. The Congressional Budget Office found that similar policies would reduce expected returns by 15% to 20%, which in turn would adversely impact research and development of new drugs; in particular up to 34 fewer drugs in the third decade thereafter. Surely, no one should be deprived of medicine that cures or alleviates an illness or saves a life because the price of the medication is beyond their means. However, the problem can be overcome by changes in government and private insurance rather than deprive pharma manufacturers of the funds needed for research and development of new drugs. Some foreign countries refuse to pay high prices for American brand name prescription drugs, but that decision may be counterbalanced by the cost of hospital stays for those who might have been cured earlier by modern but expensive drug treatment. Litigation expense and the cost of settlements enter into the equation. The Rezulin cases, which I describe here, provide some insight into the impact of litigation on the health-care system in America.

Numerous lawsuits were filed by patients who had taken or were taking Rezulin. The company settled cases filed by patients who suffered permanent or temporary harm to their livers. But plaintiffs' lawyers advertised that they could get compensation for all Rezulin users. As a result, the lawsuits flowed in. I was retained as National Coordinating Counsel together with the Arnold & Porter (A&P) law firm in Washington D.C. William Vodra, who was the A&P partner in charge, specialized in dealing with the Food and Drug Administration, and had keen insights into the scientific issues. Bill was a Civil War buff who spent his vacations touring war sites. I recall that before deciding to eat potato chips for lunch, he calculated the small and what he regarded was an acceptable percentage by which that would shorten his life span.

We put together trial teams in various parts of the country. This time we moved to have the cases transferred by the Multidistrict Panel to a single judge. There were so many cases that depositions and document production would be impossible to manage individually. The cases were transferred for pretrial proceedings to Judge Lewis Kaplan, a former litigating partner at the law firm of Paul, Weiss, in the Southern District of New York, my home court.

These cases opened a window into problems with the American judicial system. State court judges are usually elected in political campaigns, where attorneys who appear before the judges contribute to their campaigns. This can be pernicious. Many state judges had been plaintiff's contingency, personal injury lawyers before ascending the bench and maintained their membership in the bar association of such specialists. Federal judges are appointed by the president for life, but even their decisions can be influenced by preconceived ideological views. We learned that there were counties in the South where a defendant, particularly a corporation, and more particularly a "Yankee" corporation, meaning from "up north," could not expect to win a case in state court no matter what the merits.

We were told by our Mississippi counsel that in rural areas, a plaintiff's lawyer would fly into town on his Lear Jet on a Sunday, and preach at the local church against the evil corporations. The next day the same plaintiff's lawyer would be arguing in court before jurors who attended the Sunday service. While the jurors were deliberating, the lawyers could hear through the cracks that they were singing hymns from the Sunday service. A tour of the countryside revealed many homes that were little more than shacks. However, in the midst of that poverty, there might be a modern upscale ranch home built by a plaintiff who recovered a large sum in a personal injury or product liability case. The neighbors on a jury might hope that someday they could own such a home. There were billboards advertising product liability lawyers including the message: "One call, that's all."

At a meeting of a group of our trial teams at a Jackson, Mississippi, bed and breakfast where we were all staying, the breakfast consisted of biscuits and gravy. Our Alabama attorney turned to the New York contingent and warned, "You had better eat those or they will think you're a Communist."

Most of the Rezulin cases were filed in state courts. Our goal was to get as many cases as possible transferred to the Southern District of New York. In that way, the pretrial discovery and motions could be handled in one court. Otherwise, the defendant would be burdened with repetitive discovery in numerous jurisdictions. In effect this would be death by a thousand needles. The procedure was to remove cases, which had been filed in state court, to federal court located in the state, which would then be asked to effectuate the transfer to the multidistrict judge.

Federal courts only have jurisdiction where there is diversity of citizenship, meaning that the plaintiff and defendant have to be citizens of different states. So, a case filed in state court by a Mississippi plaintiff against a New York-based corporation, could be removed to federal court and then transferred to federal court in New York. To evade this rule, plaintiffs' lawyers would often name as a defendant a local drugstore, which was a citizen of Mississippi, thus destroying diversity of citizenship and avoiding transfer to the multidistrict court. We argued that this strategy resulted in fraudulent joinder because the local drug store clearly had nothing to do with any alleged defect in Rezulin. One drugstore in Mississippi was named so many times that the cost of defending the lawsuits caused it to go out of business. The local federal courts were divided on how to deal with this issue. So, we suggested that our local Mississippi counsel urge the local courts to effectuate the transfer and let Judge Kaplan decide if there had been a fraudulent joinder, and whether he had jurisdiction based on diversity of citizenship. Judge Kaplan consistently ruled in favor of retaining the transferred cases in the Southern District of New York.

Another anticorporation, antidefendant jurisdiction was the West Virginia state court. We had to take deposition testimony from plaintiffs around the state. Our team of lawyers drove from one town to the other; plaintiffs' lawyers flew in their Lear Jet. Most of the plaintiffs testified in depositions that their experience with Rezulin was positive. Their blood sugar was under control for the first time and they had no side effects. Their physicians told them to keep taking the drug. When asked why they joined the lawsuit, they responded that they had seen ads on TV and the lawyers suggested that they join the litigation at no cost and with the prospect of a windfall recovery.

We stayed in Beckley, a town with a population of about seventeen thousand. At a diner with our local counsel, the waitress asked him when she was going to get her money. He asked what she was talking about. She replied that she took Rezulin for diabetes, smoked cigarettes, and took diet drugs, all of which were in litigation. The food was mostly greasy, fried dishes. We heard that one of the plaintiffs' lawyers had part of his intestines removed as a result of this diet. One of our lawyers asked the waitress: "What was in the fruit cup?" She replied that she didn't know because "no one had ever ordered that before." The streets of the town were marked by boarded-up shops except for law offices. There were monuments to miners who died in mine accidents. All in all, this was a sad commentary on life in West Virginia, which might explain the antipathy that the courts and juries had toward corporations, and the desire of citizens to get some money by joining in lawsuits against them.

I argued in the state trial court in Beckley that a class action should not be certified because of the lack of common issues. The trial court agreed. For the appeal to the West Virginia Supreme Court, my team and I wrote the briefs but thought it prudent to have local counsel argue. That court was dominated by anticorporate judges. One judge, who had been fair in the past, had to recuse herself because plaintiffs' lawyers retained her husband as one of the attorneys of record on appeal, even though he had played no significant role in the litigation. There was a group of high school students observing the appellate arguments. At the outset, the chief judge addressed the students and told them they were about to witness how evil corporations would be brought to justice. The court reversed the lower court and ordered statewide class certification in an opinion that ran counter to a long line of precedents including the AMS case which I argued in the Sixth Circuit in Ohio.

Plaintiffs in the multidistrict proceedings before Judge Kaplan also moved for class certification. I cited my arguments, derived from the Sixth Circuit decision, that individual patients had different medical experiences and were suing under different state laws, so there was not the requisite predominance of common fact and legal issues. Judge Kaplan denied the plaintiffs' motion for class certification.

Preemption

In a case known as *Buckman,* decided in the year 2000, plaintiff alleged that the defendant had made fraudulent misrepresentations to the Food and Drug Administration (FDA) to secure fast approval of a defective medical device that caused personal injury. The U.S. Supreme Court ruled that plaintiff could not legally sustain such a claim. In a unanimous decision, the Court concluded that the FDA has exclusive jurisdiction over claims of misconduct before the agency. Otherwise, the Court reasoned, judges and jurors in fifty states could set their own different rules for regulating conduct before the agency. Hence, state law claims for fraud on the FDA were "preempted" by federal authority.

Michigan enacted a statute that narrowed the immunity from suit that the *Buckman* decision had granted. Under the Michigan statute, the plaintiff could recover upon a showing that the manufacturer misrepresented or withheld material information that would have altered the FDA's approval of the drug or device. A plaintiff in the Rezulin cases filed suit under the Michigan provision. I moved to dismiss on the ground of preemption. Judge Kaplan dismissed the complaint. Judge Kaplan applied the reasoning of *Buckman* that uniform federal regulation of such claims would avoid the havoc of numerous state court rulings. He also relied on a decision of the Sixth Circuit, which had jurisdiction over Michigan. That court ruled that such claims were preempted despite the Michigan statute. I argued the appeal from Judge Kaplan's preemption ruling to the Second Circuit before a panel that included my old friend from Yale Law School, and now Judge, Guido Calabresi. Being grilled by Judge Calabresi was, to say the least, challenging. The Second Circuit reversed. Judge Calabresi wrote the opinion. He concluded that this plaintiff's claims were not for fraud on the FDA, which were held to be preempted in *Buckman*, but rather were common law claims for misrepresentation.

With the help of my partner Steve Glickstein, we crafted a petition to the Supreme Court for a writ of certiorari citing a conflict between the Second and Sixth Circuit Courts of Appeal. The Supreme Court granted the writ and agreed to hear the case. Despite my Supreme Court experience, the client decided to retain Sidney Phillips, a Washington lawyer who specialized in Supreme Court arguments. The Supreme Court divided 4–4, with Justice Roberts having recused himself. In these circumstances, the Court does not render an opinion. The result was to leave the Second Circuit's decision intact. Judge Calabresi later told me that he thought the Supreme Court would reverse apparently because his opinion undermined the rationale of the Supreme Court in *Buckman*.

Strategizing with Partners Steven Glickstein and Alan Goott

Silent Injury

In order to recover from the ingestion of a prescription drug, the plaintiff must prove a physical injury that was proximately caused by the drug. Some plaintiffs had symptoms not known to be caused by Rezulin in any of the clinical trials or from adverse event reports that physicians had to file with the FDA. Some of these plaintiffs relied on what physicians called "differential diagnosis." Under that theory, if a patient had certain symptoms that could not be attributed to any known cause, by a process of elimination their condition could be attributed to a drug they were taking. There was legal precedent supporting this theory in the Southern District of New York, which was contrary to the rule in other jurisdictions. Differential diagnosis was commonly used by physicians in deciding how to treat patients. I convinced Judge Kaplan that the prior cases in his district were in error because they ignored the requirement that remained after other causes had been eliminated, that is, that there must be a scientific basis for concluding that the drug in question caused the symptoms. Afterward, Bert Slonim and I published an article explaining our legal analysis. I followed the practice initiated by Handler of including colleagues as coauthors of scholarly articles.

In this litigation, most plaintiffs had no symptoms or evidence of an adverse effect. Nevertheless, plaintiffs' attorneys found scientific experts who were prepared to testify at trial that a patient who had no visible adverse symptoms could nevertheless recover money damages because of what they called "silent injury." From the outset, this claim seemed far-fetched. Nevertheless, a significant amount of briefing and court hearings were required to address the theory.

The next step on the road to trial involved hearings as to whether the parties' expert witnesses satisfied the Supreme Court's so-called *Daubert* standard, which required a showing that the experts' opinions were not based on junk science. Judge Kaplan held a lengthy hearing in which both sides' experts testified and were cross-examined. I conducted some of the direct and cross-examination, which required less medical knowledge. To cross-examine the more technical witnesses, I brought in Pamela Yates, a product liability lawyer from our Los Angeles office, who was knowledgeable on the science.

We asked Judge Kaplan if he would like to invoke the rule allowing a court-appointed expert to advise the judge on interpreting expert scientific testimony. Judge Kaplan told us that he had been a premed student in college; hence he was familiar with biochemistry and was capable of understanding the expert testimony. Plaintiffs' experts testified that even though there was no visible or treatable injury, Rezulin eroded the patients' mitochondria, which are membrane-bound cell organelles that generate most of the chemical energy needed to power the cell's biochemical reactions. I was not even sure what that means. Our experts concluded that the silent injury theory was sheer fiction. Judge Kaplan rendered a lengthy opinion finding that plaintiffs' expert opinions were too flimsy to allow submission to a jury. Interestingly, Judge Kaplan went back to ancient English common law to characterize the plaintiffs' experts:

> "These 'experts' thus are loosely analogous to compurgators, also known as oath helpers, in that they lend their credentials and reputations to the party who calls them without bringing much if any relevant knowledge to bear on the facts actually at issue."

At this point, we concluded that we were at our strongest. We did not want to risk an appeal from Judge Kaplan's decision. Moreover, Judge Kaplan only had the cases for pretrial proceedings. Despite his favorable ruling, there was a risk in having to try individual cases that would be sent back to the courts where they were originally filed. So, we undertook a program of settling some three-thousand cases for modest sums. The plaintiffs presented their claims in bulk, which included many claimants who did not have elevated enzymes. We left it to the plaintiffs' lawyers to distribute the settlement funds on an equitable basis.

There came a time when we purchased a second home in Florida. I was semi-retired but felt an obligation to finish off the Rezulin cases. I had a computer with a Cisco system provided by the office, which enabled me to make phone calls using earphones and indicating that the call was coming from my office phone number. I gave an associate an assignment over this phone and she said she would like to come up to my office to discuss it. I replied that I was very busy and could not meet, while of course I was actually miles away in Florida. The next group of multi-district product liability suits involved women's hormone medications. These cases were transferred to a judge in Little Rock, Arkansas. I was not going there. When the last Rezulin case was settled, I officially retired.

Lessons Learned

The lesson from pharmaceutical product liability litigation is that there are many effective drugs or devices but none is totally free of adverse side effects in some patients. At the same time, there are products that should not have been sold, or should have had more prominent warnings. Those injured by such drugs or devices should surely have the right to sue and be compensated not only because they are deserving, but also such claims serve as a deterrent to companies who are negligent or reckless. Tobacco and Diet Drug cases are examples of worthy endeavors by plaintiffs' lawyers. Baseless suits resulting in large verdicts or settlements as well as expensive legal fees contribute to the high cost of safe and effective drugs.

There have been some legal reforms to even the playing field including limits on class actions and enhancing the right to remove cases to federal court. Just as the sale of medicines and devices requires the balancing of risks and rewards, the judicial system must achieve a fair balance to protect legitimate claims and avoid frivolous litigation. Congress is now so partisan and unable to agree on legislative proposals that it is difficult to provide legislation to achieve this balance. State legislatures vary between corporate control and influence of the plaintiffs' bar.

• • •

Chapter XXVI
A NEW LAW PROFESSOR

I learned the value of teaching from the lawyers who taught me. One of the most satisfying aspects of my career was teaching others what I had learned.

Trial Training for Government Lawyers

When Judge Walsh was Deputy Attorney General, he recognized that lawyers in the Antitrust Division were expert in antitrust theory and economics but lacked trial experience. He proposed rotating antitrust lawyers into the Criminal Division of the Department. Later, the Antitrust Division of the U.S. Department of Justice and the Federal Trade Commission decided that they could not effectively enforce the antitrust laws unless their lawyers were better at trying cases. The government asked Columbia Law School to establish an antitrust trial training program when school was out in the spring. I was asked to organize and teach at the program together with Maury Nessen, who had been an Assistant U.S. Attorney in the Southern District of N.Y. and a well-known trial lawyer with the firm of Kramer Levin.

We prepared extensive materials including a mock statement of facts for teaching trial skills. We invited trial lawyers and judges from around the country to participate as faculty. The government lawyers, who were the students, were divided into groups of two, each of which would conduct a mock antitrust trial. One faculty member would act as judge while the other sat in the back of the classroom and commented on the performance as it proceeded. The program was conducted over a five-day workweek. For seven years, we ran the program every May. Due to its popularity, Columbia opened the program to the private bar. I observed that the Texas lawyers and judges on our faculty were the most proficient in trial technique. As young associates, in contrast to those in large New York firms, the Texans were assigned to try small cases where they developed their skills.

One evening, I gave a demonstration of how to cross-examine an economic expert on antitrust issues. In my practice, I often retained National Economic Research Associates (NERA), which consisted of economic experts in various subfields including antitrust. I was also consulted by NERA as their attorney. The President of NERA was Dr. Irwin Stelzer, who wrote learned articles and a column in the press. In preparation for the mock cross-examination of Dr. Stelzer, I researched his prior writings, which I would have done in a real trial situation. I found inconsistencies between what he had written in the past and his proposed testimony in the mock trial. When I confronted him on the witness stand with his contrary writings, to avoid embarrassment he changed the facts midway through the cross-examination. It was all in fun and I hope valuable to our students.

Dr. Stelzer had a vacation home in Aspen and ran an antitrust symposium for selected antitrust lawyers every summer. I was a regular lecturer at these events. Fran and I enjoyed the Aspen trips where we were able to hike in the mountains and enjoy the company of my colleagues. We were invited to cocktail parties at Stelzer's home whose previous occupant was Claudine Longet, formerly the wife of the singer Andy Williams. The home was famous as the place where Longet shot and killed Olympic skier, Spider Sabich, in the bathtub. A highlight of the cocktail parties was to view the huge bathtub in the home. Later,

NERA shifted the venue of the lectures to Santa Fe, New Mexico. One summer, Fran and I took a train to New Mexico so I could write my lecture without interruption. We enjoyed these trips to Santa Fe where we attended the outdoor opera, as well as touring the Los Alamos atomic laboratories and Native American ruins.

Rutgers and Miami University Law Schools

After years of calling Handler "the Professor," it was fun to be addressed as professor by law school students. For six years, I taught a class entitled Complex Litigation at Rutgers Law School, in Newark, New Jersey. My friend and law school classmate, Steve Weiner, told me about such a course that he was teaching at Brooklyn Law School. The original idea came from a published casebook of that title, authored by Professors Richard Marcus of Hastings College of Law, Edward Sherman of Tulane Law School and Howard Erichson of Fordham Law School. I did not require my students to purchase the casebook, but it was a valuable tool. Much of the curriculum was what I had done in practice including class actions, multidistrict procedures, and expert opinion qualification. My classes were well attended by students in their second and third years of law school. At the end of a semester, one of my students told me: "I don't know why you choose to do this, but I am glad that you do." I also helped students with job hunting including, for one student, securing a clerkship with the New York State judge in charge of mass tort cases. The experience provided much gratification.

I assigned cases to read, which the students could access on line with the Lexis system that contained all published case law. In this way, I could assign recent cases, particularly Supreme Court decisions, which a casebook would not yet have republished. I gave a two-hour, ten-question final examination consisting of mock statements of the facts of a motion or appeal, which the students were to decide as if they were judges.

I devoted one class to brief writing. At my law firm, good brief writers were scarce even among those who came from good law schools with good grades. During my years as a practicing partner, I devoted time to teaching associates brief writing skills. Maris Veidemanis was a talented brief writer whose mother was an English teacher in Oshkosh, Wisconsin. Each year, Maris and I would teach a course to the summer associates on brief writing. I advised that the first step to effective writing was to read, and to concentrate on the style you were reading. This required carefully reading well-written sources like the *New Yorker* magazine, and focusing on their style. I transmitted the tips for brief writing from my own experience, and what I learned from Handler and Kunen of our law firm. It has been gratifying to hear from former partners and associates who expressed appreciation for how much they learned from working with me.

After I retired from practice, Stuart Deutsch, who was Dean of the Rutgers School of Law, recommended me to the University of Miami Law School. I taught there for three years. The school had a drop-add period at the outset of the semester, which allowed students to switch courses. I inquired of some students as to their reasons for dropping my class. They told me that other professors gave take-home exams or accepted papers instead of a final exam. In contrast, I was known to give a tough in-class exam. I complained to Dean Patricia White that this practice was a race to the bottom. She informed me that academic freedom precluded her interference. Notably, Rutgers had more minority students than most national law schools. My students there never complained about the exams.

In every class at both law schools, there were some students who were more attentive and better prepared than others. Interacting in class with these eager students made the effort worthwhile. I received a call from one of my former Miami Law students saying that she had just left a conference of partners who were brainstorming a class action strategy. She said that based on what she had learned in class; she was the only one to come up with the right answer. The dean in charge of adjunct faculty at Miami Law audited the class once a semester. He complimented me on the students' attention. I asked how he knew that. He told me that students all have their laptops on their desks. In many classes they play computer games, while in my class, the students were taking notes on the lesson.

There came a time when the enrollment at law schools dropped dramatically. Dean White informed me that other law schools tried to make up for the drop in admissions by lowering their standards, or raiding lesser law schools for students entering the second year who had done well in first year. To her credit, she refused to do that. So, the school had to make sure there was work for the full-time faculty. My class was taken over by a bright young Yale Law graduate who taught Complex Litigation even though he had probably never tried a case.

•　•　•

Chapter XXVII
LAW FIRM MANAGEMENT

For eight years, I was the Chair of the Executive Committee of Kaye Scholer, LLP. The firm was founded about a hundred years ago by Benjamin Kaye. He was a "man about town," a lyricist for a Broadway play with music by Richard Rodgers, and a tax lawyer. He partnered with Jack Scholer, whom he took on because he liked the way he dressed and kept his wax mustache. When I first associated with the firm, Mr. Kaye invited me to lunch; he showed me a picture of his Columbia Law graduation class, which included President Roosevelt. He took me to an upscale French restaurant, The Brussels, where he was warmly welcomed as "Monsieur Kaye." I was impressed.

One of my early assignments was to defend an antitrust suit against a women's wear company that was a client of Jack Scholer. I advised on the substance of the Robinson Patman Act and our potential defenses. At the end of our meeting, the client insisted that I file a counterclaim for malicious prosecution by the plaintiff in filing its antitrust claim. I advised to the contrary. The client then insulted my abilities. When I reported back to Scholer, he immediately phoned the client and said that if he ever spoke that way again to one of the firm's lawyers, he would pull the files and withdraw our representation. I was pleased by Scholer's moral compass.

In its early days, the firm's main client was the Phoenix Bank, which was Jewish owned. During the Great Depression, J.P. Morgan asked the major banks to chip in to help the failing banks. Phoenix refused and Morgan is said to have put it out of business. The firm turned to representing a bus company in accident cases. Harold Fierman was a partner who married Minnie Sarnoff, who was the brother of General David Sarnoff, the President of RCA. He told me that when the firm lost the Phoenix bank as a client, he and others had to represent a bus company in slip and fall cases. Later, he formed a consortium of investors in distressed companies, which, after the depression, became corporate clients of the firm.

The next generation of partners, including corporate lawyers Fred Fishman and Bill Nimkin, and litigator Jim Oliensis, had been associates at the so-called white-shoe Wall Street firms. While they were bright and talented, they were passed over for partnership at their old firms, and were taken in as partners by Kaye Scholer where they formed the backbone of the firm. Jim Hays ran the firm with an iron hand. For example, coffee makers were prohibited because a spill would spoil the carpeting. Herb Greene, one of my colleagues from the U.S. Attorneys' office, was chastised by Hays for growing a mustache, so he quit and went in-house at Xerox. Hays had a shock of white hair that made him look wise. He believed in relations with families whom the firm could advise, which was an archaic view of the role of the modern large law firm.

When I became an associate, the firm had six or seven "managing partners," who had special privileges like signing for lunch at nearby upscale restaurants. When I became a partner, I was the youngest member of a committee charged with democratizing the firm. With the advice of Price Waterhouse Consulting, we abolished the concept of managing partner and established an Executive Committee elected by the partnership: one partner, one vote. We also created an elected committee to decide annually on the partnership percentages. I served on that committee for a number of years—it was not fun.

After my term on the compensation committee ended, I had to appear annually to plead my own case. After showing that I had collected large sums for several years, which would seem to justify an increase in my percentage of profits, the chairman told me that he thought it was a "spike." I was not happy. But no one should expect that working for any law firm will always be smooth sailing. My dissatisfaction came to a head when I had a dispute with the Executive Committee over a conflict of interest between a prospective client and a client in a case I was litigating. I entered into discussions with my old friend from the U.S. Attorneys' office, Sheldon Elsen, to join his three-partner firm and bring with me the lawyers with whom I principally worked at Kaye Scholer. Fran and I took a vacation on Cape Cod where I thought about this move while sitting on the beach. In the end, I decided that I would not be happy sharpening my own pencils and decided to stick it out at Kaye Scholer. It turned out to be a wise decision as I attracted important clients and challenging cases that I might not have done at a small firm.

Management Meeting with Partners Michael Blechman, Susan Rahm, and Andy MacDonald

When I was elected as Chair of the Executive Committee, I was faced with the dilemma of not wanting to give up my litigation activities, which I found satisfying and which the firm needed. Fortunately, we had a partner in the firm, Barry Willner, who was a talented litigator but also adept at firm management. Barry had unique insights into what was going on in the firm beneath the surface. He had the ear of the younger partners who—in any firm—are often disgruntled for one reason or another. Barry also had an eye for seeing through the sales tactics of lateral recruiters who hyped their candidates. For these reasons, I named Barry the "Managing Partner" and he did a superb job of holding the firm together.

Despite Barry's help, I found that management responsibilities posed inescapable burdens. I had to be a combination of psychiatrist and social worker. Younger, ambitious partners had to be persuaded that they had a good future. Loyalty to a single firm was no more a guiding principle than remaining with your home baseball team when better offers beckoned. Potential lateral hires had to be persuaded that switching to Kaye Scholer was in their best interest. We interviewed a capable prospect for our office in Frankfurt, and I had to make sure certain partners did not question him about his grandfather's politics. I also had to show the face of management at some of our far-flung offices. We took advantage of the demise of the Dewey Ballantine firm to take over its office in Silicon Valley. I flew to California where I interviewed patent lawyers for the new Silicon Valley office. Typically, they came to the interviews in T-shirts, jeans and tennis sneakers. The manager of our D.C. office communicated the importance of my visits to her office as our lawyers were bombarded with competing offers. These visits gave me the opportunity to see my son, Jordan, who was working in D.C. as a tax lawyer. In order to meet these challenges, I read a number of books on the management of professional firms including one slim volume called *Herding Cats,* an apt name for dealing with lawyers. We also had a firm retreat at a hotel run by a team of management experts. I was pleased that our compensation system was rated highly by the partners.

We faced complaints about the absence of women partners in management. I named Nancy Fuchs, a corporate lawyer with finance firms as clients, to the Compensation Committee and others to the Executive Committee and to head a department. I nominated the first Black woman for partnership. Aaron Rubinstein, the Litigation Department chair, told me that a partner complained that I was diminishing the firm's quality. I replied that if that partner wanted to improve the firm, he should quit. This new partner, Sheila Boston, became a successful litigator and a leader in bar associations. Her father, who was a pastor, sent me a fruitcake every Christmas with a nice note thanking me for helping his daughter.

The firm closed for a number of holidays including the Jewish High Holy Days. An African American partner in our Los Angeles office telephoned to urge me to make Marin Luther King Jr. Day a firm holiday. He sent me a biography of Reverend King. I decided to announce ten closing holidays, which partners could choose to observe, but MLK Day was mandatory. Ultimately it became a federal holiday.

Kaye Scholer had a Hong Kong office. Foreign law firms initially were not permitted to have offices in Beijing, the capital of the People's Republic of China. To avoid this restriction, the firm, like others, rented hotel room space in Beijing. During the Tiananmen Square demonstrations in 1989, a paralegal was leaning out of the hotel room window to watch the events. She was shot and killed.

A Kaye Scholer tradition was that the resident partner in the Hong Kong office would invite the incoming chair of the executive committee to visit and take a personal tour of the office and the city. I received such a call from Franklin Chu, the resident partner, who was an American of Chinese descent who spoke fluent Mandarin. He had run the Hong Kong office from its inception, more than ten years earlier. I told Franklin that before accepting his invitation, I would like to know the profitability of the Hong Kong office. He informed me that in the past ten years the firm had made a profit in Hong Kong in only one year. I thought about this in light of the fact that we had recently opened an office in Shanghai, which was a commercial center. Our partner in Shanghai was Yingxi Fu Tomlinson. She was a native of China, and had a law degree from a Chinese law school as well as a JD from Washington State Law School. Her husband had been employed by Boeing, but when they moved to Shanghai, I heard that he became "Mr. Mom." Peter Fishbein, one of my predecessors as chair of the firm's Executive Committee, told me that he kept the Hong Kong office open in the face of financial losses because it added "elan" to the firm. Given the firm's current financial situation, and considering that we had "elan," as well as the ability to service clients from our Shanghai office, I decided to close the Hong Kong office. Mr. Chu left the firm. Fran and I never got to Hong Kong.

When I took over as chair, Kaye Scholer was not in a competitive financial position, and we feared an exodus of young partners. The firm had just paid a huge sum of money to the federal Office of Thrift Supervision (OTS). The OTS had sued the firm because a partner had asserted the attorney-client privilege as a ground for refusing to produce documents in a criminal investigation of Lincoln Savings & Loan, which was involved in the savings-and-loan scandal in the 1980s. Subsequently, the American Bar Association found that the privilege was properly asserted. At the time, an overly zealous general counsel of OTS induced a court to freeze the firm's bank accounts, and it had no choice but to settle. As a result, the firm's finances were tenuous. Some partners left the firm. I was told later that Hank McKinnell, the CEO of Pfizer, had privately decided that if the firm folded, he would have set me up in my own firm in order to continue servicing his company. That was a great compliment.

A group of young partners told me they would resign if I did not merge Kaye Scholer with another law firm. I consulted with McKinsey & Co., a firm client, who advised against a merger because of the social problems involved. Instead, McKinsey suggested recruiting new partners in specialties that other firms might lack. I went through the motions of pursuing mergers but none were appealing. A California firm, Gibson Dunn and Crutcher, which had recently opened a New York office, asked how one gets business in New York. The managing partner of another firm had told them that to develop clients in New York they should become active in UJA. Gibson's partner then asked, "What is UJA?" Not having heard of the ubiquitous charity, United Jewish Appeal, this out-of-town firm was not for us. Other firms, which seemingly had good profitability, were found upon examination to lack sufficient malpractice insurance or pension arrangements for nonlawyer personnel.

At the same time, I employed headhunters to find the new specialists. We hired partners who specialized in outsourcing of business, windmills for electric power, Defense Department approval of mergers with foreign companies, aviation acquisitions and a former FTC official who dealt with pharmaceutical mergers. Eventually, I brought the firm for the first time into the list of top 25 best per partner profit firms in New York City. We replaced Fried, Frank, where Leon Silverman had been a managing partner.

• • •

Chapter XXVIII
WHEN NOT AT WORK

Hiking

Hiking has been one of Fran's and my favorite vacation activities. On our trips to Aspen, Colorado, where I was lecturing at the NERA antitrust seminars, we hiked the Rocky Mountains. A favorite four-hour hike was to Maroon Bells, a lake at the base of a mountain where skiers, without tows, climbed the mountain to ski in the height of summer. In a new national park in Nova Scotia, we selected a midlevel hike with colored markings on trees as a guide. The rangers informed us that the exit for the hike was the beach at the Bay of Fundy where the tide comes in at 3:00 p.m. That tide is known to be one of the fastest in the world, which, according to the rangers, "neither man nor beast could outrun." After several hours of hiking, we realized that we were even with the tree line and were not descending, as we needed to do in order to beat the tide. We pictured a news clip saying that a couple had disappeared on the mountain and their car was found abandoned in the parking lot. Our mobile phones did not work during our stay in this area. In desperation, I tried to reach the rangers by phone. Miraculously I got through to the park headquarters. They explained that I had misread the color code. We had taken the most difficult path. The rangers guided us down just in time to beat the incoming tide.

On a hike up the mountain overlooking Lake Louise in the Canadian Rockies, I rang bells as we turned a corner. Our guide asked what that was for. I explained that on the way in, we stopped in the town of Banff and purchased bear bells, which, we were told, would scare off grizzly bears. I was concerned as a Kaye Scholer associate had been killed by a grizzly bear in Alaska when he tried to protect his wife and children from an attacking mother bear, whom they accidentally accosted while she was caring for her cubs. The guide advised that the bells were really dinner bells for bears. He asked why I had not purchased bear spray which he carried on his belt. I replied that the bells cost four dollars while the spray cost about fifty dollars. The guide asked whether my life was worth fifty dollars. A guide in Yellowstone National Park told us about a foreign tourist who thought that bear spray was like sunscreen. He had to be hospitalized after spraying himself. We hiked in the National Parks including the Grand Canyon, Bryce, Zion, The Grand Tetons, Acadia, in the Green Mountains of Vermont, and the Berkshires in Massachusetts, as well as on glaciers in Alaska.

Alaska

Golf

The comedian, Larry David, quipped that when he gets to heaven, he will be asked why he wasted so much time playing golf. It is a nontaxing exercise that is particularly enjoyable as you grow older. It is an activity that Fran and I engage in together. And it requires total concentration so as to keep the world's troubles at bay while playing. I was fortunate to have attended a summer camp that had a crude nine-hole golf course. The only reason the pro was not on the PGA tour was his love of alcohol, but in the morning when he taught the kids he was in good shape. In college, I arranged my courses to end on Thursday, and left Friday free for golf with friends. I also played with my father-in-law on weekends at municipal courses.

My son, Matthew, who has a single-digit handicap, and I were invited to play at the pro-am of a PGA tournament sponsored by Greg Norman, the Australian pro known as "The Shark." We played with Kenny Perry, who won the tournament, and Stewart Cink, who had won the U.S. Open. On the first

With Stewart Cink, PGA Champion

green, Cink asked me if I had the line (for the putt). I innocently replied, "I hope so." Matthew grabbed me aside and explained that he was trying to help me and next time I should ask where Cink thinks I should line up the putt.

Tennis

At a reunion of my Yale Law class, we each had to make a short statement of what we were doing in retirement. At our last reunion, my classmate,

Stanley Sporkin, who was a fearsome chair of the Securities & Exchange Commission and a federal judge, was telling me that he continued to go to the office four days a week. At the same time, his wife told Fran that he goes in once or twice and has little to do. Others told similar tales. I told my classmates that my ambition in retirement was to achieve an official USTA tennis ranking.

When Fran and I and our young son moved to Westchester County in New York, I joined the New Rochelle Tennis Club, where the motto was "Every game is a match." "A"-ranked players were just short of qualifying for the U.S. Open, so I was proud to have won the "B" tournament one year. The tennis club was run by a former pro. I could call him from the office at 4:00 p.m. on a workday and he would arrange a game for later that afternoon. That is how I met one of my oldest and dearest friends, Dr. George Ovanesian, Chief of Anesthesia at our local hospital. He had been on the Romanian Olympic water polo team. He regaled me with tales of how his East German coach would hurl the ball at his head if he lifted it out of the water. His Communist training gave him intense concentration, which he used to advantage in our tennis matches. I recently received a call from a lawyer who had worked for me as an associate. He recalled

East Coast Swing USTA Tournament

how I would give him an assignment to be completed by the next day. When he inquired of my secretary where I was in the late afternoon, she responded that I had gone to court. She meant the "tennis court."

In my retirement, I have continued to play singles tennis. I entered USTA tournaments and obtained a ranking of 12 in Florida in my age group. To achieve this goal, I was helped by a tennis professional who teaches at the local city courts in Boca Raton. He taught me what he called the modern game of tennis, which no longer requires the player to turn sidewise, bend your knees and hit low to high. Instead, like Rafael Nadal, I changed my 1950s tennis style to have an open stance (easier for older players as well), change my grip and hit topspin. I learned court strategy including the drop shot and the high lob, which were more effective than a blazing forehand drive. In any activity, there is no end to learning to improve, whether practicing law or tennis.

My daughter-in-law, Stephanie, was captain of the Princeton tennis team, and my son, Matthew, was captain of his high school tennis team. Jordan was ranked #1 in his age group in Florida and his wife, Debbie, also plays. Fran and I have enjoyed playing tennis with them and our grandchildren in what they have come to call "family dubs," meaning doubles. Jordan often tells fathers, whom he sees yelling instructions at their children on the tennis court, that I left our sons' instruction to professionals. For that reason, we are still playing together many years later.

Throughout my description of litigating in numerous cities, I referred to opportunities to play tennis with colleagues from my law firm, cocounsel, clients and even strangers at nearby resorts. Tennis helped to keep me in shape, but also to maintain mental acuity, to have some fun, and to make friends. I recommend strongly that a budding lawyer adopt some form of enjoyable and energetic form of exercise to stay in shape while trying cases, and to fall back on during retirement. My son, Ethan, ran marathons and now runs 5Ks. Fran was the captain of the "A" tennis team in Scarsdale, New York, where we lived, and she still plays tennis with me and her friends.

Travel

People ask why we do not travel more extensively in retirement. The answer is that during my years of practicing law, I argued motions and appeals and tried cases in practically every major city and in most states. I did not want to spend my retirement in airports. Nevertheless, we did enjoy some travel before and after retirement.

Kennedy Memorial—Israel

We always traveled with our children when they were young. A journey to Israel was a highlight. We visited sites that are no longer safe for visitors such as Hebron and Jericho. Our Israeli guide paved the way, speaking with the Palestinians whom he described as "our cousins." While traveling along the Jordan River, I asked our guide if he was armed. He did not reply. But when we were on the highway from Haifa to Tel Aviv, he asked if I was more comfortable. A few weeks later, we read that the PLO had landed in life rafts at that very spot, killed a niece of my law partner, Senator Abe Ribicoff of Connecticut, and hijacked a bus. We visited the Holocaust Remembrance Center called Yad Vashem. We were amazed when we overheard conversations by those near us on line, at how many young people had no idea of the concentration camps and gas chambers. We had previously visited the Holocaust Museum in Washington, D.C. There we viewed video of Murray Gurfein, the judge before whom I tried the bananas case, examining witnesses at the Nuremberg Trials. On our last day in Israel our guide, Ari, took us to the top of Mount Olive to say a "proper goodbye" to the City of Jerusalem. He gave each of us a simple but appropriate gift. When I offered to pay for the trip to the airport, he just asked that we send him customers as he was only busy a small percentage of his time.

Family in Rome, Italy

When Ethan was studying at Kings College in London in his junior year, we took the other two children to London, and then the family to Italy. In Florence, we were saddened by the bullet holes in the synagogue from Nazi occupation. With the children, we visited Mont-Tremblant, in Canada, where a raft trip across the lake led to a forest where we could drink the water from a waterfall. At that time, there were no roads from the lake to the North Pole.

On my first trip to France after graduation from law school, I attempted to use my high school French to check into an inexpensive hotel on the Left Bank. The proprietor asked, *"Parlez-vous Francais?"* to which I replied, *"Un peu."* Disdainfully, she responded, *"Un petit peu."* Years later,

Fran and I traveled to Paris and the Loire Valley for our fiftieth wedding anniversary. Before the trip, I took a fifteen-hour, no English spoken, refresher course at Berlitz. It came in handy when we needed directions at a truck stop on a highway. Otherwise, most everyone speaks English. At one chateau, the proprietor was offended when I shifted from her English to French. We also toured Barcelona, the Spanish gold coast, southern and western France. In the Basque country, I took a lesson in *pelota*, which we call jai alai. And we danced with the local folks in a village in the Vosges Mountains.

Louvre Musee, Paris

Recently, Fran, Jordan, Matthew, and I took a trip to Scotland where we played golf on the Old Course at St. Andrews. Locals use the course on Sundays to stroll and walk their dogs. The grass is not like the manicured fairways on American courses. But it reeks of history, as golf has been played there since the fifteenth century. We also played the more modern Kingsbarn course from which there are spectacular views of the North Sea from every hole. On that trip, Fran and I also attended the Wimbledon tennis tournament on the outskirts of London. It was a more civilized event than the many U.S. Open tournaments we had witnessed. In particular, the tennis matches were sideshows compared with an elegant luncheon in a tent, where the men wore jackets and ties, and the women wore flowered dresses. After the matches, of course, we had strawberries and cream.

Park Guëli Designed by Antoni Gaudi, Barcelona

• • •

Chapter XXIX
LOOKING BACK

In retirement, I often have dreams that I am trying a case, or preparing to do so. Applying Freud's theory that dreams are often based on wish fulfillment, I suppose I miss my trial and appellate work. But like Derek Jeter, shortstop for the N.Y. Yankees, it is wise to hang up your spikes while you are still on top of your game. Looking back, my most exciting experiences were the criminal jury trials and appeals argued to the eminent judges of the Second Circuit Court of Appeals. The most satisfying experiences were the pro bono cases, including the Supreme Court death penalty arguments, which also provided an opportunity to give back to society some of what I did for profit. Teaching was gratifying, and also hearing from former students that what they learned in class was useful in their practice.

To readers who might seek the same satisfactions in the practice of law, I can only say that—like everything else in the world—the legal profession has undergone changes. Oral argument of motions and appeals is often no longer a challenging experience. In some courts, "And you shall be heard" has become an empty euphemism. Many judges have little time or interest in oral argument. Rather, they depend on their law clerks to read the briefs and draft opinions weeks or months after the argument. During argument, they might ask some perfunctory questions supplied by their law clerks. This differs from my experience in arguing before the famous Judge Learned Hand, who never read the briefs in advance. He would spontaneously question me or other advocates in a Socratic way until he got to the logical end of his probing. Then he would turn his chair around and say in substance: "Thank you, counsel. Now I will go back to my chambers and read your briefs." Moreover, due to partisan fighting in Congress, there have been delays in filling judicial positions, so the remaining judges are often overburdened and have little patience for oral argument.

Large law firms today are less social and intimate than in my early days at Kaye Scholer. As I grew up in the firm, the partners socialized, and were invited to our children's bar and bat mitzvahs and weddings. Each summer, we hosted a swim and cocktail party for the summer associates and the lawyers with whom I worked. With a thousand lawyers in a firm, those social contacts have diminished. I recall attending an elaborate firm dinner celebrating the seventy-fifth anniversary of the founding of Kaye Scholer, and honored senior partners Milton Handler and Stanley Waxberg, the chair of the firm's banking and finance department. It was a moving ceremony. Thereafter, paralegals set about writing the history of the firm in anticipation of its one-hundredth anniversary. But it was not to be.

After I retired, the firm's lease at 425 Park Avenue expired and it moved to the West Side of Manhattan in space it could ill afford. It merged with Arnold & Porter, a Washington, D.C. based firm, to form a thousand-lawyer firm. Apparently a five-hundred-lawyer firm was no longer economically viable. Arnold & Porter was larger and so dominated management. Retired partners were no longer honored, but we were removed from the website, and later the email system. Arnold & Porter abandoned the Kaye Scholer name after a year. That was the end of the firm I worked to sustain and build for almost fifty years.

Clients have also changed. Costs have overcome loyalties, and sometimes competence, in choosing outside counsel. After I retired,

Randy Sherman, a litigation partner in the firm, told me that he was on a corporation's "A list" for outside counsel; and he had recently won a case that was identical to a new matter. Rather than retain him outright, the client asked him to submit a Request for Bid to be considered with competing firms on the basis of cost. Corporations often refuse to pay for services by first-year lawyers whom they consider useless, which, surely, they are not. The clients may insist on caps on the total cost of a lawsuit, even though it is impossible to predict the course of litigation, which depends on many factors including how vigorously opponents pursue their case. Assistant U.S. Attorneys do not try as many jury cases as they did in my day. When faced with stiff mandatory minimum sentences imposed by law automatically upon conviction, the accused will often prefer to negotiate a plea deal for a lesser offense rather than take a chance on conviction after trial.

❖ ❖ ❖

Chapter XXX
LOOKING FORWARD

While future lawyers will undoubtedly face different challenges than those described here, there always will be room in the profession for stimulating and exciting experiences. But in the end, what is noble about practicing law is not the thrill of trying a jury case or the intellectual challenge of arguing an appeal before eminent jurists. It is about "being heard" and participating in a process, however imperfect, that is designed to achieve justice—a goal to which there are varied paths.

The experiences that I have described here have focused principally on being heard by judges and jurors in the context of judicial proceedings. There is also a moral aspect to being heard within the broader community. Who else "shall be heard"? The answer is: our children, grandchildren, spouses and other family members as well as friends; the poor and hungry, the homeless, refugees seeking asylum, oppressed minorities, the mentally ill, and other disadvantaged persons. Hearing and listening, directly and indirectly, can influence our charitable donations, our votes, our professional and commercial activities, and interpersonal relationships. My hope is that I have moved the needle, however slightly, so that more people, whether seeking justice or to satisfy personal needs, "shall be heard."

The End

• • •

ACKNOWLEDGMENTS

I am grateful to my wife, who is a grammarian, and was most helpful in reviewing and editing the text. I was aided by comments from my three sons, Matthew, Jordan and Ethan, each of whom took time from their busy professional duties to review the text. My daughters-in-law, Stephanie and Lauren, and my son, Jordan, did yeoman work in searching for and arranging photographs. My daughter-in-law Debbie was very helpful in using the resources of her law firm to track down

Front Row: Bryce, Camden, Emmett. Back Row: Debra, Jordan, Stephanie, Matthew, Shayna, Fran and me, Lauren, Judah, Shula, Jaime, Ethan.

published cases on which I worked. My cousin, Richard Wax, who is not only a renowned biophysicist but is also well-published, provided useful comments. After winning tennis matches, John McEnroe often thanked his parents for "having me." I also thank my mother and father who must have done something right in inculcating the values that enabled me to succeed honorably. I also want to thank my friend, Dr. Perry Hookman, an eminent gastroenterologist, whom I had helped with a book he wrote on medical expert testimony, and he returned the favor by reading an early draft and encouraging me to develop the narrative into a book. Dr. Richard Lahey, former Dean of Nuclear Engineering at RPI and our expert in the TMI trial, reviewed the transcript and ensured the accuracy of the description of the accident and the trial. I also wish to thank the entire team at 1106 Design, who facilitated the publication of this memoir, for their excellent technical advice and encouragement and most of all their patience with my seemingly endless edits and additions.

•   •   •

APPENDIX

Publications and Lectures

Buckman Preemption Revisited, Lecture, *Food Drug & Cosmetic Div. of NYS Bar Assoc.* (January 31, 2008)

Fraud on the FDA: The Fallout from *Warner Lambert v. Kent*, Lecture, *Am. Cf. Inst.* (2008)

NYU Law School on Federal Preemption of Fraud on the FDA Claims, Guest lecture (2008)

Physicians' Differential Diagnosis as Causation Proof: Recent Case Law Holds the Line in Requiring Daubert Reliability, *BNA Product Liability Reporter and BNA*

Expert Evidence Report (November 14, 2005)

The Class Action Fairness Act of 2005, *New York Law Journal* (March 8, 2005)

Beyond CAFA: Other Recent Class Action Reforms, Panelist, *Class Action Fairness Act, The Explanation & the Implications, Association of Corporate Counsel of America* (2005)

Removal and Remand in Federal Courts, Panelist, *Advice from Experts, Successful Strategies for Winning Cases in Federal Courts, NYS Bar CLE program* (2004)

The Corporate Governance Environment Post-Sarbanes-Oxley, Lecture, *American Corporate Counsel Association* (2003)

Techniques for Expediting and Streamlining Litigation, *Chapter in Commercial Litigation in New York State Courts, West Services Inc.* ((2003 and periodic updates)

Some Experiences with ADR in Antitrust and Other Complex Disputes, *BNA Alternative Dispute Resolution Report, Vol. 3, No. 10, p. 172* (May 11, 1989)

Balancing the Benefits and Detriments of Private Antitrust Enforcement: Detrebling, Antitrust Injury, Standing and Other Proposed Solutions, *Cardozo Law Review, Volume 9, Issue No. 3* (March 1988)

New Methods of Dispute Settlement in the United States, *Carl Heymann Verlag KG, p. 73* (1985)

Aftermath of Boulder—Developments in the Application of the State Action Doctrine, *A New Era in Antitrust, New York State Bar Association, Antitrust Law Section Annual Meeting* (1984)

The Economic Expert in Antitrust Cases, *American Bar Association Monograph, contributing author, Introduction, Chapters One and Two* (1983)

Antitrust Violations as a Crime, *Chapter in White Collar Crime, ALI* (1980)

The "Trial of an Antitrust Case" (1977), "Non-Jury Trials" (1978), "The Expedited Trial" (1979), *ALI/ABA Tapes*

Trial Advocacy in an Antitrust Case for Government Lawyers program (1977); Cochair and lecturer (1978–1984), *Columbia Law School, faculty of Continuing Legal Education*

Scientific and Technological Issues in Modern Litigation: Proof of Overcharges in a Price-Fixing Case, *Columbia Law School, Eighteenth Annual Symposium* (1977)

Bull's Eyes and Carom Shots: Complications and Conflicts on Standing to Sue and Causation Under Section 4 of the Clayton Act, *Volume XVI The Antitrust Bulletin, The Journal of American and Foreign Antitrust and Trade Regulation* (Summer, 1971)

State Control Over Political Organizations: First Amendment Checks on Powers of Regulation, *The Yale Law Journal*, Vol.66, Issue No. 4 (Feb. 1957)

INDEX